Dr Jacobs

Ganiot sto book!

Affanno
Cras
IHCR
Epso

October '99

THE
Millennium
CHAMPAGNE
& SPARKLING WINE GUIDE

DORLING KINDERSLEY

LONDON • NEW YORK • SYDNEY • MOSCOW

A DORLING KINDERSLEY BOOK

Project Editor Rosalyn Thiro
Art Editor Anthony Limerick
Senior Designer Tessa Bindloss
Editors Lesley McCave, Clare Pierotti
DTP Designer Lee Redmond

Maps Chris Orr
Map of Reims Stephen Conlin .
Additional Illustrations Sarah Young

Reproduced by Colourscan

Film outputting bureau Graphical Innovations

Printed and bound by Wing King Tong, Hong Kong

Copyright 1998 © Dorling Kindersley Limited, London

Text copyright 1998 © Tom Stevenson

Visit us on the World Wide Web at http://www.dk.com

A CIP catalogue record is available from
the British Library.

ISBN 0-7513-1096-4

*To A. R. for suggesting SuperFizz,
which evolved into this guide.*

*This first edition is also dedicated to the
memory of the father of California sparkling
wine: Jack Davies, who died after a
short illness in 1998.*

CONTENTS

Street name in Hautvillers.

Poster for Veuve Clicquot.

Pop Art bottle design
by Ferrari.

Vineyard planted for sparkling wine in the Marlborough region of New Zealand.

FOREWORD

So now we know: the Titanic was not launched with a bottle of Champagne, and the rest is history, as they say. What is it about sparkling wine that possessed the first person to crack a bottle on the bow of a ship? The bubbles! The same bubbles that spout a fountain over the winner of a Grand Prix. When a glass is raised, it is the incessant froth that makes sparkling wine such a wonderful *joie de vivre*, the ultimate drink with which to celebrate and toast.

Yet, as we approach the Millennium, which promises the mother of all parties, rumours are rife that real Champagne is about to run dry! In just five years, the industry has lurched from an economic depression that created a crisis of mounting stocks to talk of a shortage.

More corks will fly at midnight on 31 December 1999 than at any previous time, but the celebrations do not start or end there. The millennium effect will last for three years, with the end of century festivities in 1999, the inevitable celebrations in 2000, and a year later for those who recognise 2001 as the true Year One of the new millennium, just as AD 1 was.

However, it will not be from individuals cracking open a few bottles at midnight on three consecutive New Year Eves that stocks will be tested. The biggest guzzlers will be crowds at major social, sporting and anniversary events around the world that happen to coincide with one of the three millennial years, giving their organizers the excuse to make the events that much bigger and more special than usual. More likely than not, it will be genuine Champagne that flows freely at such times. But fear not. This enormous demand will affect supply, but there is no real likelihood of Champagne disappearing from the shelves. After a few years of plummeting sales, stocks grew to one billion bottles, and production now averages over a quarter of a billion bottles each year. Furthermore, over the last decade production has exceeded demand, so that there are still about a billion bottles in stock.

Champagne *per se* will not run out. Moreover, sparkling wines from other parts of the world have never looked so exciting, with a new quality-minded generation in Germany, and South Africa about to join the ranks of established fizz industries in France, Italy, Spain, the USA and Australasia. However, special vintages and *cuvées* are always in high demand and will certainly be depleted over the next few years. Hence, *The Millennium Champagne & Sparkling Wine Guide* has been conceived to help you choose the very best fizz, whether you want to drink some now or lay some down for those once-in-a-lifetime occasions.

Champagne Vilmart looks to the Third Millennium with its 1990 Cuvée Création.

INTRODUCTION

A brief history of sparkling wine, how it
is made, how to store and serve it, and
what style to choose.

A BRIEF HISTORY

Wines have accidentally effervesced since biblical times, as shown by "wine…when it moveth itself" (Proverbs) and "neither do men put new wine into old bottles, else the bottles break" (Matthew). But as a deliberate style, sparkling wine dates only from the 17th century.

The Champagne Riots of 1911 were all about protecting the quality of this frothy, frivolous wine *(see p20)*.

AN ENGLISH INVENTION

Until the end of the 17th century the wine made in the Champagne region of France was a murky *rosé* colour, and it was still, not sparkling *(see p18)*. The first French document that mentions sparkling Champagne, dated 1718, refers to the emergence of this style "more than 20 years earlier". As French glass was too weak for fizzy wine before about 1695, and an efficient seal such as a cork was not available, sparkling Champagne's debut in France must have been between about 1695 and 1698.

The English, by contrast, already had the technology – their glass was coal-fired and strong, and they had cork – and there is proof that they used it to make still wines sparkle at least 30 years before the French. At the Royal Society in 1662, a Dr Merret stated that "our wine-coopers of recent times use vast quantities of sugar and molasses to all sorts of wines to make them drink brisk and sparkling". There is also evidence that the English deliberately put a sparkle into the imported still wines of Champagne. In 1676 the dramatist Sir George Etherege wrote that "sparkling Champaign…makes us frolic and gay, and drowns all sorrow".

The Joy of Fizz

No other drink has developed such a hedonistic image as Champagne. Winners, lovers and revellers of all kinds have been drenching themselves with it throughout the 20th century as well as imbibing it. And aficionados happily spend small fortunes to savour a great *cuvée*.

GROWTH OF AN INDUSTRY

Even if the Champenois did not invent sparkling wine, they began to capitalize on their *terroir's* unique suitability *(see p16)* to the style in the 18th century. Markets were found across Europe, and Americans took to it soon after George Washington served it in 1790. In the 19th century sparkling Champagne was exported under the *marques* (names) of famous houses, and most of the civilized world began to drink it in quantity.

The secret of sparkling wine-making leaked out to other wine regions in France and Germany by the 1820s, as far as America by the 1840s, and all the way to Australia by the 1850s. At the turn of the 20th century Champagne was enjoying its Golden Era, turning over 30 million bottles a year compared to 600,000 a hundred years earlier. The technology to produce sparkling wine on a vast commercial scale was available to all wine-producing countries, and the world was awash with bubbles.

Champagne is so extraordinary a wine that its greatest role has become one in which it is not drunk at all, but dashed against the side of a ship about to be launched.

Sparkling wine's most powerful image has long been that it is a drink for the exuberant and extrovert.

Ideas have changed over the years of how best to enjoy your fizz – taking it through a straw was in vogue a century ago.

Some brand names have become world famous.

Louis Roederer, whose monogram this is, was the favoured *grande marque* of those famous hedonists, the Russian tsars. That some of their Communist usurpers also drank Champagne is not so well known.

HOW IT IS MADE

The theory behind sparkling wine is simple. Fermentation converts sugar into alcohol and carbonic gas – if the gas is set free the wine is still, if not, it is sparkling. To capture the gas, the wine undergoes a second fermentation in a sealed container. The gas gushes out in the form of tiny bubbles when the container is opened.

THE GRAPES
Various grapes are used, but Chardonnay and Pinot Noir are best for premium quality sparkling wine – they are relatively neutral, with a good balance of sugar and acidity when ripe.

CUVE CLOSE METHOD
Most cheap fizz is produced by *cuve close* (or "Charmat" or "tank" method). Both fermentations take place in large vats, then the wine is bottled under pressure. As *cuve close* is a bulk-production method it attracts low-calibre base wines, but the speed and minimum yeast contact makes it perfect for sweet, aromatic fizz such as Asti *(see pp50–51)*.

MÉTHODE CHAMPENOISE
The greatest *brut*-style (dry) sparkling wines are made by *méthode champenoise*. As in *cuve close*, the first fermentation takes place en masse, some-times in oak *barriques*, but the second takes place in the actual bottle in which the wine is sold.

In the European Union the term *méthode champenoise* is reserved for Champagne. However, the terms below are all synonymous with *méthode champenoise*:

ENGLISH-LANGUAGE
COUNTRIES

Traditional Method

FRANCE

Méthode Traditionnelle
Méthode Classique
"Crémant" appellations

SPAIN

The "Cava" appellation

ITALY

Metodo Classico
Metodo Tradizionale
Talento

GERMANY

Flashengärung nach
   dem Traditionellen
   Verfahren
Klassische Flashen-
   gärung
Traditionnelle Flashen-
   gärung

SOUTH AFRICA

Cap Classique

FABRICATION DU CHAMPAGNE · REMUEUR · DÉGORGEUR · MÉLANGEUR

There are 250 million bubbles waiting to gush out of the average bottle of sparkling wine.

Three winemakers capture the sparkle of twice-fermented grape juice.

MALOLACTIC CONVERSION

Most fizz undergoes "malolactic", a natural process of fermentation that converts hard malic acid into soft lactic acid and adds creaminess to the wine. Of the few producers who prevent the malolactic, Bollinger, Alfred Gratien, Krug and Lanson are the most famous. In the New World the malolactic is often overworked because grapes are picked early, and have higher levels of malic acid.

BLENDING AND THE PRISE DE MOUSSE

The blending *(assemblage)* of the base wine is undertaken after the first fermentation. The Champenois are the masters of this, and may create a non-vintage *cuvée* from as many as 70 base wines. Sugar, selected yeasts, yeast nutrients and a clarifying agent are then added to induce the mousse. The second fermentation is often referred to as the *prise de mousse*, or "capturing the sparkle", and it can take months to complete. In contrast to the first fermentation, which should be relatively fast and warm, the second is slow and cool.

AUTOLYSIS

When the second fermentation is complete, the yeast cells undergo an enzymatic breakdown called autolysis, which is epitomized by an acacia-like flowery finesse. Good autolysis adds complexity.

REMUAGE AND DISGORGEMENT

In *méthode champenoise* only, the yeast deposit created during the second fermentation is encouraged down the neck of the inverted bottle into a small plastic pot held in place by a crown-cap. *Remuage* (or riddling), as this is called, takes eight weeks by hand, or eight days by machine. The sediment is removed (disgorged) by immersing the bottle in freezing brine, and ejecting the semi-frozen pot without losing too much wine or gas.

THE DOSAGE

Before corking, the *liqueur d'expédition* is added. In all cases except *extra brut* (very dry), this will include some sugar. The younger the wine, the greater the dosage of sugar required.

THE MAIN STAGES OF MÉTHODE CHAMPENOISE

First fermentation en masse in oak or stainless steel.

Bottled with sugar and yeast for second fermentation.

Sediment collected by the *remuage* method.

Disgorging the sediment for a crystal-clear wine.

The internal pressure in a bottle of sparkling wine is equivalent to the pressure of a double-decker bus tyre.

STORING AND SERVING

Most fizz is best drunk within a year or so. Only a few *cuvées* are capable of developing truly complex aromas and flavours after disgorgement.

WHY STORE?

Typically, Chardonnay turns "toasty" and Pinot Noir "biscuity", although the reverse is possible and even a whiff of clean sulphur can contribute to the toastiness of a wine. Some first-class Chardonnays develop specific, complex aromas such as flowery hazelnuts, creamy brazil nuts, and mellow walnuts. The greatest Champagnes can age gracefully for decades, to create rich nuances of macaroons, coconut, cocoa and coffee.

A wide, shallow glass is not the ideal vessel for drinking sparkling wine – the mousse goes flat too quickly. However it is perfect for those special occasions when you want to stack them high and watch them froth.

HOW TO STORE

Fizz is more sensitive to temperature and light than other wines, but there should be no problem keeping it for a year or two at any fairly constant temperature between 12 and 18°C (40–60°F). Higher temperatures increase the rate of oxidation; erratic temperatures can seriously damage the wine. If you do not have a cellar, keep it in a cool place inside a box. Very long-term storage should be at 9–11°C (48–52°F) in total darkness. There is no reason why bottles should be stored horizontally apart from to save space: the CO_2 in the bottle neck keeps the cork moist and swollen even when upright. Some Champagnes have retained their sparkle for a century under ideal conditions.

Some Champagnes, such as Roederer Cristal, are shipped with a yellow, anti-UV wrapping, which you should leave on while storing. Brown-glass bottles offer better protection against ultra-violet than green-glass, and dead-leaf or dark green is better than light or bright green.

Champagne *cuvées*, boxed up and ready for shipment.

Chilling

Temperature determines the rate at which bubbles in a sparkling wine are released. Bubbly should not be opened at room temperature – the wine will quickly froth up and go flat. Chill it, ideally down to 4.5–7°C (40–45°F), the lower temperature for parties and receptions where the room temperature is likely to rise.

It is okay to chill wine in a refrigerator for a couple of hours, but try not to leave it longer than a day because the cork might stick or shrink. Emergency chilling of a sparkling wine by putting it in the coldest part of a deep-freeze for 15 minutes is fine.

A bucket of ice and water (never just ice) is still one of the quickest ways to chill a bottle of fizz, but faster still are the gel-filled jackets that are kept in the deep freeze and slip over the bottle for about six minutes. Invert the bottle gently a couple of times before opening to help chill the wine in the neck.

Gel-filled jacket for efficient, fast chilling.

Opening

Remember that the secret of success is to try and prevent the cork from actually coming out.

Remove the foil to begin, or simply score around the base of the wire cage. Then gently untwist the wire and loosen the bottom of the cage, but don't remove it. Hold the bottle with a cloth if you are a novice, and completely enclose the cork and cage in one hand (the right, if you are right-handed). Holding the base of the bottle with your other hand, twist both ends in opposite directions, backwards and forwards.

The "Champagne Star", made by Screwpull. Designed specially to open a bottle of fizz, it is the best bet for a stubborn cork.

As soon as you feel pressure forcing the cork out, try to push it back in, but continue the opening operation ever more gently until the cork is released from the bottle with a sigh, not a bang.

Pouring

Pour a little into each glass first to allow for the foam, then go back and top up each one to between two-thirds and three-quarters of the vessel. Do not tilt the glass and pour gently down the inside, it is not lager!

A steel wire cutter and grip for the cork – a more basic way of opening bottles.

Untwist the wire and loosen the cage.

Twist cork and bottle in opposite directions.

Allow the cork to be released with a sigh.

STYLES

D ry *(brut)* is a classic style of bubbly, while *sec* and *doux* indicate a rising scale of sweetness. Other categories of style include the basic division of vintage and non-vintage, grape variety, colour and degree of mousse.

WHAT'S IN A VINTAGE?
A Champagne vintage implies that the harvest was exceptional, while for most other fizz "vintage" is best regarded as a statement of age, not quality. Vintage Champagne must be 100 per cent from the year, but elsewhere it varies (95 per cent in California; 85 in Australia). Store vintage Champagne for 8–10 years from the date of harvest. The term non-vintage (NV) sounds derogatory to many people, but wines from various years can be skilfully blended to create some of the finest *cuvées* available.

COLOUR
Pure Chardonnay *blanc de blancs* (white wine made from white grapes) make good *brut*-style sparkling wines, and the best come from the Côte des Blancs in Champagne. In the New World, *blanc de noirs* (white wine made from black grapes) can be various shades, but in Champagne the skill is to produce as white a wine as possible from Pinot Noir or Meunier, and the most famous is Bollinger's Vielles Vignes Françaises. Champagne *rosé* can be made by blending white wine with a little red. Sparkling red wines are also available, such as Australian Sparkling Shiraz.

CRÉMANT
The *crémant* style has a soft mousse, and few producers outside France have a reputation for it. Normal fizz has a pressure of 5–6 atmospheres, while *crémant* has 3.6. To be a true *crémant*, the mousse must unfold slowly, leaving a creamy cordon in the glass. Mumm de Cramant (sic) is the best known.

*P*restige *cuvées* are particular wines that producers feel best epitomize their style. Examples are Dom Pérignon (made by Moët & Chandon), Cristal (by Louis Roederer) and

Belle Epoque (by Perrier-Jouët). They are produced in tiny quantities, and it is their rarity value that determines the high price. The selection of base wines is the most significant defining factor in any prestige *cuvée*.

THE WORLD'S BEST PRODUCERS

An overview of Champagne, other parts
of France, and Spain, Germany, Italy,
the USA, Australia, New Zealand
and South Africa.

FRANCE
THE CHAMPAGNE REGION

The world's finest *brut*-style sparkling wine is created from Chardonnay, Pinot Noir and Meunier grapes grown on the pure chalk hillsides of the Champagne region in northern France. A fizz from anywhere else, including other parts of France – no matter how good – is simply not Champagne.

Chardonnay, whose acidity is well suited to Champagne, is cultivated across about a quarter of the AOC area.

A UNIQUE VITICULTURAL REGION
Elsewhere in the world sparkling wine producers have to work hard to produce decent fizz, but the Champenois can make it almost without trying. The region is in a viticultural twilight zone where the vine struggles to ripen each year. Grapes eventually ripen at a relatively low alcoholic strength, ideal for a second fermentation, and have a very high level of ripe acidity, which is necessary for the wine to age well in bottle.

It is true that Chardonnay and Pinot Noir can be grown almost anywhere, and vines thrive on chalk hillsides in many places, but only in the Atlantic-influenced north of France (the country's northernmost winemaking region) do these and other factors come together, albeit precariously, with a climate that is barely on the right side of the knife-edge between success and failure. Yet the risks are deemed worth taking because, when all goes well, the result is undoubtedly the world's finest sparkling wine.

The harvest brings Champagne to life in the autumn. Even grapes from lesser years can make good Champagnes.

Veuve Clicquot *(see p34)* is one of the largest and best-loved houses, exporting its top-notch fizz to scores of countries.

AOC DISTRICTS

Five main Champagne districts, encompassing some 32,000 hectares of vineyards, lie within the AOC (Appellation d'Origine Contrôlée) delimited region. Reims and Épernay are the area's main towns.

Paris

FRANCE

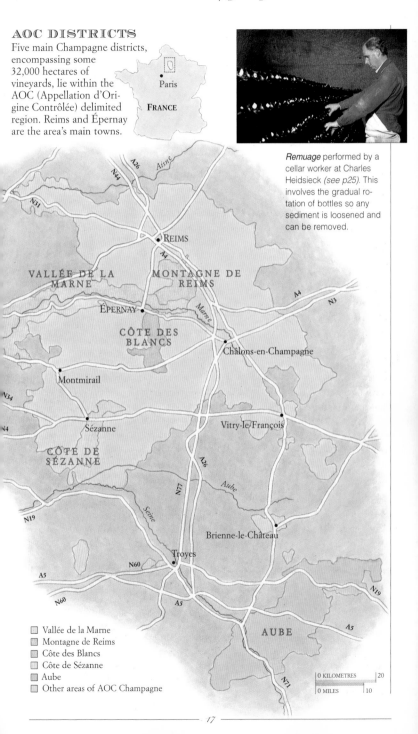

Remuage performed by a cellar worker at Charles Heidsieck *(see p25)*. This involves the gradual rotation of bottles so any sediment is loosened and can be removed.

Aisne

A26

N44

A26

N31

REIMS

VALLÉE DE LA MARNE

MONTAGNE DE REIMS

A4

ÉPERNAY

Marne

A4

N3

CÔTE DES BLANCS

Châlons-en-Champagne

Montmirail

N34

N4

Sézanne

Vitry-le-François

CÔTE DE SÉZANNE

A26

N77

Aube

Seine

N19

Brienne-le-Château

Troyes

N60

A5

N19

N60

A5

A5

AUBE

N71

☐ Vallée de la Marne
☐ Montagne de Reims
☐ Côte des Blancs
☐ Côte de Sézanne
☐ Aube
☐ Other areas of AOC Champagne

| 0 KILOMETRES | 20 |
| 0 MILES | 10 |

CHAMPAGNE – A STILL WINE?

It may seem strange to us now, but the wine of Champagne was originally still, not sparkling. It was introduced in this form to the French Court – traditionally the domain of Burgundy – in the 15th century. Merchants from around Europe took this still wine to other parts of France, Spain, Italy, England and the Low Countries.

The English are known to have put a sparkle into imported Champagnes in the 17th century *(see p8)*. Dom Pérignon (1639–1715), a monk at Hautvillers Abbey, near Reims, is widely thought to have invented sparkling Champagne, but there is little hard evidence to support this. Most French gourmands despised the idea of fizzy Champagne at the time. However, in the 18th century the habit of drinking sparkling as well as still Champagne spread across Europe and as far as Russia.

Iron sign in Hautvillers, Vallée de la Marne.

Ruinart, in Reims, was the first Champagne house.

THE FIRST CHAMPAGNE HOUSES

Ruinart *(see p30)*, the first proper Champagne house, was founded in 1729. Others soon followed, though the vast majority of Champagne produced was still, and this remained the situation up to the end of the 18th century. Several houses started out as textile firms, offering gifts of Champagne to customers, until demand for the gifts outstripped that for the textiles.

Many firms hired German salesmen, renowned for their linguistic and commercial skills, some of whom later set up their own firms in the Champagne region (such as Krug and Bollinger).

Le Monopole c'est moi

CHAMPAGNE *Heidsieck & C.*
Monopole MAISON FONDÉE à Reims en 1785

Heidsieck & Co Monopole was founded in 1834 by Henri-Louis Walbaum, a member of the famous Heidsieck family.

Best Houses

GRAND CRU AREA

The *crus* of Champagne are 300 or so villages whose vineyards are rated according to a percentile system called the Échelle des Crus. Of the villages surrounding Épernay and Reims, 17 have *grand cru* status – the quality of their grapes is rated 100 per cent.

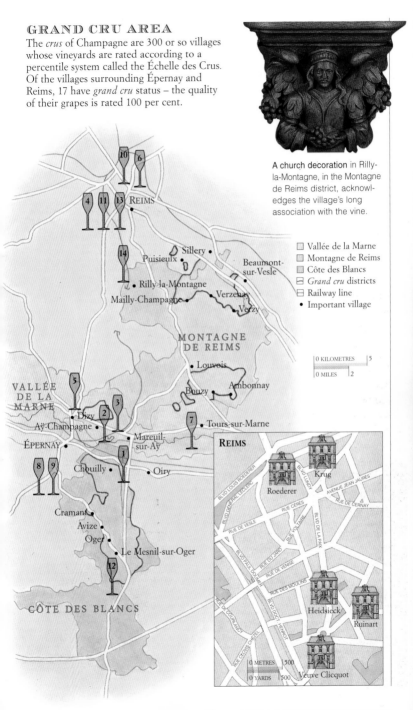

A church decoration in Rilly-la-Montagne, in the Montagne de Reims district, acknowledges the village's long association with the vine.

☐ Vallée de la Marne
☐ Montagne de Reims
☐ Côte des Blancs
⊟ *Grand cru* districts
⊟ Railway line
• Important village

Sillery
Puisieulx
Beaumont-sur-Vesle
Rilly-la-Montagne
Verzenay
Mailly-Champagne
Verzy

MONTAGNE DE REIMS

Louvois

VALLÉE DE LA MARNE
Dizy
Aÿ-Champagne
ÉPERNAY
Bouzy
Ambonnay
Mareuil-sur-Aÿ
Tours-sur-Marne
Chouilly
Oiry
Cramant
Avize
Oger
Le Mesnil-sur-Oger

CÔTE DES BLANCS

0 KILOMETRES 5
0 MILES 2

REIMS

Roederer
Krug
Heidsieck
Ruinart
Veuve Clicquot

BLVD LOUIS ROEDERER
BLVD GÉNÉRAL LECLERC
BLVD LUNDY
AVENUE JEAN JAURÈS
RUE DE CERNAY
RUE CÉRÈS
RUE DE VESLE
RUE VOLTAIRE
BLVD DE LA PAIX
RUE DU JARD
RUE DE VENISE
BLVD PAUL DOUMER
RUE DES MOULINS
BLVD DIEU LUMIÈRE
RUE DE COURLANCY
RUE CROIX CORDIER
BLVD HENROT

0 METRES 500
0 YARDS 500

Moët & Chandon produces more than 13 per cent of all *négociant-manipulant* (house) Champagne.

CHAMPAGNE TAKES ON THE WORLD

It was not until the early 19th century, when the entrepreneurs of the most famous houses hawked their brands to all four corners of the globe, that the production and therefore name of the Champagne region became synonymous with sparkling wine. The English and Americans, especially, took to Champagne's natural appeal as a wine to celebrate with, and were drinking themselves under the table by the mid-19th century. Surprisingly to us now, it was a sweet wine that they were imbibing. At the turn of the century one in ten bottles was as sweet as the dessert wine Sauternes.

In the early 20th century, as increasingly more land in the Champagne region was given over to viticulture, and the quality of the wine grew ever higher, the Champenois started to quarrel over the Champagne name. Not only were other nations calling their own sparklers "Champagne" but some houses were using grapes from other parts of France. The Champagne Riots of 1911 brought the issue to a head, with growers from the Marne and Aube fighting in the streets of Aÿ. Worse still, the vineyards were the scene of trench warfare a few years later as German forces swept into Champagne.

Exports suffered after World War I, as the Russian market collapsed and Prohibition took America (see p54) and parts of

*S*ince the Americans christened Charles-Camille Heidsieck *(see p25)* "Champagne Charlie" and George Leybourne hit the boards with his celebrated song *(see p29)*, Champagne has been affectionately referred to by some slang-name or other. In England, the Victorians were the first to call it fizz. The Edwardians knew it as bubbly, in the 1960s and '70s it was champers, and in the '80s it became known as shampoo.

The world's most prestigious wine has long been associated with celebration, romance and general *joie de vivre*.

THÉOPHILE ROEDERER & C?
MAISON FONDÉE EN 1864.

Théophile Roederer was once a separate company from Louis Roederer *(see p31)*, but was purchased by the latter in 1907.

Scandinavia out of the equation. Domestic sales increased, however, and the Appellation d'Origine Contrôlée (AOC) rules for Champagne were drawn up in 1927. In World War II the cellars came under German control and only just escaped being blown up as the Germans retreated.

Many new markets have developed since the 1950s, but at the Millennium France is drinking almost twice as much Champagne as the rest of the world put together.

There are over 9,000 brands of Champagne marketed by 2,500 houses, growers and cooperatives. Also, there are 3,000 buyers'-own-brands, making a total of more than 12,000 seemingly different brands. With each offering an average of four *cuvées*, there are thus about 50,000 "different" Champagnes!

THE CHAMPAGNE QUALITY

The Champagne name is considered such a guarantee of quality that it is the only AOC wine not obliged to mention AOC on the label. The Champenois are not only blessed with perfect growing conditions for sparkling wine, but they have also spent centuries perfecting their art. It is they who developed the *méthode champenoise* and who take the *assemblage* more seriously than other producers.

WHO ARE THE PRODUCERS?

A Champagne "house" is a *négociant-manipulant* (NM on labels) – it makes and sells Champagne using its own vineyards and buying extra grapes from small growers. There are over 250 houses, producing about 70 per cent of the wines and nearly all exports. The biggest house is Moët & Chandon. Some small growers and cooperatives, collectively known as the *vignoble*, also make their own wines, mostly for the domestic market. On pages 22–35 we take a closer look at the best houses.

Gosset *(see p24)* started to make Champagne in the 16th century, though it was a still wine at the time.

BILLECART-SALMON

A SMALL, family-owned house that produces Champagne of great finesse, Billecart-Salmon is famous for its delicate *rosé*, which represents one-fifth of all it sells.

Nicolas-François Billecart established the house in 1818 with the help of his brother-in-law Louis Salmon, in Mareuil-sur-Aÿ, where his family has lived since the 1500s.

Founded in 1818, the firm says its wine "crosses the centuries...".

Billecart-Salmon's entire range will delight those who enjoy a purity and ripeness of fruit in their Champagnes, yet also want them to be able to age well. Billecart-Salmon was exceptional 20 years ago, but due to the acquisition of another ten hectares of vineyards and a constant upgrade in grapes, the wines are even better today.

The essence of the Billecart-Salmon style has always been its meticulous production, from the double *débourbage,* or cleansing of the must, through the use of its own cultured yeast (from natural yeasts of Avize, Cramant and Verzenay), to its long, slow, very cool fermentation. This regime was formulated by James Coffinet, the *chef de caves* under Jean Roland-Billecart until the mid-1980s. That Coffinet was head-hunted by Pol Roger *(see p30)* is a testament to his winemaking skill and reputation. The fact that his successor, François Domi, has made even better wines under François Roland-Billecart should reassure aficionados of this house.

Billecart-Salmon quickly gained a worldwide reputation but nearly went bust just 12 years after being founded, when an American agent lost the company a staggering 100,000 golden francs.

The Billecart house has an attractive English-style garden and the only Chasselas vine in Champagne.

Building on its reputation for *rosé*, Billecart-Salmon introduced a superb new wine with its 1988 vintage Cuvée Elizabeth Salmon.

BOLLINGER

The Bollinger house in the village of Aÿ was spared from destruction during the Champagne Riots of 1911. A growers' uprising had started when the government tried to bring in strict laws to control the Champagne name.

T HE KEY TO "Bolly's" success is its 140 hectares of top-rated vineyards, providing some 70 per cent of its needs compared with 12 per cent for the average house. The keys to its style are judicious selection of grape juice, the use of oak *barriques*, minimal malolactic and extraordinary reserve wines.

*W*ho drinks Bolly? James Bond, Prince Charles; and Joanna Lumley's Patsy thinks it's Absolutely Fabulous.

Jacques Bollinger first sold wines in 1822 for Müller-Ruinart (now Henri Abelé) and seven years later formed a company with Paul Renaudin, using the vineyards of the Comte de Villermont. The house was called Renaudin Bollinger until 1984.

Bollinger's vintage Champagnes are all 100 per cent barrel-fermented, whereas its non-vintage Special Cuvée is 50 per cent. Reserve wines are bottled in magnums with a tiny dosage of sugar and yeast, which helps to keep them fresh, or *pétillant* (lightly sparkling). There are some amazing Bollinger reserves up to 80 years old, although 15 years is usually the limit set for commercial use.

Reserve wines are bottled in magnums, and some are left undisturbed literally for decades.

*L*ily Bollinger (1899–1977) was responsible for Champagne's most famous quote. When asked how she enjoyed a glass of Bolly she replied: "I drink it when I'm happy and when I'm sad. Sometimes I drink it when I'm alone. When I have company I consider it obligatory. I trifle with it when I'm not hungry and drink it when I am. Otherwise I never touch it – unless I'm thirsty of course."

GOSSET

JEAN GOSSET was Seigneur d'Aÿ in 1531, and his son Claude was a vigneron in 1555, but there is no proof that they traded wine, thus the honour of founding the house goes to Pierre Gosset in 1584.

As mayor of Aÿ between 1584 and 1592, Pierre had the privilege of receiving Henri IV, who in all probability drank Gosset's wine, though it was still, not sparkling, at the time. (Ruinart was the first Champagne house on record to produce sparkling wine.)

In 1992 Gosset became the first new *grande marque* (literally "famous name") for more than 30 years, though ironically the Syndicat des Grandes Marques de Champagne was disbanded in 1997.

In 1994, after 410 years of family ownership, Gosset was sold. While this was very sad, at least it was not taken over by one of the large groups. It is owned by the Cointreau family, under the direct control of Béatrice Cointreau. The *chef de caves* and oenologist remain the same at Gosset, as do the winemaking techniques, which involve the use of some wood and an avoidance of malolactic fermentation . The production level is also unchanged, at just over 500,000 bottles (similar in size to Krug). Small is indeed beautiful at Gosset, where the Grande Réserve, Grand Millésimé, Grand Millésimé Rosé and Celebris consistently rank among the best wines made in Champagne.

The temperature inside stainless steel fermenting tanks is checked by Jean-Pierre Marson of Gosset.

An extremely large bottle of Champagne was produced by Gosset in 1986 to celebrate the 100th Anniversary of the Statue of Liberty. Called a "Salomon" and made of pure crystal, it held the equivalent of 24 bottles of Champagne, and was 20 per cent larger than a Nebuchadnezzar size of bottle.

Béatrice Cointreau, who has breathed some fresh air into the Champagne trade, enjoying Gosset.

CHARLES HEIDSIECK

THERE ARE THREE Heidsiecks in Champagne: Charles Heidsieck, Piper-Heidsieck and Heidsieck & Co Monopole, and all three claim roots back to the Heidsieck firm established by Florens-Louis Heidsieck in 1785.

Daniel Thibault justly won the award of Sparkling Winemaker of the Year in 1994 for his contribution to non-vintage Champagne.

The first two belong to Rémy-Cointreau, a French family-owned group that includes Krug. The best of the three is Charles Heidsieck, established in 1851 by Charles-Camille Heidsieck, a grand-nephew of Florens-Louis. He was known as "Champagne Charlie" in America in the late 1850s through his flamboyant and daring lifestyle, which landed him in prison in 1861 for smuggling French company contracts through enemy lines to the Confederates.

Charles Heidsieck Reserve has been the most consistent and best-value non-vintage Champagne since the late 1980s, when master blender Daniel Thibault transformed the brand. Its rich, complex flavour is tinged with oak-like vanilla, though the stainless-steel fermented *cuvée* has never seen so much as a stave of oak.

Much is made of Thibault's extensive use of reserve wines, but it is his philosophy of Champagne's *crus* (Champagne-producing villages) that has had the greatest influence. Thibault insists on emphasizing the individual characteristics of each village, by allowing the fermentation to progress as naturally as possible. He wants a palate of the purest colours when he paints his blend on the canvas of a *cuvée*. To his mind, he cannot possibly produce an expressive Champagne blend if each component part has not been allowed to express itself.

*C*harles-Camille Heidsieck inspired George Leybourne's famous

1860s music-hall song "Champagne Charlie". For a shilling, however, Leybourne would insert the name of any other Champagne firm in his song. The most quoted version is for Moet and Shandon (sic), so Moët must have had more shillings than anyone else, even then.

JACQUESSON & FILS

The label of the 1985 Dégorgement Tardive ("late disgorgement") depicts the gold medal awarded by Napoleon after he visited the cellars in 1810.

IT WAS NOT UNTIL 1974, when Jacquesson was purchased by the Chiquet family of Dizy, that the foundations of the superb quality we know today were laid down.

The firm was established in 1798 by Claude Jacquesson and his son Memmie. They built ten kilometres of magnificent cellars in Châlons-sur-Marne (now called Châlons-en-Champagne). The "richness and beauty" of these cellars prompted Napoleon to award the house a special medal.

In 1834 Jacquesson employed a young German by the name of Joseph Krug, who later left the company to set up his own house. By 1867 Jacquesson was selling in excess of one million bottles, but after Adolphe Jacquesson died in 1875, his family chose other careers and sales dwindled. In the 1920s Jacquesson was bought by a broker called Léon de Tassigny, who moved the firm to Reims. The Chiquet family, who have owned it since 1974, have been growers for generations (their cousins, in Dizy, sell under the *récoltant-manipulant* Champagne Gaston Chiquet label).

Some of Jacquesson's base wines are vinified in large oak *foudres* (large wooden casks or vats), which are also used to store the reserve wines. This factor contributes to the great complexity that these Champagnes can have.

On 4 July 1849, the *Niantic* dropped anchor in San Francisco Bay, and her crew deserted to join the gold rush. The abandoned, beached ship was used as a warehouse then hotel for a few years. When the hotel was demolished in the 1870s some 35 baskets of wine labelled Jacquesson were found. Newspaper clippings report this wine was "so completely covered as to be almost excluded from the air, and some of the wine effervesced slightly on uncorking, and was of a very fair flavour".

The Chiquet family's vineyards in Aÿ, Dizy, Hautvillers and Avize provide the heart and soul of the Jacquesson style.

KRUG

AS FAR AS wine investors are concerned, Krug is the only blue-chip Champagne on the market: it never fails to attract bidders at auction.

Ever since the house was founded in 1843 by the Mainz-born Joseph Krug, the family has put quality first, regardless of popular taste or production costs. No better example exists of the extraordinary lengths Krug goes to than Krug Grande Cuvée, which is fermented in small oak *barriques*, receives 35 to 50 per cent of reserve wines from six to ten different vintages, and spends about five to seven years on its yeast. With the possible exception of the tiny house of Salon *(see p33)*, this sort of quality is not equalled by any other producer, although it could be if others were willing to sell tiny quantities at extremely high prices.

Not everyone appreciates the Krug style, but that merely makes Krug drinkers more elitist. The problem is that it is the world's most famous yet least-consumed Champagne, so it gets deified on the one hand, and vilified on the other.

Most regular wine drinkers have never drunk Krug, and even the wine trade and wine writers rarely have a chance to taste it. Happily I have tasted Krug countless times and can honestly say that I have detected a drop in quality just twice in over 20 years: namely Clos du Mesnil 1980, and a very green Grande Cuvée that was circulating in 1988, and in the twilight zone of Champagne that is as close to perfection as you can get.

Krug's house in Reims *(top)* was used as a hospital during World War I. Jeanne Krug was one of the last women to evacuate the heavily shelled city. The family has its own philosophy for making wine, such as using small oak *barriques (bottom)*.

Krug is served at some of the most fashionable social events in England. Guests at the annual bash of novelist and politician Jeffrey Archer are greeted with a plate of shepherd's pie and a glass of the bubbly.

LAURENT-PERRIER

Bernard de Nonancourt's Château de Louvois was built in 1680 by Louis XIV's Secretary of State for War, on the site of a ruined castle. It is said to be haunted.

THE LAURENT FAMILY were coopers in the village of Chigny-les-Roses, when in 1812 they tired of seeing other people's wines in their own casks, and set up a house in the remains of an abbey at Tours-sur-Marne.

Eugène Laurent married Mathilde Émile Perrier, but they died without heirs. Marie-Louise de Nonancourt, one of the Lanson family *(see A–Z listing)*, bought the firm in 1938, keeping the name Laurent-Perrier. It became really successful under her son Bernard and is now ranked in the top six houses. The Laurent-Perrier group also includes De Castellane, Delamotte, Lemoine, Joseph Perrier and Salon *(see p33)*.

The general house style leans towards light and elegant, but the vintage is fuller, while the prestige *cuvée* Grand Siècle can be almost sumptuous in its richness, attaining great complexity and finesse with age. Laurent-Perrier is also famous for its *rosé*, and it is one of the few houses to make it by the *saignée* method, whereby surplus liquid is drawn off from the fermenting vat. The non-vintage *rosé* with the salmon pink label is the best known, but the vintaged Grand Siècle Cuvée Alexandre is a class apart. Bernard de Nonancourt named it after his daughter, and no doubt his winemaker, Alain Terrier, did not dare produce anything but the best.

In the 1980s there was a trend for non-dosage (extremely dry) Champagnes, which died a quick death, to the relief of many. But few people knew that Laurent-Perrier had sold a "Grand Vin Sans Sucre" a century earlier. In 1893 the firm described it as: "The natural highest class Champagne of remarkably fine flavour, taste and bouquet, without any added sugar or alcohol, shipped by Laurent-Perrier & Co. A wine of marvellously clean taste, invigorating and exhilarating properties, superior to all Champagnes containing sugar."

MOËT & CHANDON

WHILE Napoleon's patronage laid the foundations for Moët's early success, what has sealed this firm's fortune is a marketing vision that keeps it several steps ahead of the rest of the pack.

That Moët & Chandon is Champagne's largest and best-known producer is due to ceaseless

Jean-Rémy (1758–1841), grandson of the founder, Claude Moët, had one great claim to fame: his friendship with Napoleon, which had begun when the young Bonaparte was still at military school in Brienne. The Emperor would stop off at his old friend's cellars on his way to war with Prussia.

marketing strategies. From making ephemera, such as this 1920s fan, to sponsoring international sporting events, Moët has made itself a household name in the wine-drinking world (though few people realise they should pronounce the "t" of Moët!).

After Jean-Rémy retired in 1832, control of the house went to his son-in-law Pierre Gabriel Chandon. Later, the firm started to associate itself with another historical figure, Dom Pérignon, the 17th-century Benedictine monk from the Abbey of Hautvillers, who is credited (wrongly) with inventing Champagne *(see p18)*. Moët had the foresight to purchase the Abbey back in 1823 and happily fostered the legend. The crowning glory of this association was the use of Dom Pérignon's name for the very first prestige *cuvée*. The name had already been registered by Mercier, but had never been used. Moët purchased it in 1930 and used it in 1936 to launch their 1921 vintage (a 15-year-old wine speaks volumes of the sort of maturity expected of Champagne in those days). So successful was it that Moët was able to return to Mercier in 1970 and purchase the entire company. Moët & Chandon is now part of the LVMH (Louis Vuitton-Moët Hennessy) group.

By 1900 Moët & Chandon's small army of workers was enjoying company rights and benefits, such as sick pay, that at the Millennium are still denied in many industries around the world.

POL ROGER

Churchill said of Champagne that "In victory we deserve it, in defeat we need it". His favourite Pol Roger vintages were 1928, 1934 and 1947. At the launch of the firm's Cuvée Sir Winston Churchill in 1984, Lady Soames said

of her father's passion for Pol Roger, "I saw him many times the better for it, but never the worse".

P OL ROGER was only 19 when he founded the house in 1849. His son Maurice took control in 1899 and built up the firm's reputation, particularly between the two wars in England, where it became the top-selling brand.

Maurice changed the family name from Roger to Pol-Roger. He was Mayor when the Germans occupied Épernay for seven days in September 1914, during which time he withstood German threats to shoot him and burn the town to the ground. His grateful fellow townsmen voted him Mayor at every subsequent opportunity.

The most famous admirer of Pol Roger was Winston Churchill, and he proved to be the firm's greatest promoter. In November 1944, just three months after the liberation of Paris, he met Odette Pol-Roger at a luncheon party and was so captivated by her wit, charm and intelligence that he named one of his racehorses Odette Pol-Roger (although it always ran simply as Pol-Roger). He even ordered his supply of Pol Roger to be bottled in imperial pints, so that he could drink it even when alone.

This family-owned house continues to produce the classic quality and style that Churchill adored. These Champagnes nearly always last longer and remain fresher than those of any other house.

Churchill once dubbed this château "the most famous address in Europe". It is still owned by the Pol-Roger family.

LOUIS ROEDERER

THIS IS THE MOST profitable house in Champagne, and as such should be an object lesson for those houses that count success in the number of bottles they sell rather than the money they make.

Jean-Claude Rouzaud knows not to exceed 2.5 million bottles a year, lest the brand's quality and exclusivity are compromised.

The Roederer house style is typified by a creamy-biscuity complexity, which is usually apparent in its non-vintage Brut Premier but can take two to three years after disgorgement to evolve in the vintage *cuvées*. The house is famous for its Cristal prestige *cuvée*, which sells like hot-cakes in the US, while its least-known gem is its Blanc de Blancs. Cristal was originally produced exclusively for the Russian Imperial Court, until the Revolution of 1917 left the firm in dire straits. Unlike today, Cristal was made very sweet to suit the palate of the tsars. The first commercial vintage of Cristal was in 1945.

Nowadays, the key to true success in Champagne, as owner Jean-Claude Rouzaud demonstrates, is an impeccable reputation to secure a premium price, enough vineyards to guarantee quality for a production that is sufficient to rake in the money, yet the self-discipline not to go beyond this turnover. Rouzaud does not, however, like to see his capital lie idle, which is why he took over Deutz *(see A–Z listing)*. That Roederer is not in hock to the bank, when most Champagne houses have overdraft facilities, also helps. Rouzaud's biggest financial worry has been deciding when the exchange rate might be best to transfer 15 million dollars from California to France. A problem others would love to have.

This diploma of the Tsar of Russia was issued to Louis Roederer in 1908.

*L*ouis Roederer also owns the lesser-known Théophile Roederer, which has always been a good value Champagne brand; Château Haut-Beauséjour in St-Estèphe; Roederer Estate in California; and the Port house of Ramos-Pinto in Spain.

A Methuselah of Cristal 2000 is opened by one of Roederer's winemakers.

RUINART

THIS HOUSE WAS founded by Nicolas Ruinart on 1 September 1729 and is the oldest house to trade in sparkling, rather than still, Champagne. Nicolas's uncle, Dom Thierry Ruinart, was a contemporary of Dom Pérignon *(see p18)*.

Ruinart actually started trading in linen goods, rewarding loyal customers with bottles of his Champagne, but the wine was so good that he had more orders for it than the linen, and gradually it took over his business. Nicholas's grandson Jean-Irénée was active in selling Ruinart Champagne to such famous customers as Joseph Bonaparte, King of Spain, Joachim Murat, King of Naples, and Talleyrand. He also sold wine to the Empress Josephine, but she refused to pay her bills after the divorce. Jean-Irénée was ennobled as Vicomte de Brimont by the decree of Louis XVIII, and, as Deputy of the Marne and Mayor of Épernay, he received the Empress Marie-Louise and, later, Charles X.

This high-quality Champagne has never been produced in large amounts. Even though sales quadrupled jsut before its purchase by Moët & Chandon in 1963, and have almost trebled since, Ruinart's turnover is still below two million bottles, which positions it between Bollinger and Louis Roederer in size. Ruinart is known for its stunning Dom Ruinart in both *blanc de blancs* and *rosé* styles, but its basic "R" de Ruinart range is all too often overlooked, and amazing value.

Rheims, the old-fashioned English spelling of Reims, is sometimes still used by Ruinart on its labels.

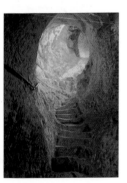

The firm's cellars *(left)*, a series of Gallo-Roman chalk pits, are officially classified as a historical monument. You must write for an appointment to visit Ruinart, but it is worth the effort to see the magnificent *crayères*.

SALON

Maxim's Restaurant in Paris chose Salon's vintage *blanc de blancs* – the only style of Champagne that Salon has ever produced – as its house wine in the 1920s.

SALON SHOT TO FAME during the 1920s and '30s, when it was the house wine at Maxim's in Paris, but after the death of its founder in 1943 it declined into obscurity.

Eugène-Aimé Salon (1867–1943) spent much of his boyhood assisting his brother-in-law Marcel Guillaume, the *chef de caves* of a small firm producing a single vineyard Champagne called Clos Tarin. Later he purchased five hectares of vines at Le Mesnil-sur-Oger where, in his spare time, he set about realising a youthful ambition: to create a perfectly balanced Champagne from a single growth and from just one grape variety, Chardonnay. He used only the best fruit and exclusively the *vin de cuvée* or first pressing, selling off the rest. Furthermore, he produced only vintage Champagne. Through such strict measures, Salon mastered *blanc de blancs* and appears to have been the first to exploit this style commercially, founding the House of Salon in 1921.

Salon was taken over by Besserat de Bellefon in 1963, but its existence remained low-key until Besserat was in turn purchased by Pernod-Ricard. Paul Bergeot, the new chairman, took an active interest in Salon, relaunching it as Salon Cuvée S in 1976. Salon was acquired by Laurent-Perrier in 1989, and run for eight years by Bertrand de Fleurian, who did all he could to assure the ascendancy of this minute, yet extraordinary Champagne house.

*P*aul Bergeot was so impatient to relaunch Salon in a new, fatter bottle, he ordered what remained of the 1971 and 1973 vintages to be decanted, mixed with a light *liqueur de tirage* and re-bottled. This caused a third fermentation and was illegal, but no one realised at the time. Thus it is possible to find "old" and "new" versions of these two vintages.

Salon, relaunched in 1976, is one of the few Champagnes that does not undergo malolactic.

VEUVE CLICQUOT PONSARDIN

The **Hôtel du Marc**, Veuve Clicquot's house in Reims, was bequeathed by Madame Clicquot to her business partner, Édouard Werlé.

THE NAME AND IMAGE of Veuve Clicquot Ponsardin are still identified with its illustrious 19th-century owner, the Grande Dame of Champagne, and quality is still surprisingly high for such a large operation.

*W*hat did Pushkin, Chekhov, Ian Fleming, Alfred Hitchcock, Jules Verne, the Bourbons, Romanovs, Hapsburgs, Bonapartes and every British monarch after Edward VII have in common? They all drank Veuve Clicquot.

It is true that a satisfying quality is simpler to achieve in a full-bodied and characterful wine like Clicquot's than it is in a lighter one (because the lighter the style, the easier it is to discern the slightest flaw). It is much harder, however, to achieve finesse in a full-bodied style. Nonetheless, what comes across about Clicquot is that it is not just big but also beautiful.

Widowed at the age of 27 ("Veuve" means widow), Nicole-Barbe Clicquot-Ponsardin had become the Grande Dame of Champagne by the time of her death, over 60 years later.

The house was founded in 1772 by Philippe Clicquot-Muiron, but it was his daughter-in-law, who took over in 1805, who really established Clicquot as one of the truly great houses. She was aided by a man named Bohne, who at first criticized the mousse of the Champagne, notably claiming "this is a terrible thing that gets up and goes to bed with me: toad's eyes!" Heeding this, she employed winemaker Antoine Müller. It was through the pair's enterprise that *remuage*, a process that draws out sediment, became widespread.

VILMART

Bottles of Champagne undergo *remuage (see p11)* while resting at a 45° angle in V-shaped *pupitres* in Vilmart's cellars at Rilly-la-Montagne.

VILMART DATES BACK to 1890, but its breakthrough as one of the great houses of Champagne was very recent – it was only in the late 1980s that the owner, René Champs, started to make a brilliant wine.

The Champs family have always owned Vilmart, and René's son Laurent now assists his father. The location of the firm's vineyards in Rilly-la-Montagne is responsible for the fullness and complexity of its Pinot-driven style. But Vilmart's quality is less due to the vineyards' location than their low yield, which means the wine is rich and balanced by abundant ripe acidity.

Oak is another major factor. Most of the wines are fermented in large wooden ovals more reminiscent of Alsace than Champagne, but the top *cuvées* are all fermented in small oak *barriques*. Indeed, Vilmart has spearheaded a mini-trend in Champagne to return to fermenting in new oak *barriques*. The policy has been implemented with too much zeal at times – the 1991 Coeur de Cuvée and the 1990 Cuvée du Nouveau Monde are too oaky.

The Champs have learned from such experiences, however, and had they not been aiming so ambitiously high in the first place, Vilmart's wines would not be as great as they are today.

René Champs is an exceptionally talented man who has designed and built his own home as well as creating a first-class Champagne. The stained-glass window showing the traditional way to crush Chardonnay grapes is just one of the building's many delightful flourishes.

This and other panes each took René Champs about 200 hours of patient and meticulous work to create.

FRANCE SPARKLING WINE REGIONS

Best Producers
1 Aigle (Domaine)
  Roquetaillade
2 Baumard
  Rochefort-sur-Loire
3 Bouvet
  St-Florent
4 Deliance
  Dracy-le-Fort
5 Die (Cave
  Cooperative)
  Die
6 Dopff Au Moulin
  Riquewihr
7 Gratien & Meyer
  Saumur
8 Picamelot
  Rully
9 Sieur d'Arques
  Limoux
10 Wolfberger
  Eguisheim

Sparkling wines have been produced in parts of France outside of the Champagne region since at least 1820. There is a tendency to overlook French fizz alternatives, yet, of the two billion bottles of bubbly produced globally each year, the rest of France accounts for about an eighth.

APPELLATIONS
There are 50 French sparkling wine appellations. Of these, Saumur, in the Loire, is the most important and Limoux the most intriguing, but the Burgundy and Alsace appellations are more rewarding for quality and range. From the tiny region of Die comes Clairette de Die Méthode Dioise Ancestrale, one of the world's finest sweet fizzes.

ALSACE
Crémant d'Alsace, the sparkling wine appellation of the Alsace region, is dominated by the producers Wolfberger, Laugel and Dopff Au Moulin. Dopff effectively established the sparkling wine business in Alsace in 1900. Early-picked Pinot Blanc is the most popular style. Pinot Gris makes a more superior *cuvée*, but the higher price of this grape has prevented its widespread use. Riesling is also sometimes used. *Crémant rosé* is the region's most underrated fizz: an elegant, pure Pinot Noir wine with soft strawberry or cherry fruit. Note that these wines seldom improve beyond 18 months.

Crémant d'Alsace was the first French sparkling wine appellation to adopt the term *crémant* in 1976.

Some producers in the wine villages of Alsace make use of the extra richness and higher acidity of Pinot Gris, but the grape costs 40 per cent more than Pinot Blanc.

SPARKLING WINE APPELLATIONS

Most of France's sparkling wines come from the north and central part of the country – southern regions such as Provence are not known for fizz, although Limoux is interesting. There are appellations for sparkling wine in regions such as Bordeaux, but the best ones are in Alsace, Burgundy and the Loire.

☐ Major sparkling wine appellations
☐ Champagne *(see pp16–21)*

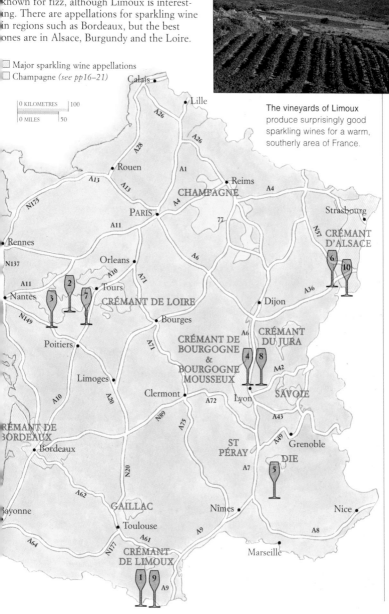

The vineyards of Limoux produce surprisingly good sparkling wines for a warm, southerly area of France.

Calais

Lille

0 KILOMETRES 100
0 MILES 50

A26

A28

A26

Rouen

A1

Reims

CHAMPAGNE

A4

A13

A13

Strasbourg

N175

PARIS

A4

77

N57

CRÉMANT
D'ALSACE

Rennes

A11

Orleans

A6

6

10

N137

A10

A71

A36

A11

2

Tours

Dijon

Nantes

3

7

CRÉMANT DE LOIRE

N149

Bourges

CRÉMANT DU JURA

Poitiers

A71

CRÉMANT DE
BOURGOGNE
&
BOURGOGNE
MOUSSEUX

A6

4

8

A42

Limoges

A10

A20

Clermont

A72

Lyon

SAVOIE

N89

A73

A43

RÉMANT DE
BORDEAUX

ST
PÉRAY

A49

Grenoble

Bordeaux

N20

DIE

5

A62

GAILLAC

Nîmes

A7

Nice

Bayonne

A64

Toulouse

A61

A9

A8

Marseille

N177

CRÉMANT DE
LIMOUX

1

9

A9

BURGUNDY (BOURGOGNE)

There are three major production centres of sparkling wine in Burgundy: the Yonne or Chablis district, the Region de Mercurey or Chalonnaise district, and the Mâconnais. The appellation for sparkling Burgundy is Crémant de Bourgogne, which has now superseded the term Bourgogne Mousseux for all but fizzy red Burgundy.

There are some very good Crémant de Bourgogne wines, but the average quality is not as good as it should be because too many producers rely on buying grapes that are sold off cheaply after being rejected for still Burgundy. Such wines suffer from excessive sulphur levels. The sparkling wine industry in Burgundy has yet to understand that grapes must be cultivated specifically for sparkling wines if serious progress is to be made across the board.

However, when Crémant de Bourgogne is good it is usually very good and almost always a bargain. The best are invariably made purely from Chardonnay grapes. Styles range from full and toasty (often from Yonne), through rich and smooth (usually from the Chalonnaise) to fresh, light and vivacious (mainly Mâconnais). *Crémant rosé* from Burgundy is not usually interesting, unless made from 100 per cent Pinot Noir grapes. Most good quality Crémant de Bourgogne is best consumed within three years of purchase.

The best producers include Caves de Bailly, André Bonhomme, Deliance, Picamelot, Roux Père, Simonnet-Febvre and Caves de Viré.

*T*he thrill of effervescing sweet wine was such a vogue in France in the 1870s that the production of another wine – sweet, still Sauternes – was under threat from the bubbly bandwagon. In *A History of Champagne* (1882), Henry Vizetelly records vast quantities of Sauternes being transported by rail to Messers Normandin Sparkling Sauternes Manufactory near Angoulême, where it was turned into award-winning sparkling wine.

Burgundy, one of France's oldest wine regions, vied with the Champagne region for royal favour in the 17th century, when both wines were still. Later, as sparkling Champagne took off, most Burgundy resolutely remained still.

LIMOUX

This small region near Carcassonne claims to have made sparkling wine more than 160 years before Dom Pérignon *(see p18)*, but this has not yet been proved. What is true, however, is that Limoux makes exceptionally fine sparkling wines for such a sunny southern location, and winemaking techniques have improved by leaps and bounds over the last decade. The style of Crémant de Limoux and Blanquette de Limoux has moved away from the distinctive character of fresh-cut grass to a much finer aroma. The best producers include Domaine de l'Aigle, Antech, Robert, Sieur d'Arques and Héritiers Valent.

Winemaking is shown in this detail of a medieval painting from the Loire.

THE LOIRE

If you are used to good-quality Champagne, you might find Loire sparklers difficult to appreciate. This is because the main grape used, Chenin Blanc, is too aromatic for a classic *brut* style.

Saumur is the largest French sparkling wine appellation outside of Champagne, and were it restricted to Chardonnay and Pinot Noir it would be the best. Saumur Mousseux *Rosé* can be made from several varieties, but many are pure Cabernet Franc, and the best are some of the most thrilling raspberry-flavoured fizzes in the world. Some pure Cabernet Sauvignon *rosés* can also be very good, in a smoother, less overt way.

Sparkling Vouvray and, particularly, Montlouis are hard to find, but can be delightfully fresh, smooth and elegant, especially when *pétillant*. Touraine and Crémant de Loire can be good value, but too many poorly made, cheap fizzes have debased those appellations. However, there are numerous good producers throughout the Loire – too many to name here.

The appellation Blanquette Méthode Ancestrale, from Limoux, is made by *méthode rurale*. There is no second fermentation, which most other sparkling wines undergo. Instead, the wine is bottled before the first alcoholic fermentation is over. In the 19th century, all Blanquette de Limoux was produced in this fashion.

Bouvet, one of the best Saumur producers, associates itself with the sport of motor-racing.

SPAIN

Cava has been widely exported since the mid-1970s and is now the world's second largest bottle-fermented sparkling wine appellation. The industry is dominated by two houses: Codorníu, the oldest, largest and most innovative firm, and Freixenet, which is probably the best known.

Freixenet (pronounced roughly "freh-zhe-net") delights in a fun-loving image for its Cava.

WHAT IS CAVA?

Cava is the generic name for bottle-fermented Spanish sparkling wine; it simply means "cellar". It was devised in 1970 for all Spanish sparkling wines made by the *méthode champenoise*, regardless of where in Spain they are made. However, when Spain joined the Common Market in 1986, Cava became subject to the EC wine regime, which is based on the integrity of origin. The EC made the Spanish choose between confining the Cava name to a geographical appellation or dropping it altogether.

This demand was cruelly ironic because at the same time the EC was failing to protect the integrity of the name "sherry" – the world's oldest geographical appellation. But Spain managed to extract its revenge simply by pinpointing every known Cava producer and drawing boundaries around individual municipalities. Cava was thus transformed overnight into a "geographical" appellation scattered across half of Spain. In practice, though, most Cava comes from the Penedès region and always has done, with the area around Sant Sadurní d'Anoia producing much of the best.

CAVA COUNTRY

Penedès is Cava Country, but there are pockets of Cava production in Rioja, Navarra, Aragón and elsewhere. Thus the Cava appellation is geographical only in a loose sense.

SPAIN
Madrid

☐ Main Cava districts

Codorníu began to win gold medals for its Cava in 1888.

The Art Nouveau winery of Codorníu was designed in the late 19th century by José Maria Puig i Cadafalch and declared a National Historical Monument in 1976.

Manresa
C411
N
E
D
È
S
Bérós
A7
5 Taregga
11
Igualada
Terrassa
Sabadell
A18
A7
A19
COSTERS DEL SEGRE
6 Masquefa
A7
A2
1 2 3 Sant Sadurní d'Anoia
A2
BARCELONA
Montblanc
240
Llobregat
4 Vilafranca del Penedès
NA
Valls
A7
El Vendrell
A16
Castelldefels
Reus
Vilanova
A7
Tarragona

RAIMAT
CHARDONNAY
Brut
Méthode Traditionnelle
75 cl
CAVA DE SPAIN
12% vol.

Most famous for its Cava, the Freixenet group also includes Gloria Ferrer in California, Castellblanch and the Champagne house of Henri Abelé.

Best Producers

1 Codorníu
Sant Sadurní d'Anoia
2 Freixenet
Sant Sadurní d'Anoia
3 Gramona
Sant Sadurní d'Anoia
4 Mascaró
Vilafranca del Penedès
5 Raimat
Costers del Segre
6 Raventós Rosell
Masquefa

THE CAVA INDUSTRY

It was long widely believed that the first Spanish sparkling wine was made in 1872 by José Raventós, the head of Codorníu (a winery dating back to the 16th century), but recent research has revealed that it was "invented" much earlier by Luis Justo Vilanueva, and first produced in 1862 by Antoni Gili. This date coincides with the migration of French Champagne producers to the region. However, there was no Cava industry as such until after World War II, and until 1974 production was so small that export statistics were not even recorded.

Gramona was founded in 1881 and started to produce Cava in 1921. The wines, shown here being corked, spend five years in darkness in Gramona's cellars before being sold.

A SOFT ACIDITY

Cava is an obvious choice for buyers who find the acidity of even the best Champagnes too aggressive. For many drinkers, however, Cava suffers from being too soft. Not that softness is itself a shortcoming, but in a sparkling wine if the acidity is softer than the mousse, the dosage (*see p177*) will be minimal, making the wine short and hollow, with no potential for long-term maturation. Cavas that best manage to overcome these drawbacks include Codorníu, Freixenet, Gramona, Mascaró, Raimat and Raventós Rosell.

THE GRAPES OF CAVA

The three grapes used most in Cava are Parellada, Macabéo and Xarello, which were all growing locally when Cava was first made. According to the Cava gospel, Macabéo, which is usually the base of a Cava *cuvée*, provides the fruit, Xarello the strength and body, and Parellada the softness and aroma. However, each of these grapes is problematic in sparkling wine.

The best Parellada grapes come from the highest vineyards, where they take longer to ripen.

*S*ome of the Spanish *méthode champenoise* wines started production after the Cava boundaries were drawn up and therefore do not come under the Cava appellation. They include Xamprada (León), Oriella (Madrid), Juan de Arges (Valencia), Montsec and Ibón (Zaragoza), El Grifo (Lanzarote) and Cantares and Mantolán (Ciudad Real).

Macabéo is not bad as a base wine, having good fruit and decent acidity, and Xarello is useful in small amounts, but Parellada has very little acidity and is prone to an internal rot that is hard to detect.

Freixenet's headquarters are at Sant Sadurní d'Anoia, the most important Cava town in Spain, in the heart of the Penedès region.

IN SEARCH OF BETTER GRAPES

Given that it took the Champenois 250 years to settle on the best three grapes for Champagne, the Cava industry has been surprisingly reluctant to try other varieties until recently. Codorníu realised the problem in the 1970s, and started cultivating Chardonnay as a quality booster. Freixenet opposed this, fearing that foreign grapes would erode Cava's Spanish character (a fair point), and this stance sparked a rift between the houses.

However, this author believes that Cava can be improved through using different native grapes, especially black grapes in a white wine blend. Codorníu was the first house to try this style, and even went to the extreme of making a *blanc de noirs*, albeit with the foreign Pinot Noir, producing the most sumptuous of Spanish sparkling wines. Freixenet is now experimenting with the native black Monastrell in a white *cuvée*, which is starting to show promise.

Trepat and Garnacha have been used in experiments with *rosé* Cava. The producer Mont Marcal has used Tempranillo, the greatest of all Catalan grapes, and Can Ràfols dels Caus has even tried Merlot, both of them for pink Cava.

The Spanish terms *Fermentación en Botella*, *Vino Espumoso Natural* and *Método Transfer* indicate the transfer method (*see p178*). Sparkling wines stating *Vino Gasificado* or *Granvás* are carbonated in the same way as lemonade or cola.

Manuel Raventós, who took over Codorníu in 1885, commissioned posters from Catalan artists such as Ramón Casas (1866–1932).

GERMANY

Sign for the town of Durbach in the southern wine region of Baden.

Sekt, the German fizz, is now the largest sparkling wine industry in the world. In some years, production tops half-a-billion bottles, which is almost twice that of Champagne. However, very little Sekt has so far been exported, making this wine practically unknown outside Germany.

A GERMAN TASTE
For most of the 20th century, the Germans have essentially made Sekt for themselves. The wine is off-dry with an unusual youthful tartness, which most sparkling wine drinkers elsewhere do not comprehend, let alone enjoy. Exports average barely eight per cent of total Sekt sales, and have dropped to as low as four per cent. Yet the Germans are drinking more and more Sekt, with per capita consumption currently running at five litres, compared with less than one litre in 1960.

EARLY ATTEMPTS
German salesmen were widely employed by the earliest Champagne houses *(see p18)*. The first attempts to make sparkling wine in Germany date back to 1783, but because the process took a while to master, the oldest commercial producer, Kessler, was not founded until 1826. Ten years later, when it became possible to measure the amount of sugar left in a wine after the first fermentation, the number of producers significantly increased.

Best Producers
1 Deis
  Mosel-Saar-Ruwer
2 Durbach
  Baden
3 Kassner-Simon
  Pfalz
4 Kirsten
  Mosel-Saar-Ruwer
5 Knyphausen
  Rheingau
6 Ratzenberger
  Mittelrhein
7 Ress
  Rheingau
8 Winzersekt
  Sprendlingen
  Rheinhessen
9 Wilhelmshof
  Pfalz
10 Zahringer
  Baden

Bremm is beautifully located by the Mosel in the Mosel-Saar-Ruwer wine region.

SOUTHERN WINE DISTRICTS

Most of Germany's QbA delimited wine districts (Qualitätswein bestimmter Anbaugebiete) are based around the Mosel and Rhein (Rhine) river valleys in the south of the country. Sparkling wine is produced in most of these regions.

☐ QbA regions

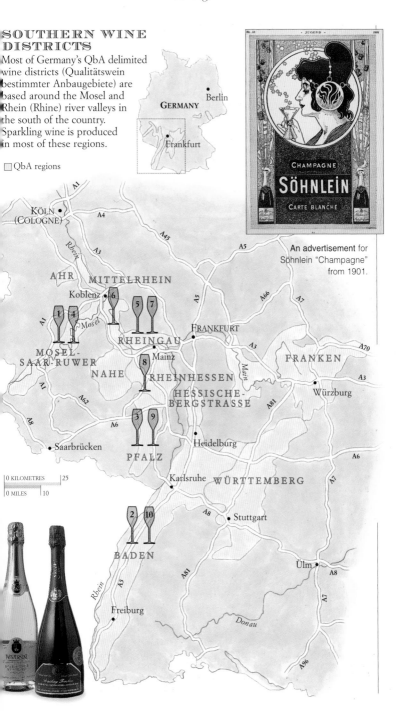

An advertisement for Söhnlein "Champagne" from 1901.

GERMANY

• Berlin

• Frankfurt

KÖLN •
(COLOGNE)

AHR   MITTELRHEIN

Koblenz • 6

1 4

Mosel

MOSEL-
SAAR-RUWER

RHEINGAU

5 7

FRANKFURT

• Mainz

8

NAHE   RHEINHESSEN

HESSISCHE-
BERGSTRASSE

FRANKEN

Main

Würzburg •

3 9

• Saarbrücken

• Heidelburg

PFALZ

0 KILOMETRES |25

0 MILES |10

• Karlsruhe   WÜRTTEMBERG

2 10

• Stuttgart

BADEN

Ülm •

Rhein

Freiburg •

Donau

"SEKT" IS BORN

A boom in sales came in the 1850s, coinciding with when the peculiar term "Sekt" is thought to have first been used. The classical German actor Ludwig Devrient was in the Berlin restaurant Lutter & Wegener one November night in 1852 and ordered a glass of

Wine presses in a museum owned by State Domaine Kloster Eberbach, in the Rheingau region.

sherry. In jocular mood, he quoted a line from Falstaff in Shakespeare's *Henry IV* to the waiter: "Give me a cup of sack, rogue. Is there no virtue extant?" Not understanding that Shakespeare's "*sack*" meant sherry (in turn deriving from the Spanish *sacar*: to take away or, less favourably, to loot – i.e. exported sherry!), the waiter brought him a glass of his usual German sparkling wine. After going the rounds of Berlin restaurants, it is thought that "*sack*" became "*sekt*" and by 1900 was widely used to refer to German sparkling wine (also known as "Champagne" at the time).

Many of the Sekt houses that sprang up from the 1850s soon disappeared, but by 1872 production had risen to four million bottles, and no fewer than 12 Sekt houses were of sufficient size and repute to exhibit at the World Exhibition in Vienna.

The sack (sherry) of Falstaff is thought to have given its name to Sekt, in a convoluted manner.

Deutscher Sekt means the wine is made only with German grapes.

Rheinhessen is one of the delimited QbA wine regions.

DEUTSCHER SEKT · S.A. RHEINHESSEN

WINZERSEKT

KLASSISCHE FLASCHENGÄRUNG

SPÄTBURGUNDER WEISSHERBST

EXTRA TROCKEN

ERZEUGERGEMEINSCHAFT WINZERSEKT GMBH · D-55576 SPRENDLINGEN

Klassische Flaschengärung is the equivalent of the French *méthode champenoise*.

*T*he language on German wine labels is notoriously complex, and Sekt is no exception. To start, Sekt is synonymous with Schaumwein. If either term is used without qualification, the wine is probably a blend of grapes from various countries. Deutscher Sekt tells you that only German grapes have been used, and Deutscher Sekt bA and Deutscher Qualitätsschaumwein both mean that the grapes come from a specified QbA region *(see p45)*.

Moving up the quality scale, Flaschengärung means bottle-fermented, while Flaschengärung nach dem traditionellen Verfahren, Klassische Flaschengärung and Traditionelle Flaschengärung are all equivalents of *méthode champenoise*. Handgerüttelt means hand-riddled, and Jahrgangsekt is vintage Sekt. At the opposite end of the scale, Perlwein is cheap, semi-sparkling wine made by carbonation.

ORDINARY SEKT

Although it started as a bottle-fermented product, virtually all Sekt is now produced by *cuve close* or tank method, and over 85 per cent is made from imported foreign base wines. Most Deutscher Sekt (sparkling wines made exclusively from German grapes) are also *cuve close* and thus little better than the ordinary Sekt of no fixed abode.

SEKT AT THE MILLENNIUM

Germany's Sekt industry underwent its largest expansion in very recent times, increasing from 200 producers in the late 1980s to more than 1,300 today. Although this represents a 650 per cent increase, total production has increased by just 25 per cent, and therein lies the clue to the radical change that has occurred at the very top of Sekt's quality scale. A small but growing band of quality-conscious estates has been crafting some truly excellent sparkling wines since the early 1990s. Most of these are small, go-ahead wine estates, rather than large, old-established Sekt factories.

The most obvious development is pure Riesling Sekt, whereas the most unlikely style evolving is pure Pinot Noir *rosé*, the quality of which should bowl over the most ardent Sekt-hater. It will not be long before specialist importers on major export markets pick up on this emerging new breed of Sekt. But although their numbers are increasing, the wines are by nature produced in such small quantities that they will remain in short supply.

Germans make merry with Sekt in this engraving from the journal *Jugend* in 1897.

*T*he best Sekt this author has ever tasted is the rare Wegeler-Deinhard Bernkasteler Doktor. Just two vintages were produced, 1978 and 1984, and, like Champagne, they were aged for three years, but in a special vat fitted with a paddle to stir the lees.

Riesling, the greatest German grape, is increasingly being used on its own to make Sekt.

ITALY

No other country has as many sparkling wine appellations as Italy, with its optional "may be *spumante*" (sparkling) clauses cluttering up more than 100 of the country's Denominazione di Origine Controllata (DOC) appellations. Yet Italy had no appellation specifically for classic *brut* sparkling wine until Franciacorta was elevated to the higher rung of Garantita (DOCG) in 1995.

Ferrari, one of the few firms to use *metodo classico*, says that it delights in "conserving the original excellence of the *spumante*."

A MYRIAD HALF-FORGOTTEN WINES

Italy's little-known sparkling wine appellations are nearly all *cuve close* (undergoing a second fermentation in a vat or tank rather than in a bottle). This is the best method for sweet sparkling wines like Asti, which has DOCG status and is Italy's best contribution to the sparkling wine world. However, *cuve close* is the worst possible method for classic *brut*. This is not because it is an intrinsically inferior method; in theory it should be able to produce *brut* sparkling wines that are every bit as good as those made in bottle, but in practice it does not. It is a bulk-production process and consequently attracts the cheapest base wines. To remedy the situation, the Italian Wine Law should require all *brut*-style DOC sparkling wines to be produced by the *metodo classico*, the Italian equivalent of *méthode champenoise*.

The view over Bellavista's aptly named vineyards in Lombardy.

NORTHERN ITALY

Sparkling wines are made throughout Italy, but the most interesting ones are made in the north. The best appellations are Asti, for sweet fizz, and Franciacorta, for *brut*-style sparkling wine.

Main wine regions

Sophia Loren drinking classic Italian *brut* at the Venice Biennale.

Best Producers

1 Banfi *Tuscany*
2 Bellavista *Franciacorta*
3 Berlucchi *Franciacorta*
4 Ca'del Bosco *Franciacorta*
5 Equipe Trentino *Trentino*
6 Ferrari *Trentino*
7 Gancia *Asti*

FRANCIACORTA

The Franciacorta appellation covers various producers with vineyards on the hills around Lake Iseo northeast of Milan. The wines are made from Chardonnay, Pinot Bianco (Pinot Blanc) and up to 15 per cent Pinot Nero (Pinot Noir). Franciacorta is still the only Italian classic *brut* appellation, the only wine that must be made by *metodo classico*.

Until September 1995, Franciacorta, like most Italian DOCs, was allowed to be still or sparkling. The still reds were in fact quite impressive. However, in a rare decision by the Italian Wine Law to put quality first, the most successful sparkling style was elevated to a super-appellation, its production restricted to the finest areas, its yield lowered, and its production method tightened up.

The *Festa dell'uva* (Grape Harvest Festival) celebrates the wines of Northeast Italy.

The still wines retain their DOC status, renamed Terre di Franciacorta. Only the sparkling wines may claim the Franciacorta DOCG. Were this uncompromising attitude applied to every appellation in the country, Italy would not only be the largest wine-producing nation in the world, as it is now, but also the greatest. With 25 months ageing on its lees (if the label says *riserva* then it is 37 months), Franciacorta has the potential for producing fine, biscuity, *brut* and lightly rich *rosé* sparkling wines. The best brands include Bellavista, Berlucchi, Ca'del Bosco and Faccoli.

The most ubiquitous cheap Italian sparkling wine is probably sparkling Lambrusco, which comes in pretty shades of red, white and *rosé*, but much the same effect for the tastebuds can be had by putting a shot of Vodka into a soft fizzy drink.

ASTI – THE SWEET FIZZ

The town of Asti in Piedmont gives its name to the local sweet fizz made by *cuve close*. The finest Asti are the greatest sweet sparkling wines in the world – a fraction of the price of *demi-sec* Champagne, but ten times the quality. It was formerly sold as Asti Spumante, but *spumante*, which like *mousseux* in France merely means "sparkling", had become tarnished by the cheap products that also use the term, thus was dropped when Asti was promoted to the status of DOCG in 1993.

Bernhard Langer is given a silver cup filled with Berlucchi after winning the Vincitore Open d'Italia golf competition in 1997.

Asti is made entirely from Moscato (Muscat) grapes, which come from 52 communes throughout the provinces of Asti, Cuneo and Alessandria. The *cuve close* method of production is well suited to an aromatic, sweet sparkling wine like Asti because its most vital quality – the freshness of its fruit – gains nothing from the extended yeast contact of *metodo classico*.

AC Milan shower themselves with the locally produced Ca'del Bosco after another historic win.

The best Asti has a fine mousse of tiny bubbles, a fresh, grapey aroma, a luscious sweetness and a light yet rich flowery-fruitiness that should be vivacious and mouth-watering. The greatest examples are reminiscent of peaches, and may even have a hint of orange. One of the most important compounds in the Moscato aroma is geraniol, which is wonderful when fresh, but with bottle-age assumes an unpleasantly pungent geranium odour. Asti is not, therefore, a wine that should be kept.

Good Asti producers include Araldica, Fontanafredda, Gancia, Giuseppe Contratto and Tosti. Gancia's special selection *cuvée*, Camilo Gancia, is a class apart.

OTHER FIZZ

After Franciacorta, Tuscany and Northeast Italy are the leading areas for *brut* sparkling wines, though grapes may be sourced from far and wide. Equipe Trentino, Ferrari (both Trentino) and Villa Banfi (Tuscany) are among the best. Of the rest, Prosecco sparkling wine is widely available but often boringly amylic. Soldati la Scola is based in Gavi and makes various sparkling wines.

*W*hile Asti is a pure Moscato sparkling wine, Moscato d'Asti is an entirely different product, which is not supposed to be fully sparkling, just *frizzantino* (very lightly sparkling), or even still. A Moscato d'Asti is easily recognized by its normal cork, which is fully inserted into the neck, with no mushroom top. If a wine simply states Moscato, it will be a cheap, fizzy blend of Moscato grapes from anywhere in Italy. Such wines rarely have the scintillating freshness of Asti, but even an average Moscato is preferable to an Asti that is too old.

Ferrari has recently diversified its image with a range of label designs inspired by Pop Art *(left)*.

THE UNITED STATES

Americans were among the first to appreciate Champagne, and have been producing their own fizz since the mid-19th century. The sparkling wines of California have come of age, but the states of Washington and Oregon possibly possess as much potential as their southern counterpart. A number of producers are the US arms of French Champagne and Spanish Cava houses.

CATAWBA AND OTHER EARLY SUCCESSES

The first American sparkling wine was made in 1842 by Nicholas Longworth, using Catawba grapes planted along the Ohio River near Cincinnati. Catawba is a native American variety with an exotic, cloying taste often described as "foxy".

The first of New York's fabled "champagnes" was made in 1865 by Joseph Masson. Five years later the Great Western Champagne brand was launched, which became the first American sparkling wine to win a gold medal in Europe. Great Western Champagnes claimed to be made in "Rheims, New York" – the winery's postroom was cunningly named Rheims for this purpose. This so-called champagne became the most important brand of sparkling wine in the country for a staggering 50 years, until Prohibition intervened.

Catawba, a native American grape used for both still and sparkling wines, was so famous by the 1850s that the *Illustrated London News* reported that "sparkling Catawba ... transcends the Champagne of France".

Hollywood, ever keen to associate itself with romance and the high life, strategically places a bottle of Mumm by Bogart and Bergman.

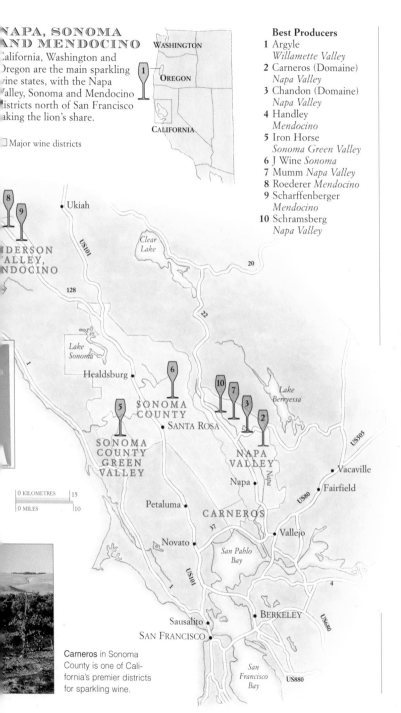

NAPA, SONOMA AND MENDOCINO

California, Washington and Oregon are the main sparkling wine states, with the Napa Valley, Sonoma and Mendocino districts north of San Francisco making the lion's share.

☐ Major wine districts

Best Producers

1 Argyle
  Willamette Valley
2 Carneros (Domaine)
  Napa Valley
3 Chandon (Domaine)
  Napa Valley
4 Handley
  Mendocino
5 Iron Horse
  Sonoma Green Valley
6 J Wine *Sonoma*
7 Mumm *Napa Valley*
8 Roederer *Mendocino*
9 Scharffenberger
  Mendocino
10 Schramsberg
  Napa Valley

Carneros in Sonoma County is one of California's premier districts for sparkling wine.

CALIFORNIA

The first California sparkling wine was made in about 1855 at the San Gabriel Winery, and various producers were making it by the turn of the century. The industry was going reasonably well until virtually all alcohol production came to a grinding halt in 1920. After Prohibition was repealed, in 1933, California's wine industry was painfully slow to re-establish itself. The only sparkling wine was cheap, bulk-produced and had little to commend it.

Schramsberg was eventually the first quality California fizz. A boost came in 1973, when Moët & Chandon chose the Napa Valley to locate its first premium quality winery outside Champagne. These

The end of Prohibition (1933) was celebrated in the most appropriate way.

companies converted a sporadic production into California's fully-fledged industry today. A flood of French-owned and Franco-American fizz ventures appeared on the scene in the 1980s, and the two giant Spanish Cava houses, Freixenet and Codorníu, also began to invest in California at this time. Technologically, California fizz came of age in the early 1990s, when the acidity became less "ribby" and more in tune with the fruit, giving the wines greater elegance than before. This was a surprising development because, as with many other New World sparkling wine areas, the climate is less than ideal. California producers are faced with two basic choices: pick ripe grapes that have too much sugar and insufficient acidity, or harvest earlier, when acidity levels are much higher and the grapes have an almost ideal sugar level. Unsurprisingly, most winemakers have chosen to harvest early, but they have to expend much effort overcoming numerous problems posed by grapes that have too much hard malic acid.

*T*he clergy, of all people, demanded wine during Prohibition (for sacramental use, of course!), so a few wineries had permits for still, but not sparkling, wine for this purpose. Not satisfied with this, the Pleasant Valley Wine Company filed a suit for the right to sell bubbly to the clergy. Amazingly, it was granted. The company enjoyed a monopoly on fizz for two years until several other wineries won the same right. The end of Prohibition closed this most peculiar chapter of American Law.

The best California sparkling wine areas already proven are Mendocino, Carneros and Sonoma, but perhaps the most exciting potential for the future is the Santa Maria Valley, which was first planted for sparkling wines in the 1960s and 1970s, long before its potential for silky Pinot Noir red wines was known.

An advert for Golden State Champagne claims that those who drink it will go "straight to heaven".

"MAD HARRY"

A few producers, like "Mad Harry" Osborne of Kristone, have decided to go the opposite route to other California sparkling winemakers and pick ripe grapes. Osborne challenges critics with such logic as "why harvest unripe grapes when they have no flavour and the wrong acidity, when you can harvest a larger crop of ripe grapes and simply add the acidity?" It is not as simple as that, of course, because they invariably contain too much sugar, but "Mad Harry" has managed to create a first-class product from truly ripe grapes (*see* Kristone in A–Z listing), and has helped New Zealanders to improve their bubbly too (*see p59*).

WASHINGTON AND OREGON

These two states are slow developers in the field of sparkling wine production, yet they may have as much potential as California. In Washington, Château Ste. Michelle's sparkling wines showed great promise in the late 1970s, but they have been disappointing ever since. Dr Michael Manz is currently making this state's most serious fizz at the Mountain Dome winery in Spokane.

Given Oregon's reputation for Pinot Noir, it is perhaps surprising that the Champenois have not shown more interest. Laurent-Perrier purchased land there in the early 1990s, but made nothing of it. Another French Champagne house, Bollinger, has a financial-only interest in Argyle, in the Red Hills of Dundee, which is owned by Croser in Australia and is Oregon's best fizz by far.

It is legal in the USA to sell domestically produced sparkling wine as "Champagne", because the term has been used to describe American sparkling wine from very early days, and is thus defined as a generic name under Federal Law. However, most serious sparkling wine producers have stopped using the term.

Pinot Noir is picked by a vineyard worker for sparkling wine in the Willamette Valley in Oregon.

AUSTRALIA AND NEW ZEALAND

The climate and geography of New Zealand are very suited to sparkling wine production – maybe more so than anywhere else outside the Champagne region. By contrast, a vast expanse of Outback makes Australia one of the least obvious countries associated with the industry. Yet Australia's winemaking history is almost as old as its colonial history, and there are many areas where excellent sparkling wine grapes can be grown.

FLYING WINEMAKERS AND OTHER FIRSTS

The concept of the flying winemaker was born in Australia: owing to the size of this continent and the staggered picking dates, consultant winemakers hop by plane from harvest to harvest. Domaine Chandon Australia (aka Green Point) has zoomed ahead of its sister company in California mainly because flying winemakers like Tony Jordan and his former partner Brian Croser have quickly identified numerous suitable vineyard areas.

Australia's first so-called Sparkling Burgundy was produced by Auldana in 1881. This was the precursor to the country's famed Sparkling Shiraz, a generic style that includes wines made from Cabernet Sauvignon, Merlot and other grapes.

Victoria's stunning mountain scenery is the setting for Great Western's vineyards.

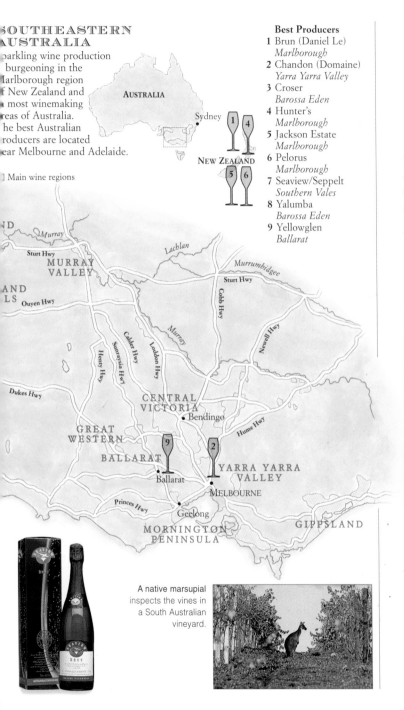

SOUTHEASTERN AUSTRALIA

Sparkling wine production is burgeoning in the Marlborough region of New Zealand and in most winemaking areas of Australia. The best Australian producers are located near Melbourne and Adelaide.

☐ Main wine regions

AUSTRALIA

Sydney •

NEW ZEALAND

Best Producers
1 Brun (Daniel Le)
   Marlborough
2 Chandon (Domaine)
   Yarra Yarra Valley
3 Croser
   Barossa Eden
4 Hunter's
   Marlborough
5 Jackson Estate
   Marlborough
6 Pelorus
   Marlborough
7 Seaview/Seppelt
   Southern Vales
8 Yalumba
   Barossa Eden
9 Yellowglen
   Ballarat

A native marsupial inspects the vines in a South Australian vineyard.

AUSTRALIAN PIONEERS

In 1843, about 50 years after the first vines were planted in Australia, the first Australian sparkling wine was made at Irrawing in the Hunter Valley, New South Wales, by James King, a free settler originally from Hertfordshire.

The Yalumba winery, founded 1849, lies in the verdant Barossa Valley.

From the late 1840s onwards, South Australian winemakers, including Patrick Auld (Auldana), Thomas Hardy, Samuel Smith (Yalumba) and Joseph Ernest Seppelt (B. Seppelt & Sons; Seppeltsfield; and Chateau Tanunda), experimented with fizz. Some of these firms are still going strong.

The main development in Australia's emerging sparkling wine industry came in the 1890s when Hans Irvine purchased Great Western. He installed specialist equipment for sparkling wine and employed Charles Pierlot, who had trained at Pommery. Irvine's friend Benno Seppelt bought the company in 1918, thus creating Seppelt Great Western, which soon dominated the Australian fizz industry.

A year later, a French cook, Edmund Mazure, left Auldana to make his own fizz under the La Perouse label. This was taken over by Wynns, and in 1975 became the famous Seaview label.

Minchinbury was the first Australian winery to utilize the transfer method, whereby wines are filtered from one bottle to another after fermenting. Many famous Australian sparkling wines are now produced in this manner rather than strictly by *méthode champenoise*, according to which the wine must be fermented in the same bottle in which it is sold.

*K*een to be acknowledged by Europe as a cultured people rather than a nation of outcasts, in 1855 James King and other Australian winemakers sent their wines sailing halfway round the world to the Paris Exposition. This was at a time before settlers had crossed Australia overland from south to north.

In their official report on the wines of New South Wales, the French judges magnanimously described the "bouquet, body and flavour" of King's sparkling wine as "equal to the finest champagnes". It was chosen as one of only two wines to be served to Napoleon III at the final banquet.

Benno Seppelt owned a wine merchant's in Broken Hill, New South Wales, before buying Great Western in 1918.

SPARKLING SHIRAZ

Sparkling Shiraz has an appealing deep purple-red colour and is made in two basic styles, oaky or fruity. When tasting a sparkling Shiraz for the first time, drinkers often complain that it tastes like a full-bodied red wine that just happens to be fizzy. However, for most people, the more sparkling Shiraz encountered, the more seriously the style will be taken. Sparkling Shiraz certainly has its place at the dinner table, particularly when partnering strong flavours such as Stilton sauce.

Pinot Noir grapes are harvested in the Brancott Valley of Marlborough for the New Zealand producer Cloudy Bay.

NEW ZEALAND'S LATE START

Sparkling wine did not became serious business in New Zealand until 1981, when industry giant Montana put its muscle behind the launch of Lindauer. One factor for such a late development was that few classic grape varieties had been planted. The collaboration between Montana and Champagne Deutz in 1988 then put this country on the bottle-fermented sparkling wine map. Also in that year, Cloudy Bay produced its first vintage of Pelorus under the wandering eye of "Mad Harry" Osborne *(see p55)*. It took one year longer for an expatriate Champenois, Daniel Le Brun, to demonstrate the Marlborough region's true potential for sparkling wine.

In the 1990s Domaine Chandon has produced a New Zealand *cuvée* using the facilities at Hunter's, which makes its own fizz too. This came of age in 1997 when Jane Hunter launched her compelling Mirru Mirru wine. Hopefully we will see more individually crafted sparkling wines from New Zealand, particularly Marlborough, which is capable of competing with Champagne in terms of quality as well as value.

Nautilus
CUVÉE MARLBOROUGH
NV BRUT
NEW ZEALAND SPARKLING WINE

*M*ate Selak made New Zealand's first fizz in 1956, although he was unable to market it at the time. The Chasselas grape he used did not work well, and, most alarmingly, many of the bottles exploded. It took 15 years of experimentation before Mate could launch his bubbly. He died in 1991, and there is now a top-of-the-range Blanc de Blancs named after him.

Jackson Estate takes its distinctive 50-ft high inflatable bottle and tent to wine festivals.

SOUTH AFRICA

The ostracism of South Africa during the final phase of its apartheid period stifled developments in the wine industry. However, in the 1990s, after the country finally embraced a multiracial democracy, world markets suddenly opened up, and a fledgling sparkling wine industry gained strength.

Nelson Mandela drinks to the post-apartheid era.

THE FINE FRUIT OF THE CAPE

Wineries are concentrated in the delimited Wine of Origin (WO) districts around Cape Town. Many produce sparkling wine, though at the moment much of it is merely fruity fizz. However, there is a fine structure and a certain delicacy of fruit about Cape grapes that promise an interesting future. The best sparkling wine brands include Graham Beck, Krone Borealis (made by Twee Jongegezellen), Jacques Bruère (made by Bon Courage), Pierre Jourdan (made by Clos Cabrière), Oak Village (made by Vinfruco) and Villiera.

FIRST PRODUCERS

The first South African sparkling wine was made by the Stellenbosch Farmers' Winery in 1929.

Called Grand Mousseux Vin Doux, it was simply a still wine that had been carbonated like a fizzy soft drink. Made from the grape varieties Chenin Blanc and Clairette Blanche, Grand Mousseux Vin Doux was the market leader for 60 years, and is still a big success today, particularly in neighbouring Namibia. Nederburg Première Cuvée, a *cuve close* fizz, was launched in 1945.

Main map
☐ Wine of Origin
(Wyn van Oorsprong) district

CAPE WINE DISTRICTS

Although wine is also made in areas between
Cape Town and Pretoria, sparkling wine
production is confined to the
main swathe of wine regions
within 100 miles of Cape
Town. Terminology on
labels is increasingly in
English, or both English
and Afrikaans. A few have
just the Afrikaans terms.

SOUTH AFRICA

LESOTHO

Cape Town

Best Houses

1 Beck
  Robertson
2 Bon Courage
  Robertson
3 Clos Cabrière *Paarl*
4 Oak Village
  Stellenbosch
5 Twee Jongegezellen
  Tulbagh
6 Villiera *Paarl*

| 0 KILOMETRES | 50 |
| 0 MILES | 25 |

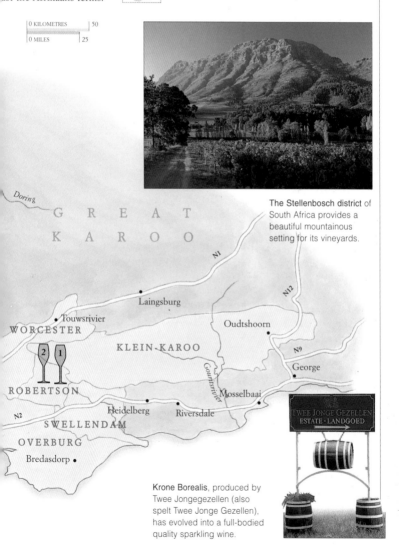

The Stellenbosch district of
South Africa provides a
beautiful mountainous
setting for its vineyards.

Doring

G R E A T

K A R O O

N1

N12

Laingsburg

• Touwsrivier

WORCESTER

Oudtshoorn •

N9

KLEIN-KAROO

George •

Gouritsrivier

ROBERTSON

N2

Heidelberg •   Riversdale •

Mosselbaai •

SWELLENDAM

OVERBURG

Bredasdorp •

TWEE JONGE GEZELLEN
ESTATE · LANDGOED

Krone Borealis, produced by
Twee Jongegezellen (also
spelt Twee Jonge Gezellen),
has evolved into a full-bodied
quality sparkling wine.

Labels of South African wines sometimes mention a night harvest – a wise way to overcome the problems of a hot climate on newly picked grapes. Grapes harvested at night tend to produce fresher, more aromatic and livelier wines compared with those picked in the day.

FIRST HINTS OF QUALITY

The first South African *méthode champenoise* sparkling wine was made by Frans Malan at Simonsig in 1971. This was called Kaapse Vonkel and was originally made primarily from Chenin Blanc, though it is now made from Pinot Noir and Chardonnay. Such was the grip of low-priced wines on the domestic market that this remained the only bottle-fermented South African wine until Boschendal produced its first *cuvée* in 1979.

The international sanctions imposed on South Africa during the 1980s affected wine exports. However, in 1984 Jeff Grier of Villiera entered into a fruitful ten-year partnership with the French winemaker Jean-Louis Denois, originally from Cumières (where his family still makes Champagne), but now one of the most innovative producers in Limoux. Since the end of apartheid, Champagne Mumm has collaborated with Nicky Krone of Twee Jongegezellen, producer of Krone Borealis, one of South Africa's best sparkling wines.

*M*ost South African fizz is made by the *cuve close* (tank) method, and some is even made by carbonation, including virtually all those described as *perlé* or *perlant*. For higher quality fizz, look out for the words Cap Classique on the label: this has been the South African term for *méthode champenoise* since 1992.

The Cabrière Estate in the Paarl region is run by Achim von Arnim, and it owns the phenomenally successful Pierre Jourdan brand of sparkling wine.

THE CAPE COMES OUT OF ISOLATION

In the early 1990s, as a new South Africa began quickly to re-establish and forge new export links with other countries, it became clear that the Cape's vineyards were in a rather poor state after lengthy international isolation, and the country's viticultural knowledge was lagging ten years behind the rest of the winemaking world. The Cape wine industry, however, was eager to learn, and started this process in the winery, where

TRADITION

fairly instantaneous results could be achieved simply through a stricter selection of grapes and also a massive investment in new wood and better winemaking equipment. More importantly, a visionary scheme called the Vineyard Improvement Programme (or VIP for short) was set up soon after sanctions were lifted, and this is being funded by a substantial proportion of South Africa's growing export income from wine.

THE FUTURE

Phase One of VIP, involving clonal selection and rootstock improvement, is underway. Nevertheless, a vine needs three years before it yields a crop, and five years before its true potential is known, thus the earliest effects of Phase One are only just now being seen.

Phase Two of the programme, which is to test the suitability of Phase One clones and rootstock in the different *terroirs* of the Cape, is a very long-term project.

Thus, although a number of South African still wines have already noticeably improved through the better winery practices, the real expected leap in quality will not start to show for a decade or so. Moreover, the learning curve for sparkling wine vinification is taking longer than for still wine. A winemaker can see the result of his or her work on a still wine within a year of its harvest, but it takes at least two years, often three, and sometimes even longer, before a serious-quality sparkling wine can be taken off its yeast lees.

The Cape winelands generally have a Mediterranean climate, which lends itself more to still wines than sparkling wines, but the idea that South Africa is simply too hot for sparkling wine is an exaggeration. Coastal regions have a much higher rainfall and are chilled by the icy Benguela current from Antarctica. In some places it is impossible for grapes to ripen properly, which is ideal for sparkling wine production, and the South African fizz industry will eventually gravitate towards such areas rather than rely on the inappropriate balance of early-harvested grapes.

Villiera has gone from strength to strength in the 1990s and now exports around the world as well as selling from the cellar door.

OTHER COUNTRIES

Fizz is made in several other countries. None has the sophistication of the industries already covered, but some have great potential.

Countries such as Switzerland and Austria produce surprisingly little fizz given the potential of their *terroirs*, but Nyetimber has recently emerged as the UK's first world-class sparkling wine. All East European countries produce some bubbly, usually the disappointingly bland product of the Russian Continuous system. Hopefully, the same miracle that transformed Portuguese table wines will soon occur with Portuguese sparkling wines.

Harvesting Chardonnay in Argentina, a country that is likely to produce much better fizz in the next millennium.

In Canada, the Brights-Cartier group has produced top-scoring wines and now has the pioneering Inniskillin winery. British Columbia's bottle-fermented Blue Mountain is world-class, and Colio's *cuve close* Chardonnay Lily is worth trying.

South American potential is barely tapped. In Chile, Mumm's new fizz shows promise, and Miguel Torres has recently returned to form. Moët & Chandon makes a reasonable quality fizz in Brazil, but less so in Argentina, although huge new plantations of Chardonnay and a change of emphasis from *cuve close* to *méthode champenoise* will transform this firm's South American sparkling wines over the next decade. On the other side of the world, the best Asian fizz, Omar Khayyam, has been made in the Sahyadri Mountains, east of Bombay, for more than ten years.

Good bottle-fermented fizz includes Nyetimber and Omar Khayyam, from England and India respectively.

Cricova in Moldova is the most intriguing sparkling wine facility in Eastern Europe. An underground "city" with 40 miles (65 km) of roads and enough cellars to store a billion bottles, it was clearly built for more than just the two million bottles of fizz that it now produces. Who might have installed such opulent reception halls and marble-clad men's rooms, and a series of steel doors that could withstand a nuclear blast? Who but the now defunct Politburo!

A–Z Listing

An alphabetical listing of recommended producers and over 900 individual Champagnes and sparkling wines.

INTRODUCTION TO THE A–Z LISTING

SCOPE OF THE LISTING

Almost all the wines in the listing are recommended by the author; those without a score are in an unusual developmental phase and cannot be fully judged yet, but are likely to be good when ready. Most wines were tasted blind (with labels covered) at a professionally equipped facility, where producers submit samples. Champagnes had to score 80 or above (on a scale of 100) to qualify for this guide; other sparkling wines had to score 70 or above. Producers without any qualifying wines are not included, no matter how good their range has been in the past. The inclusion of a particular *cuvée* in the listing is not a guarantee of its availability in the UK: for a guide of where to buy popular brands in the UK see pages 180–91.

HOW THE SPARKLING WINES ARE JUDGED

Three elements are essential in sparkling wine: bubbles, acidity and fruit.

Bubbles are the most obvious factor affecting quality. The strength of mousse can range from very soft at the lowest level of effervescence, to firm at the highest. Most people prefer a softer mousse, but the longer you intend to cellar a wine, the firmer the mousse should be. The smaller the bubbles, the smoother the mousse feels, whether it is soft or firm, and this smoothness enhances the perception of creaminess on the finish. The only way to assess the quality of a mousse is in the mouth, not by looking at it in the glass.

Acidity maximizes finesse, gives persistence to the flavour and is vital for graceful ageing. Without sufficient acidity, a sparkling wine will either be heavy if full-bodied, or hollow and short if light-bodied. The right balance of acidity can give even the most light-bodied sparkling wine a long and persistent flavour. Without acidity the toasty and biscuity bottle-aromas that develop will lack finesse, while other finer, more complex aromas will be restricted.

Fruit is essential, although in lighter, more elegant styles this can start out as a floweriness, and may develop fruitiness only after "ripening" in bottle. Simple fruity fizz is fine if it is cheap.

The tell-tale amylic aroma of peardrops or banana has a banal effect. Dominant buttery or butterscotch aromas indicate an overuse of malolactic *(see p11)*. A tiny whiff of free sulphur may eventually evolve into a pleasant toastiness, but leave an overtly sulphurous wine alone.

HOW THE WINES ARE DESCRIBED

The glossary *(see pp176–8)* includes tasting terms such as amylic, toasty and oxidative. Besides these, I may also give two or three fruits or flowers to describe a sparkling wine. Besides aroma and taste, I tend to focus on the balance and finesse, the acidity and the basic style of the wine; for example, light-bodied or full, fruit-driven or complex. When it is obvious to me, I say how a wine will develop over the next few years.

FINDINGS FOR THE MILLENNIUM EDITION

With wines recommended for more than 140 producers, Champagne trounced all opposition, and so it should, having a *terroir* uniquely suited to classic *brut*-style sparkling wine. I was saddened that only a third of the wines from Alsace, Burgundy, Bordeaux and the Loire qualified. The success rate for Cava – 23 per cent – was about as expected, but I was startled by Germany's 20 per cent

success rate as I had expected it to be much lower! Some small estates have started producing quality Sekt not just from Riesling, as might be expected, but also from Pinot Noir in an elegant *rosé* style. I was also amazed by the number of Italian sparkling wines to qualify for this first edition – the Franciacorta appellation turns out to be of exceptional high quality.

As for the New World, quality is high and the rate of improvement is staggering. South Africa has come up so quickly that its sparkling wines now vie with those from California. There is still a lot of fruity fizz about, particularly in Australia, but at least these wines are clean and cheap.

How the Listing Works

KEY

- ☐ Real Champagne
- ☐ Sparkling wine
- 🟢 Tom Stevenson's overall score
- ⊖ Overall score impossible to judge yet
- ❗ Ready to drink now until year indicated
- ▬ Preferably store until years indicated

PRICE BANDS

The publishers have provided price bands in the A–Z listing because it is impossible to indicate exact prices for different outlets in numerous markets for an international publication.
- ⓕ Up to £9.99
- ⓕⓕ £10–£19.99
- ⓕⓕⓕ £20–£34.99
- ⓕⓕⓕⓕ £35 and above

PRICE IN FRENCH FRANCS

🍾 The price in French Francs is for vineyard/cellar door sales, and given only for real Champagne, where available from the producer.

HOW TO FIND A WINE

Producer names are simplified and indexed according to wine cataloguing conventions. This is usually by family name: for instance, you will find Graham Beck under "B" for Beck, not "G". Cross-references are provided where brand names differ significantly from producer names, or where confusion may arise. Contact details are given for real Champagne producers (dark-tinted boxes). Below each producer box are the full names of recommended *cuvées*. Note that some producers named elsewhere in this book do not appear in the A–Z listing, as none of their wines has qualified this year.

THE 100-POINT SCORING SYSTEM

The 100-point scale, by which a critic makes an overall judgement on a wine, is now globally recognised.

- **70** The point at which any sparkling wine other than Champagne becomes interesting.
- **75** A reasonably good score for a sparkling wine.
- **80** Because Champagne has such advantages over sparkling wines produced in less favourable *terroirs*, this is the level at which it qualifies for inclusion in this guide.
- **85** If a non-Champagne sparkling wine scores this high, it is of exceptional quality.
- **90** A top-quality vintage or prestige *cuvée* Champagne, which will probably need three to five years' extra cellarage to achieve its full potential.
- **95** Only the greatest Champagnes score this high or above. Most could be left forgotten in a cellar for ten years.

ABBATIALE

See Locret-Lachaud

ADAM

Alsace, France

An underrated producer of varietal wines and a passable *crémant*.

**JEAN-BAPTISTE ADAM NV'
CRÉMANT D'ALSACE,
EXTRA BRUT**

Light and elegant, yet really quite rich on the nose and finely structured.
❚ On purchase ⓔ

**JEAN-BAPTISTE ADAM NV
CRÉMANT D'ALSACE BRUT**

Although this has the straw-like character that detracts from so many sparkling wines, not just Crémant d'Alsace, there is a good mouthful of fruit on the palate, making it more satisfying than most.
❚ On purchase ⓔ

ADAM-GARNOTEL

15 rue de Chigny, 51500 Rilly-la-Montagne
☎ (326) 03.40.22 ℻ (326) 03.44.47

A small house with some important vineyards, but only the non-vintage *cuvée* survived the test.

**ADAM-GARNOTEL NV BRUT
EXTRA QUALITY, 1ᴱᴿ CRU**

Deeper and richer than most non-vintage *cuvées*, with some sprightly fruitiness on the finish.
❚ On purchase ⓔⓔ ♚79F

AGRAPART

57 avenue Jean-Jaurès 51190 Avize
☎ (326) 57.51.38 ℻ (326) 57.05.06

The Demoiselles Rosé and vintage Blanc de Blancs are reliable, but several other *cuvées* failed the test.

**AGRAPART & FILS NV CUVÉE DES
DEMOISELLES BRUT ROSÉ**

Pale peach colour. Extremely fruity, but developing complexity and richness.
❚ Now–2000 ⓔⓔ ♚93F

**AGRAPART & FILS 1989
L'AVIZOISE, BLANC DE BLANCS
BRUT, GRAND CRU**

The malolactic is too creamy-buttery for a classic *brut* style. This robs it of finesse, but it is full of smoky-creamy-rich flavour.
❚ Now–1999 ⓔⓔⓔ ♚135F

**AGRAPART & FILS 1988
MILLÉSIME BLANC DE BLANCS
BRUT, GRAND CRU** 89

Mellow creamy-biscuity aroma now, but promises to go toasty as well.
❚ Now–2000 ⓔⓔⓔ ♚93F

ALBERT

See Baron Albert

ALDRIDGE

See Cranswick

ALIGUER

See Torelló

ALLIAS

Loire, France

**VOUVRAY BRUT, ALLIAS
PÈRE ET FILS**

This soft and easy-drinking fizz scrapes in as one of the Loire's top ten per cent.
❚ On purchase ⓔ

ANDERSON VINEYARD

Napa, California, USA

S. ANDERSON 1993 BRUT

Zesty, crisp-sherbetty aromas, with a long, fine and delicate fruit, and a very fresh finish that is developing some complexity.
❚ Now–2000 ££

S. ANDERSON 1993 ROSÉ

Salmon-coloured, with big aromas and real flavours. Serious, complex, long, deep and beautifully balanced.
❚ Now–1999 ££

ANGAS
See Yalumba

ANTEO
Oltrepò Pavese, Italy
Specializes in Pinot Noir fizz, using "almost organic" methods.

ANTEO BRUT, METODO CLASSICO NV PINOT NERO, OLTREPÒ PAVESE

Streets ahead of Anteo's non-vintage Anteo Brut, which is rather mean and made by the *metodo martinotti (cuve close)*. This is a more mature and more serious *cuvée* with some malo-complexity on the nose and creamy fruit on the palate.
❚ On purchase £

ANTEO ROSÉ BRUT NV PINOT NERO, OLTREPÒ PAVESE

Pale in colour, with very little on the nose, but quite an intense, firm-style flavour.
❚ On purchase £

ANTEO SELEZIONE DEL GOURMET NV PINOT NERO, OLTREPÒ PAVESE BRUT

Hinting of almonds on the nose, with rich, almost unctuous fruit. Good structure and intensity of flavour.
❚ On purchase £

ANTICA CANTINA FRATTA
Franciacorta, Italy

ANTICA CANTINA FRATTA NV BRUT, FRANCIACORTA

Very creamy nose, with succulent fruit on the palate and a pungent strawberry aftertaste. Too sweet for a true *brut,* otherwise it would have scored higher, but those who drink *sec* in preference to *brut* should add on a few points.
❚ On purchase £

ANTINORI
Tuscany, Italy
Large, aristocratic Chianti producer.

MARCHESE ANTINORI NV NATURE BRUT

Fresh, light and elegant.
❚ On purchase £

MARCHESE ANTINORI 1993 BRUT MILLESIMATO

Lemony aroma following onto the palate, with good balancing acidity on the finish.
❚ On purchase ££

ANTOINE
See Marne et Champagne

(D')ARCO
Trentino, Italy

CONTI D'ARCO 1993 RISERVA NICOLÒ D'ARCO BRUT, TRENTO

Lively fruit acidity gives this a heightened freshness and a tingly, crisp finish.
❚ Now–1999 ££

(D')ARENBERG
South Australia, Australia
D'Arenberg has made sparkling Shiraz on and off since the 1960s but now mostly concentrates on the Chambourcin grape, a hybrid of uncertain parentage.

D'ARENBERG 1996 THE PEPPERMINT PADDOCK CHAMBOURCIN

Fresh, light and creamy, with a simple but enjoyable raspberry flavour. Not one of the greatest wines in this book, but one of the most interesting, this red fizz is D'Arenberg's first vintage of Chambourcin. It is not allowed into EU countries because it is made from hybrid grapes.
❦ On purchase ⓔ

ARNOULD

28 rue de Mailly 51360 Verzenay
☎ (326) 49.40.06 ℻ (326) 49.44.61

Michel Arnould specializes in pure Grand Cru Champagne from Verzenay.

MICHEL ARNOULD & FILS NV BRUT, GRAND CRU **86**

Has a rich, biscuity complexity, yet still with the potential to develop.
❦ Now–1999 ⓓⓔ 🍷72F

MICHEL ARNOULD & FILS NV RÉSERVE BRUT, GRAND CRU **88**

Richer and softer than the above, with vanilla-finesse and a lovely cushiony mousse.
❦ Now–2002 ⓓⓔ 🍷76F

MICHEL ARNOULD & FILS NV CUVÉE AN 2000 BRUT GRAND CRU **90**

Slow-building complexity of high finesse.
❦ Now–2005 ⓓⓔⓕ 🍷121F

ARQUES

See Sieur d'Arques

ARUNDA

Alto Adige, Italy

ARUNDA RISERVA NV EXTRA BRUT, SÜDTIROLER SEKT – ALTO ADIGE

Tangy fruit, solid and fat, but good acidity.
❦ On purchase ⓔ

ASCOT

See Thames Valley Vineyard

AURIGNY

See Devaux

BACKSBERG

Paarl, South Africa

Made famous by the late Sydney Back, who was three times Champion Estate Winemaker, Backsberg continues to produce some of South Africa's most consistent and classy wines.

BACKSBERG BRUT 1991 CAP CLASSIQUE

The nose is still developing, but the quality of the light yet rich, creamy-biscuity fruit was evident on the palate.
❦ On purchase ⓔ

BALARD

Bordeaux, France

This brand is used by the Union Vignerons d'Aquitaine cooperative.

BALARD NV CRÉMANT DE BORDEAUX

Crisp, refreshing fizz.
❦ On purchase ⓔ

BANFI

Tuscany, Italy

Immaculate vineyards and a high-tech winery help to make Villa Banfi one of Italy's more consistent producers of sparkling wine.

BANFI BRUT PINOT NV VINO SPUMANTE

A fresh, light and fruity, everyday fizz.
❦ On purchase ⓔ

BANFI 1992 BRUT, TALENTO

Fat but very fresh aroma, with soft vanilla fruit lifted by the fizz on the finish.
❚ On purchase ⓔ

ACQUI BRACHETTO D'ACQUI 1997 BANFI, VINO SPUMANTE DOLCE

Big, blowsy Pinot aromas followed by soft, sweet strawberry fruit on the palate.
❚ On purchase ⓔ

BANFI ASTI NV VINO SPUMANTE DOLCE

Sweeter than most Asti, with very fresh, light and fluffy fruit.
❚ On purchase ⓔ

TENER SAUVIGNON-CHARDONNAY, BANFI NV VINO SPUMANTE BRUT

A fresh, crisp wine with a light balance, this is dominated by Sauvignon and has little Chardonnay input.
❚ On purchase ⓔ

BARANCOURT

Place Tritant, 51150 Bouzy
☎ (326) 53.33.40 ⠇FAX (326) 53.33.41

Once an interesting range, especially of mono-*cru* Champagnes, but now mostly disappointing, with a dull marzipan flavour. Devotees of the mono-*cru* should now try Delbeck or Brice.

BARANCOURT 1989 BRUT

Very elegant for such a full-bodied style.
❚ Now–2000 ⓔⓔⓔ

BARNAUT

13 rue Pasteur, 51150 Bouzy
☎ (326) 57.01.54 ⠇FAX (326) 57.09.97

The grapes here are harvested later than the norm for Bouzy and always by a succession of sweeps to pick out only the ripest and healthiest grapes.

E. BARNAUT NV SELECTION, EXTRA BRUT, GRAND CRU

A serious old classic of some complexity.
❚ On purchase ⓔⓔ ❦91F

E. BARNAUT NV CUVÉE DOUCEUR, SEC, GRAND CRU

Biscuity with sweetish fruit.
❚ Now–1999 ⓔⓔ ❦85F

BARON ALBERT

Grand Porteron, 02310 Charly-sur-Marne
☎ (23) 82.02.65 ⠇FAX (23) 82.02.44

Claude Baron is an enthusiastic producer who is restricted by the limitation of his vineyards on the western outskirts of Champagne.

BARON ALBERT NV BRUT ROSÉ

Pale peach colour and a fresh amylic aroma. Acidity is very good.
❚ On purchase ⓔⓔ ❦71F

BARON ALBERT NV CARTE D'OR BRUT

Still lacks finesse, but has improved and picks up with food.
❚ On purchase ⓔⓔ ❦74F

BARON ALBERT 1991 BRUT

Firm, young and lean, but will it develop any finesse?
 Wait and see ⓔⓔⓔ ❦79F

BARON B.

See Chandon

BARON DE HOEN

Alsace, France

BARON DE HOEN NV CRÉMANT D'ALSACE BRUT

Lovely ripe fruit and a succulent finish that is not too *brut*. I much preferred this to Baron de Hoen's Blanc de Noirs.
❚ On purchase ⓔ

BARON ZU KNYPHAUSEN

See Knyphausen

BARRAMUNDI

See Cranswick

BAUCHET

Rue de la Crayère 51150 Bisseuil
☎ (326) 58.92.12 ℻ (326) 58.94.74

One *cuvée* qualifies, but there is a general lack of finesse on the nose.

SAINT NICAISE NV BRUT ROSÉ 1ᴱᴿ CRU, BAUCHET

This apricot-gold coloured Champagne just scrapes in out of curiosity: like an old Burgundy with fizz. Definitely dry, but not at all dried out, this *cuvée* has a long flavour, some aged complexity, and is definitely a food wine.
🍷 On purchase ⓔⓔ ⬦84F

BAUMARD

Loire, France
Before his retirement Jean Baumard was the Loire's greatest exponent of Chenin Blanc. He was a rare, gifted winemaker who could make this grape sing, even in the driest still wines, and his son Florent shares some of his father's magical abilities.

BAUMARD 1993 CRÉMANT DE LOIRE

Mature, fresh and clean, although there is no real substance for a top score.
🍷 On purchase ⓔ

BAUMARD, CARTE CORAIL NV CRÉMANT DE LOIRE BRUT

Nice dry, easy-going and accessible, with a perfumed aftertaste. The deliciously tangy fruit is as clean as a whistle, making this *rosé* a delight to drink.
🍷 On purchase ⓔ

BAUMARD, CARTE TURQUOISE NV CRÉMANT DE LOIRE BRUT 🄱🄽

Drier than the Carte Corail, with less perfume and a more food-wine structure.
🍷 On purchase ⓔ

BAUR

Alsace, France
This Eguisheim grower consistently produces elegant Riesling Gewurztraminer from Grand Cru Eichberg, and is becoming adept at crémant.

CHARLES BAUR 1994 CRÉMANT D'ALSACE BRUT

With such lovely intensity of fruit in this Crémant d'Alsace, you can taste the quality of the grapes used. They have obviously been selected, rather than utilizing underripe leftovers.
🍷 Now–1999 ⓔⓔ

BEAUMET

3 rue Malakoff, 51207 Épernay
☎ (326) 59.50.10 ℻ (326) 54.78.52

Flagship brand from the same stable as Jeanmaire and Oudinot.

BEAUMET 1990 CUVÉE MALAKOFF, BLANC DE BLANCS BRUT

Cuvée Malakoff has a soft and easy style that does surprisingly well with food. Fine cushiony mousse.
🍷 On purchase ⓔⓔⓔ

BEAUMONT DES CRAYÈRES

64 rue de la Liberté,
Mardeuil 51318 Épernay
☎ (326) 55.29.40 ℻ (326) 54.26.30

This Champagne cooperative often outperforms the classification of its *crus* (villages) because all its members have tiny vineyards they attend to like gardens at weekends.

BEAUMONT DES CRAYÈRES NV CUVÉE DE PRESTIGE BRUT

The non-vintage Cuvée de Prestige is fatter and has more ripeness and finesse than the basic Cuvée de Réserve made by Beaumont des Crayères.
🍷 On purchase ⓔⓔ ⬦99F

BEAUMONT DES CRAYÈRES NV CUVÉE DE RÉSERVE BRUT

Classic, lean and biscuity.
❚ On purchase ⓔⓔ ☜85F

NOSTALGIE 1990 BRUT, BEAUMONT DES CRAYÈRES

Rich and complex, yet packed with fruit.
❚ Now–2000 ⓔⓔⓔ ☜160F

NOSTALGIE 1988 BEAUMONT DES CRAYÈRES, BRUT

Acidity is the defining factor of this
beautifully mellow, toasty rich *cuvée*.
It will just get better and better and will
never go blowzy.
❚ Now–2002 ⓔⓔⓔ

CHARLES LEPRINCE NV GRANDE RESERVE BRUT

Has some maturity already, but is only
just beginning to build biscuit richness
and has the structure for further development. A Pinot-dominated food-wine style.
❚ Now–2000 ⓔ

JACQUES LORENT NV CUVÉE TRADITION BRUT

This will develop a nice biscuity richness
after a year or two in bottle.
➤ 1999–2000 ⓔ

BEAUREGARD

See Château de Beauregard

BECK

Robertson, South Africa
Graham Beck produces budget fizz
under the Mandeba label and
reserves his eponymous brand for
more serious Cap Classique with a
very stylish presentation.

GRAHAM BECK BRUT NV CAP CLASSIQUE 🔢

Slightly amylic, but the fruit on the palate
is very elegant, fresh and fluffy. With a
year in bottle this *cuvée* usually goes
zesty-toasty.
❚ Now–1999 ⓔ

GRAHAM BECK CHARDONNAY SUR LIE NV CAP CLASSIQUE

Again slightly amylic, but again the fruit
on the palate is very elegant, only this
time it has a more sherbetty feel.
❚ Now–1999 ⓔ

GRAHAM BECK BLANC DE BLANCS BRUT 1993 CAP CLASSIQUE 🔢

Nothing amylic here, so unless Beck puts
his non-vintage *cuvées* through a colder
first fermentation, the peardrop character
will work its way out of these wines given
sufficient time. This has lovely lemony-
toasty fruit, like a good mature
Chardonnay, but with bubbles.
❚ Now–2000 ⓔⓔ

GRAHAM BECK BLANC DE BLANCS BRUT 1992 CAP CLASSIQUE 🔢

There's no getting away from the New
World origins of this citrussy-creamy-
oaky humdinger.
❚ Now–1999 ⓔⓔ

BELLAFON

See Besserat de Bellafon

BELLAVISTA

Tuscany, Italy
For many years this has been one of
my favourite Italian sparkling wine
producers, and Bellavista's 1993
Gran Cuvée Brut Rosé is the greatest
dry Italian fizz I have ever tasted.

BELLAVISTA NV CUVÉE BRUT, FRANCIACORTA

A restrained nose with delicately ripe
fruit on the palate and a fine, cushiony
mousse. An elegant wine of some finesse.
❚ On purchase ⓔ

BELLAVISTA 1993 GRAN CUVÉE BRUT ROSÉ, FRANCIACORTA

A lovely golden-sunset colour here, with
delicious cushiony fruit supported by
lively acidity. A mini classic!
❚ Now–2001 ⓔⓔ

BELLAVISTA 1992 GRAN CUVÉE BRUT, FRANCIACORTA

Biscuity aroma, with a rich fruit flavour and good acidity for more development.
❚ Now–2000

BELL DUC

See CIGRAVI

BELLEI

Emilia Romagna, Italy

FRANCESCO BELLEI 1994 BOMPORTO, EXTRA CUVÉE BRUT

The mousse has a noticeably low pressure, but very fine bubbles. There is something missing from the mid-palate, but the wine has nice vanilla finesse and complexity on the finish.
❚ On purchase

FRANCESCO BELLEI NV LAMBRUSCO DI SORBARA ⓗ

If only all Lambrusco were of this quality, it would not have the bad name that it does. Deep, dry, intense, seriously flavoured sour-cherry fruit.
❚ On purchase ⓔ

BENNWIHR

Alsace, France

BENNWIHR RIESLING NV CRÉMANT D'ALSACE ⑦

I much preferred this to Bennwihr's other two *brut cuvées*, even though the structure is not quite right and this particular *cuvée* needs a slightly higher dosage.
❚ On purchase ⓔ

BERGKELDER

Stellenbosch, South Africa

Large winery that has the Fleur du Cap, Stellenryck and Pongrácz labels.

PONGRÁCZ BRUT NV CAP CLASSIQUE ⑦

A youthfully oxidative aroma coarsens the rich, complex flavours in this wine.
❚ On purchase ⓔ

(FRATELLI) BERLUCCHI

Franciacorta, Italy

Pia Berlucchi produces Franciacorta and traditionally packages his wine. Note that Fratelli Berlucchi is distinct from the best-selling, plain Berlucchi brand blended from various sources, and run by Pia's cousin Guido. The latter has been good in the past, but none passed the test this year.

FRATELLI BERLUCCHI 1993 BRUT, FRANCIACORTA ⑦

Fresh, easy-drinking fizz with a sweet twist of almondy fruit on the finish.
❚ On purchase

FRATELLI BERLUCCHI 1993 BRUT, FRANCIACORTA ROSÉ ⑦

The deepish colour could be brighter, but the fruit-acidity balance makes this a nice, easy drinking fizz.
❚ On purchase

FRATELLI BERLUCCHI 1993 BRUT, FRANCIACORTA ⑦

This wine has oxidative complexity on the nose, but no such development, as yet, on the palate, which has lovely, soft vanilla fruit on the finish.
❚ Now–2000

BESSERAT DE BELLEFON

19 avenue de Champagne, 51205 Épernay
☎ (326) 59.51.00 ℻ (326) 59.51.19

Owned by Marne et Champagne and made at Marne's mega-winery.

BESSERAT DE BELLEFON NV CUVÉE DES MOINES BRUT ⑧

Fresh aromas of some finesse and plenty of flavour on the palate, but a touch green on the finish.
❚ On purchase

BILLECART-SALMON

40 rue Carnot, 51160 Mareuil-sur-Aÿ
📞 (326) 52.60.22 📠 (326) 52.64.88

A small family-owned house of
unimpeachable quality, Billecart-
Salmon is currently offering one of
the strongest ranges of high-quality
Champagnes available.

BILLECART-SALMON BRUT RÉSERVE

A beautifully elegant non-vintage with
gentle, ripe-apple fruit and soft, cushiony
mousse.
❚ Now–2000 ££

BILLECART-SALMON BRUT ROSÉ

Delicate, pale-peach colour, with very
fresh, elegantly perfumed aromas and soft
red fruit flavours.
❚ Now–1999 £££

BILLECART-SALMON BLANC DE BLANCS 1989 BRUT

Fine acacia aroma of fresh disgorgement,
with a gentle richness of creamy fruit on
palate. It is exceptionally fresh for the
vintage and promises to develop a creamy
Brazil nut and walnut complexity.
❚ Now–2010 £££

BILLECART-SALMON CUVÉE NICOLAS-FRANÇOIS 1990 BRUT

Very fresh, acacia-like aromas, with lots
of Chardonnay richness currently dominating the palate, and such a ripeness of
fruit on the finish that it is really quite
peachy. The acidity and extract is so
intense on the finish that you know this
wine has a million places to go before it
reaches its peak. I cannot guess what it
will be like when it gets there, except that
I know it will be sensational.
━━ 2000–2015 £££

BILLECART-SALMON CUVÉE NICOLAS-FRANÇOIS 1989 BRUT

Predictably broader in style than the
1990, and developing much more quickly,
but a deliciously rich and complex *cuvée*.
❚ Now–2002 £££

BILLECART-SALMON CUVÉE NICOLAS-FRANÇOIS 1988 BRUT

The 1988 has a sumptuous quality that is
rare for the year. The palate is heaped
high with creamy-walnutty fruit, and the
creaminess pervades everything, from the
nose through the finish to the aftertaste,
yet it has excellent 1988 acidity to
guarantee a lovely long life.
❚ Now–2010 £££

BILLECART-SALMON GRANDE CUVÉE 1988 BRUT

No surprise here; this really does have
1988 typicity, with tightly-sprung concentrated fruit and high acidity waiting to
unleash into creamy-nutty richness.
━━ 2000–2010 ££££

BILLECART-SALMON GRANDE CUVÉE 1985 BRUT

At least as rich and as tightly sprung as
the 1988, with promises of even greater
complexity to come.
━━ 2000–2012 ££££

BILLECART-SALMON, CUVÉE ELIZABETH SALMON ROSÉ 1988

The first vintage of this *cuvée* was
launched to build on Billecart-Salmon's
great reputation for its non-vintage Rosé
Brut wines, which account for an amazing
one-fifth of all this producer's output.
Elizabeth Salmon was immediately
impressive for its creamy summer fruit
notes, which made it a touch riper and
richer than its non-vintage sister wine,
but every bit as delicate due to its
exquisite balance.
━━ 1999–2005 £££

BILLECART-SALMON, CUVÉE ELIZABETH SALMON ROSÉ 1989

An elegant, slow-developing *rosé* for
1989. Billecart-Salmon deliberately prevented malolactic on some of the wines
from this vintage, hence the finer balance.
━━ 1999–2005 £££

BILLECART-SALMON, CUVÉE ELIZABETH SALMON ROSÉ 1990

Billecart-Salmon continues the trend with
its 1990 Elizabeth Salmon to create a *rosé*
worth dying for. True *vin de garde*.
━━ 1999–2005 £££

BISCHÖFLICHE
Mosel-Saar-Ruwer, Germany

BISCHÖFLICHE WEINGÜTER 1993 SCHARZHOFBERGER RIESLING SEKT BRUT

Perfumed Riesling aroma with soft, peachy fruit and fine acidity for freshness.
❘ On purchase ⓔⓔ

BLANCK
Alsace, France

BLANCK 1995 CRÉMANT D'ALSACE, EXTRA BRUT

Restrained malo aroma followed by malo-dominated fruit on the palate.
❘ On purchase ⓔⓔ

BLIN
5 rue de Verdun, 51700 Vincelles
☎ (326) 58.20.04 ℻ (326) 58.29.67
A cooperative with vineyards in the *petit crus* of the Marne valley.

H. BLIN 1990 BRUT

Tony Rasselet's most stunning vintage yet.
❘ Now–2002 ⓔⓔⓔ

BLUE MOUNTAIN
British Columbia, Canada

BLUE MOUNTAIN 1993 OKANAGAN VALLEY, VINTAGE BRUT ⓻⑥

Creamy-malo nose, high acidity and an oxidative hint to finish. With some fatness in the fruit it would have been world class.
❘ Now–1999 ⓔⓔ

BODEGAS CHANDON
See Chandon (Argentina)

BOECKEL
Alsace, France

EMILE BOECKEL BLANC DE BLANCS 1995 CRÉMANT D'ALSACE BRUT ⑦②

The freshest of all the Boeckel *cuvées*, and it promises to develop some biscuity complexity with a little bottle-age.
❘ Now–1999 ⓔⓔ

BOHEMIA
Czech Republic
With more than 28 million bottles of sparkling wine, Bohemia's production dwarfs even that of the mighty Champagne house Moët & Chandon.

BOHEMIA REGAL RED SPARKLING WINE NV LA BOHEME, DEMI SEC ⑦⓪

Closer to sparkling red Burgundy than any other fizzy red wine, with light, clean, easy-drinking, cherry fruit.
❘ On purchase ⓔ

BOIZEL
14 rue de Bernon, 51200 Épernay
☎ (326) 55.21.51 ℻ (326) 54.31.83

BOIZEL NV BRUT RÉSERVE

Has fresh, fruit-driven aromas, but needs to crank up the finesse to compete with the top *marques*.
❘ On purchase ⓔⓔ 99F

BOIZEL NV CHARDONNAY BRUT BLANC DE BLANCS

Creamy and fattish, yet crisp, with plenty of ripe acidity.
❘ Now–2000 ⓔⓔ 135F

BOIZEL 1990 GRAND VINTAGE BRUT MILLÉSIME

So fruity and succulent, the wine is almost exotic on the finish, yet it has classic structure and length.
❘ Now–2002 ⓔⓔⓔ 140F

VEUVE BORODIN NV WHITE LABEL, BRUT, BOIZEL **83**

Absolutely up-front fruit-driven style without any of the amylic aromas that belittled Boizel in the late 1980s.
❗ On purchase ⓔ

VEUVE DELAROY NV BRUT **83**

This seriously fruity Champagne has the structure to develop.
❗ Now–2000 ⓔ

BOLLINGER

16 rue Jules Lobet, 51160 Aÿ-Champagne
☎ (326) 53.33.66 ℻ (326) 54.85.59

Some tips: if you prefer fruit, buy the non-vintage by magnum, and if you like the toasty complexity and mellow richness of a mature vintage, buy Grande Année and age it yourself, rather than paying for R.D. (Bolly's *récemment dégorge* trademark – "recently disgorged"). Also, look out for a special pre-Millennium release of three R.D., including one that has never been released as a Grande Année.

BOLLINGER SPECIAL CUVÉE (BOTTLES) **85**

One of the most complex non-vintage *cuvées* on the market, with a lean, austere, acidic, even unforgiving, character, and oaky echoes on the finish. Reserve wines go back 15 years or so, but most of the blend is young, thus when given two or three years further ageing, the wine becomes silky-smooth, toasty and mellow.
 2000–2001 ⓔⓔⓔ 🍷169F

BOLLINGER SPECIAL CUVÉE (MAGNUMS) **89**

Much softer, fruit-driven and more accessible than the same in bottles, yet promises to mature to great complexity and finesse over a much longer period.
❗ Now–2004 ⓔⓔⓔ

BOLLINGER 1990 GRANDE ANNÉE **92**

Big, rich and powerfully flavoured, with some vanilla on the finish. My score could be underrating this vintage: it stands for the time being, but watch this space.
 2000–2010 ⓔⓔⓔⓔ 🍷236F

BOLLINGER 1989 GRANDE ANNÉE **95**

Beautiful, creamy-vanilla fruit, with gorgeously lush finish and the tiniest of bubbles.
❗ Now–2009 ⓔⓔⓔⓔ 🍷236F

BOLLINGER 1988 GRANDE ANNÉE **93**

The 1988 is still available and now has a lovely toasty-oaky richness with a great intensity of Pinot Noir fruit.
❗ Now–2013 ⓔⓔⓔⓔ

BOLLINGER 1985 GRANDE ANNÉE **96**

Still available and if you still have the first release of 1985 nestling in your cellar, you have a wine of magnificent fruit, exuberance, complexity and finesse.
❗ Now–2010 ⓔⓔⓔⓔ

BOLLINGER 1985 R.D. **93**

Dominated by the flowery, acacia-like finesse of autolysis, which all R.D. fans love, the powerful, rich-flavoured fruit in this wine is awesome, but I still prefer the way the first disgorgement has developed.
❗ Now–2010 ⓔⓔⓔⓔ

BOLLINGER 1982 R.D. **90**

Fine, flowery, acacia-like aromas are followed by really quite spicy flavours, with dried-fruit complexity.
❗ Now–2007 ⓔⓔⓔⓔ

BOLLINGER 1989 VIEILLES VIGNES FRANÇAISES **95**

This is the wine that bred the lie that all *blanc de noirs* are big. Vieilles Vignes Françaises is big, but not simply because it is pure Pinot Noir. These particular vines are located in three minuscule parcels of ungrafted vines in the *grands crus* of Aÿ-Champagne (Clos St-Jacques, Chaudes Terres) and Bouzy (Croix Rouge). The 1989 is full, rich and complex, with broad, creamy-ripe lushness of fruit on both nose and palate, yet a structure that is firm for such a big wine, with vanilla and oak coming through on the finish.
❗ Now–2009 ⓔⓔⓔⓔ

BOLLINGER 1988 ROSÉ **89**

Fat, sassy and satisfying fruit on a classic lean structure. Ideal with pheasant.
❗ Now–2002 ⓔⓔⓔ

BON COURAGE
Robertson, South Africa

Owner Andre Bruwer was Champion Estate Winemaker in 1985–6, yet if anything the quality has gone up since son Jacques took over in 1995.

JACQUES BRUÈRE BLANC DE BLANCS NV CAP CLASSIQUE	85

Classic creamy-rich biscuity complexity.
 Now–2000 ⓔ

(ALEXANDRE) BONNET

138 rue du Général-de-Gaulle
10340 Les-Riceys
ⓒ (325) 29.30.93 ℻ (325) 29.38.65
Serge and Alain Bonnet are ambitious Aubois producers who sell under the Alexandre Bonnet label.

ALEXANDRE BONNET NV CUVÉE PRESTIGE	82

Satisfying mouthful of tingling-fresh fruit.
On purchase ⓔⓔ

ALEXANDRE BONNET 1990 MADRIGAL	86

Behind its somewhat incongruous label this is a nicely rich, but extremely tight, Champagne that needs more post-disgorgement bottle-age.
 2000–2002 ⓔⓔ

(FERDINAND) BONNET

12 allée du Vignoble, 51055 Oger
ⓒ (326) 84.44.15 ℻ (326) 84.44.19
Part of the Remy-Cointreau group since 1992, the Ferdinand Bonnet brand still represents good value and the wines improve with further bottle-age, but they will never be the same quality as the old stocks.

FERDINAND BONNET NV BRUT HERITAGE	83

Although it has wet-straw aromas now, this should go nice and toasty.
 1999–2000 ⓔⓔ 🍷99F

PRINCESSE DE FRANCE NV BRUT, GRANDE RÉSERVE DE FERDINAND BONNET	87

Made by women for women, this *cuvée* was created by Cécile Rivault and Myriam Jacqueminet, two oenologists in Daniel Thibault's highly talented winemaking team. It is elegant, but more lean than soft or delicate, which are the sort of adjectives the French use for the so-called feminine characteristics of a wine. Whatever your sex, I think you'll find that this is an excellent Champagne.
 1999–2000 ⓔⓔ 🍷96F

BREDON NV BRUT	80

Easy drinking style, with peppery fruit.
Now–1999 ⓔ

JEAN DE PRAISAC NV BRUT, F. BONNET	80

Fresh, easy-going style with some pepperiness to the fruit.
On purchase ⓔ

LOUIS RAYMOND NV BRUT, F. BONNET	80

Some green hints to the fruit, but the wine scrapes in because there is a good depth of flavour in addition to this greenness, and the balance promises a mellowing development.
Now–1999 ⓔⓔ

BORODIN
See Boizel

BOSCHENDAL
Paarl, South Africa
One of the Cape's pioneering *méthode champenoise* producers.

BOSCHENDAL LE GRAND PAVILLON BRUT NV CAP CLASSIQUE	70

I have come across several samples of the current shipment that were corked, but when on form this *cuvée* has a tangy richness of fruit, and a hint of complexity.
On purchase ⓔ

BOSCO

See Ca'del Bosco

BOTHY VINEYARD

Frilford Heath, England, UK
The irrepressible Roger Fisher and
his indefatigable wife tend this
vineyard on the outskirts of Oxford.

BOTHY VINEYARD 1991 DRY

The more I think about this wine, the
more convinced I am that it is one of the
most distinctive English sparkling wines
ever made, although the 1992 was a great
disappointment.
❚ On purchase ⓔ

BOUCHER

10 rue Pasteur, 51160 Champillon
☎ (326) 59.48.17 🖷 (326) 52.97.67

BOUCHER FILS NV CUVÉE FIN DE SIÈCLE, PRESTIGE

The concentration of flavour blows away
any lack of finesse.
▬ 1999–2001 ⓔⓔ 🍾82F

BOULARD

1 et 4 rue du Tambour
51480 La Neuville aux Larris
☎ (326) 58.12.08 🖷 (326) 58.13.02

There is an amylic tendency in too
many wines here. A slightly warmer
first fermentation is probably needed.

RAYMOND BOULARD NV RÉSERVE BRUT

A touch amylic, but overshadowed by
sprightly fruit on the palate.
❚ On purchase ⓔⓔ 🍾90F

RAYMOND BOULARD NV BRUT, GRAND CRU

Richer, more sprightly fruit than the above.
❚ On purchase ⓔⓔ 🍾99F

RAYMOND BOULARD NV TRADITION BRUT

None of the amylic aromas found in the
Réserve Brut, and more serious than the
Grand Cru, without its sprightly fruiti-
ness. Some true complexity and finesse.
❚ Now–1999 ⓔⓔ 🍾118F

RAYMOND BOULARD 1993 BRUT

Very fruity.
❚ On purchase ⓔⓔⓔ 🍾102F

BOURGOGNE

See Haute Bourgogne

BOURSAULT

See Château de Boursault

BOUTILLEZ-VIGNON

26 rue Pasteur, 51380 Villers-Marmery
☎ (326) 97.95.87 🖷 (326) 97.97.23

G. BOUTILLEZ-VIGNON NV CUVÉE PRESTIGE BRUT

Oxidative nose, but extremely rich fruit
on the palate. An extra gram of finesse
could add a kilo of quality to this wine.
❚ On purchase ⓔⓔ 🍾77F

G. BOUTILLEZ-VIGNON 1990 BRUT, 1ᴱᴿ CRU

There is a strange strength to the flavour
of this high-acid, biscuity-rich *cuvée* that
compels me to withhold judgement for at
least another year.
▬ Wait and see ⓔⓔⓔ 🍾99F

BOUVET

Loire, France

BOUVET NV SAUMUR, DEMI-SEC

Fresher and more elegant than most
demi-sec, with plenty of sweet fruit.
❚ Now–2000 ⓔ

BOUVET 1995 SAPHIR BRUT VINTAGE

Richer and softer than most Saumur, with a liquorice quality to the fruit.

❙ Now–1999 Ⓔ

BOUVET EXCELLENCE NV CRÉMANT BRUT

This has a longer finish and is more perfumed than Bouvet's basic Brut – it can be regarded as the entry level for Bouvet.

❙ On purchase Ⓔ

BOUVET LADUBAY NV TRESOR BRUT, SAUMUR

When first released, the fruit seemed much riper and more exotic, and it tasted more like an Australian Chardonnay with bubbles than anything from the Loire. People either loved it or loathed it, especially as it was expensive for a Loire fizz. Now it is half the price and dare I say half the wine, which will probably give it wider appeal, but there is nothing exotic or oaky, just peppery and firm.

❙ On purchase ⓔⓔ

BOUVET LADUBAY NV TRESOR ROSÉ BRUT, SAUMUR

The Tresor Rosé Brut shows little sign of its *barrique* first fermentation, but has delicate fruit underpinned by good, ripe acidity, which gives the wine excellent length in the mouth. Very fine mousse.

❙ On purchase ⓔⓔ

BOUXHOF

See Domaine du Bouxhof

BREAKY BOTTOM

Lewes, England, UK
Peter Hall's fizz is enjoyable enough, but has the potential for more finesse.

BREAKY BOTTOM CUVÉE RÉSERVÉE 1994 BRUT

This was very amylic at first, although this tamed down after a few months to become a good, easy-drinking fizz.

❙ Now–1999

BRÈQUE

Bordeaux, France
One of the oldest producers of sparkling Bordeaux wines.

RÉMY BRÈQUE NV CRÉMANT DE BORDEAUX BRUT

Just scraped in ahead of Rémy Brèque's prestige *cuvée*.

❙ On purchase Ⓔ

BRIANT

See Leclerc Briant

BRICE

3 rue Yvonnet, 51150 Bouzy
☎ (326) 52.06.60 ☎ (326) 57.05.07

Brice is one of the three founders of Barancourt, now doing his own thing.

BRICE NV AŸ GRAND CRU BRUT

Firm fruit, intense and long, this wine is capable of ageing.

▬ 1999–2002 ⓔⓔ ♚130F

BRICE NV PREMIER CRU BRUT

Light, elegant and stylish.

❙ Now–1999 ⓔⓔ ♚108F

BRICE NV BOUZY GRAND CRU BRUT

Ripe and juicy fruit that promises to go quite toasty.

❙ Now–2000 ⓔⓔ ♚130F

BRISON

14 Grande Rue, 10360 Noé-les-Mallets
☎ (325) 29.66.62 ☎ (325) 29.14.59

Ambitious Aube growers. Francis Brulez ferments in well-used oak casks and prevents the malolactic.

LOUISE BRISON 1994 BRUT

Dry, spicy and perfumed.

▬ 2000–2002 ⓔⓔⓔ ♚88F

LOUISE BRISON 1993 CUVÉE GERMAIN BRULEZ BRUT

Under blind conditions, I thought I detected some perfumed Meunier aromas, but after the covers came off I discovered that this *cuvée* comprises 40 per cent Chardonnay and 60 per cent Pinot Noir, with no Meunier whatsoever!

On purchase ⓔⓔⓔ 🍾200F (magnum)

LOUISE BRISON 1993 CUVÉE TENDRESSE BRUT

I found this hard, but not in a non-malolactic way, more of a hard-cum-metallic taste.

 Wait and see ⓔⓔⓔ 🍾110F

BRIZÉ

See Domaine de Brizé

BROCHET-HERVIEUX

10 rue Saint Vincent, 51500 Ecueil
☎ (326) 49.24.06 ᴀᴍ (326) 49.77.94
Current production is just 1,250 cases per year.

BROCHET-HERVIEUX NV BRUT EXTRA, PREMIER CRU ⓼⓹

Quite fat and sweet for *extra brut*.

On purchase ⓔⓔ 🍾75F

BROCHET-HERVIEUX 1990 HBH BRUT, PREMIER CRU ⓼⓹

Very rich malty-biscuity flavour.

Now–1999 ⓔⓔⓔ 🍾100F

BROGSITTER

Ahr, Germany

BROGSITTER PRIVAT SEKTKELLEREI 1995 SPÄTBURGUNDER SEKT BRUT ⓻⓺

Under this awful looking label lurks a very good Pinot Noir Sekt, with an elegant cherry fruit flavour and a soft mousse. Bottle-fermented.

On purchase ⓔⓔ

BROUETTE

Bordeaux, France
Large Crémant de Bordeaux producer.

BROUETTE ROSÉ NV CRÉMANT DE BORDEAUX BRUT

Off-putting mature-orange colour, but plenty of perfumed fruit on the palate, with a delicately fruity finish.

On purchase ⓔ

BROUETTE CRÉMANT DE BORDEAUX NV TRADITION BLANC DE BLANCS BRUT

Fresh, easy fruit, with better acidity than Brouette's prestige Cuvée de L'Abbaye.

On purchase ⓔ

BROWN BROTHERS

Victoria, Australia

BROWN BROTHERS PINOT NOIR CHARDONNAY NV BRUT

Peachy fruit with plenty of ripe acidity.

On purchase ⓔ

BRUÈRE

See Bon Courage

(CELLIER LE) BRUN

Marlborough, New Zealand
One of the New World's top sparkling wine producers, in the late 1980s Daniel Le Brun's wines began to rival the quality of good Champagne. Indeed, the 1989 Blanc de Blancs was so outstanding that it started rumours that Daniel Le Brun had imported it from his family in Champagne! The straight vintage of 1990 seemed to confirm the ascendency of this Gallic star, but Daniel flew the coop in 1996 to a new venture. Meanwhile, the priority for the new owners is surely to improve the Non-Vintage Brut.

DANIEL LE BRUN NV BRUT, MARLBOROUGH

This fresh, fruit-driven *cuvée* is the best non-vintage from Le Brun in some time.
❗ On purchase ⓔⓔ

DANIEL LE BRUN 1992 VINTAGE BRUT, MARLBOROUGH

A quick whiff of sulphur, but it is free and clean, and will therefore turn toasty with some more bottle-age. This is a rich and flavoursome wine that will gain complexity, but loses points for coconutty oak (although some people love that).
❗ Now–2000 ⓔⓔ

DANIEL LE BRUN 1992 BLANC DE BLANCS BRUT, MARLBOROUGH

The current shipment is unpleasantly oxidative, but I have tasted this vintage several times and the wine is good, so I must reserve judgement for a year or two.
➤ Wait and see ⓔⓔ

(EDOUARD) BRUN
14 rue Marcel Mailly 51160 Aÿ-Champagne
☎ (326) 55.20.11 ℻ (326) 51.94.29

EDOUARD BRUN & CIE NV RÉSERVE 1ᴱᴿ CRU BRUT

Extraordinarily fruity.
❗ On purchase ⓔⓔ ☖84F

EDOUARD BRUN & CIE NV CUVÉE SPÉCIALE BRUT

Almost as fruity as the 1ᵉʳ Cru Réserve, but not quite as rich, although it has more room for development.
❗ Now–1999 ⓔⓔ ☖76F

EDOUARD BRUN & CIE NV ROSÉ BRUT

Pale salmon colour, sprightly fruitiness, deep flavour, true *brut* dryness.
❗ On purchase ⓔⓔ ☖90F

EDOUARD BRUN & CIE 1990 CUVÉE DU CENTENAIRE BRUT

This *cuvée* does not celebrate the end of the century, but 100 years since Edouard Brun was established in 1898. I have my doubts about how this will develop.
➤ Wait and see ⓔⓔⓔ ☖119F

BRÜNDLMAYER
Austria

Vinegrowers and winemakers in Kamptal since the 17th century, the Bründlmayers currently vie with Weingut Platzer as Austria's best sparkling wine producer.

BRÜNDLMAYER 1993 BRUT

Crisp, with fine acidity, and an elegant, if slightly oxidative, complexity.
❗ Now–1999 ⓔⓔ

BUECHER
Alsace, France
The *cuvée* below is the best *crémant* from Buecher that I have tasted.

PAUL BUECHER, PRESTIGE NV CRÉMANT D'ALSACE BRUT

Rich, fruity and well-structured.
❗ Now–1999 ⓔ

BUISSE
Loire, France

PAUL BUISSE NV CRÉMANT DE LOIRE

This comes in a heavier, more expensive bottle than the so-called Prestige, and it is a richer, more succulent *cuvée*.
❗ On purchase ⓔ

PAUL BUISSE PRESTIGE NV TOURAINE BRUT

The fresh, sweet and peppery fruit in this wine is attractive, but not in the same class as the basic *brut* above.
❗ On purchase ⓔ

BUITENVERWACHTING
Constantia, South Africa
Buitenverwachting is part of the historical Constantia estate and produces many outstanding wines.

**BUITENVERWACHTING
BRUT NV CAP CLASSIQUE**

This perfumed yet rich and full sparkling
wine makes an interesting, non-classic,
almost contradicting style.
❙ On purchase ⓔ

BURGE
See Grant Burge

BURG HORNBERG
Baden, Germany

**WEINGUT BURG HORNBERG
1991 BLANC DE NOIRS
SEKT BRUT**

Made exclusively from Meunier in a true-
white *blanc de noirs* style, rather than the
New World synonym for *rosé*, this is one
of the few Sekts that could take some
ageing. Bottle-fermented.
❙ Now–2000 ⓔⓔ

CABRIÈRE
See Jourdan

CÀ DEI FRATI
Lombardy, Italy

**CÀ DEI FRATI, CUVÉE DEI
FRATI NV BRUT, LUGANA**

Rich, fruity aromas with fresh, easy-going
fruit on the palate.
❙ On purchase ⓔ

CA'DEL BOSCO
Franciacorta, Italy
Motorcycle-mad, multi-millionaire
Maurizo Zanella is one of Italy's most
consistent sparkling wine producers,
and the style is now more elegant.

**CA'DEL BOSCO NV
BRUT, FRANCIACORTA**

Fresh Mâcon-like aroma, with good, fresh
fruit and acidity on the palate, but the
bubbles could be smaller.
❙ On purchase ⓔ

**CA'DEL BOSCO 1994
BRUT, FRANCIACORTA**

Some lemony finesse on the nose, with
rich fruit on mid-palate and a creamy
finish, but the aftertaste lacks elegance.
❙ On purchase ⓔⓔ

**CA'DEL BOSCO 1993
ROSÉ BRUT, FRANCIACORTA**

A very fruity front palate, drying to a
nicely focused finish.
❙ On purchase ⓔⓔ

**CA'DEL BOSCO 1992 SATÈN
BRUT, FRANCIACORTA**

Strong but fruity volatile acidity aromas
on the nose, following onto the palate
where they add a piquancy to the fruit.
❙ On purchase ⓔⓔ

**CA'DEL BOSCO 1991 CUVÉE
ANNAMARIA CLEMENTI
BRUT, FRANCIACORTA**

A bit too rich for its balance to be
special, but this is a nice, ripe-fruity fizz
for easy drinking without food.
❙ On purchase ⓔⓔ

CALIXTE
See Hunawihr

CALLOT
100 avenue Jean Jaurès, 51190 Avize
☎ (326) 57.51.57 ℻ (326) 57.99.15
These Champagnes are fermented in
well-used, large oak barrels, with
fewer than 600 cases produced.

**PIERRE CALLOT NV BLANC
DE BLANCS BRUT, GRAND CRU**

A fruity style of some depth and the
potential to develop well.
▬ 1999–2000 ⓔⓔ ♉81F

PIERRE CALLOT NV GRANDE RÉSERVE, BLANC DE BLANCS BRUT, GRAND CRU

Not quite as overtly fruity as the standard Blanc de Blancs, but with more finesse.
1999–2001 ⓔⓕ 🍾101F

CANARD-DUCHÊNE

1 rue Edmond Canard, Ludes le Coquet
51500 Rilly-la-Montagne
📞(326) 61.10.96 📠(326) 61.13.90

This brand is practically given away in French supermarkets, but quality is better on export markets, although the Grande Charles VII Cuvée is disappointing wherever you buy it.

CANARD-DUCHÊNE NV BRUT

The Canard-Duchêne fruit-driven style plus a more classic, lean structure.
On purchase ⓔⓕ 🍾120F

CANARD-DUCHÊNE 1990 BRUT

One sample was old and past it, but the other was high quality for the price.
Now–2000 ⓔⓕⓕ 🍾150F

CAPE LEVANT

See SAVISA

CARIAD

Wales, UK

CARIAD GWRID BLUSH 1995 BRUT

Assertive jammy fruit with a firm mousse.
On purchase ⓔⓕ

(DOMAINE) CARNEROS

Napa, California, USA
The first releases were very poor but now these wines are among the best. Even the Champenois need a year or two to get it right, it seems.

DOMAINE CARNEROS 1992 BLANC DE BLANCS

Pale colour, with creamy-flowery-sherbetty aromas, fine and light fruit on the palate, very good acidity, and a soft mousse of very tiny bubbles.
Now–2000 ⓔⓕ

DOMAINE CARNEROS 1993 BRUT

Very fresh and fine, with nice acidity and a crisp mousse of tiny bubbles.
Now–2000 ⓔⓕ

CAROLINA

See Masachs

CARRINGTON

See Orlando

CASSEGRAIN

New South Wales, Australia
It was in 1980 that John Cassegrain established this winery at Port Macquarie, which some critics believe has too much of a maritime climate for viticulture. There have been some lows, but some of the highs have been very exciting, and the early sparklers are encouraging.

CASSEGRAIN 1994 BRUT

This rich, smooth, full-bodied wine is spoilt by too much sulphur, and although it is clean and not fixed, thus will turn toasty, this simply should not happen in any sparkling wine.
Wait and see ⓕ

CASTELL

Franken, Germany
Vineyard owners for 27 generations, the Castell-Castell family has produced wine since 1258, but Sekt is a relatively recent phenomenon here, with the first *cuvée* produced in 1973.

FÜRSTLICH CASTELL'SCHES DOMÄNENAMT 1993 CASTELLER HERRENBERG RIESLANER SEKT BRUT

A lees-rich petrolly Riesling style, even though this is a *Riesling x Sylvaner* cross.
❙ On purchase ⓔⓔ

(DE) CASTELLANE

57 rue de Verdun, 51204 Épernay
☎ (326) 51.19.19 ℻ (326) 54.24.81

Part of the Laurent-Perrier group, this underrated house offers brilliant value for money, with the top *cuvées* capable of very high quality indeed.

VICOMTE DE CASTELLANE NV BRUT

Fresh and fruity, with a touch of pepper.
❙ Now ⓔⓔ

DE CASTELLANE 1990 BRUT

Bit of an old bruiser last year, but the richness now hangs well on this wine's lean structure, with more development to come.
❙ Now–2000 ⓔⓔⓔ 🍾110F

DE CASTELLANE 1988 CUVÉE FLORENS DE CASTELLANE BRUT

Atypically buttery-malo on the nose, but rich fruit that will go biscuity, not toasty.
❙ Now–2000 ⓔⓔⓔ 🍾180F

CUVÉE COMMODORE 1989 DE CASTELLANE BRUT 88

Nice intensity of fruit, with a long, layered, citrussy and lime blossom complexity.
❙ Now–2002 ⓔⓔⓔ 🍾160F

CROIX ROUGE DE ST ANDRÉ DE CASTELLANE NV BRUT 84

Quite rich and full, with a fine, fluffy finish.
❙ Now ⓔⓔ

MAXIM'S NV GRANDE CUVÉE BRUT

Lush, ripe, elegant fruit with a long finish.
❙ On purchase ⓔⓔ

MAXIM'S NV PRESTIGE BRUT 84

Light and elegantly fruity style. Some pepperyness and spicy green apple on the finish.
❙ On purchase ⓔⓔ

CASTELLBLANCH
Penedès, Spain

CASTELLBLANCH 1995 CAVA BRUT ZERO

Has the terpene character of a wine that has been stored in tank prior to second fermentation, but also good enough acidity, structure and quality to qualify.
❙ On purchase ⓔ

CASTELLBLANCH 1996 CAVA ROSADO BRUT

A simple, fresh, easy-drinking style.
❙ On purchase ⓔ

CASTILLO PERELADA
See Perelada

CATTIER

6 & 11 rue Dom Pérignon
51500 Chigny-les-Roses
☎ (326) 03.42.11 ℻ (326) 03.43.13

For many years this small house has produced one of the most individual Champagnes, its single-vineyard Clos du Moulin, which is always a blend of three vintage years. The vintages are on the back label.

CATTIER NV BRUT ROSÉ, 1ᴱᴿ CRU

Pale salmon colour, sprightly fruitiness, soft and succulent, with Pinot coming through on the finish. Smooth mousse, tiny bubbles.
❙ On purchase ⓔⓔ 🍾93F

CATTIER NV BLANC DE BLANCS BRUT, 1ᴱᴿ CRU

Floral style with excellent acidity and creamy aftertaste.
❙ Now–2002 ⓔⓔ 🍾89F

CATTIER 1990 BRUT

Exotic fruit and lovely acidity, fine and refined, with tropical fruits on the finish.
❙ Now–2006 ⓔⓔⓔ 🍾93F

CATTIER 1989 CUVÉE RENAISSANCE BRUT, 1ᴱᴿ CRU **87**

Still in ultra-fruity mode, with a depth of fruit that makes its serious potential obvious, but it could well go through a less attractive phase between these two enjoyable extremes.
❢ Now–2001 ⓔⓔⓔ 🍾140F

CLOS DU MOULIN NV CATTIER BRUT, PREMIER CRU **90**

This particular *cuvée* is a blend of 1985, 1986 and 1988. It is already complex, although needs a few years post-disgorgement ageing. Having tasted future *cuvées*, I cannot wait for the amazing 1988/1989/1990 blend.
▶ 2000–2005 ⓔⓔⓔ 🍾196F

CATTIN

Alsace, France

There is some inconsistency in the style of Joseph Cattin's Crémant d'Alsace because he keeps changing the *encépagement* (blend of grape varieties), otherwise it is always an interesting wine.

BRUT CATTIN NV CRÉMANT D'ALSACE **70**

Lots of sprightly fruitiness, strawberry-like, but finishes rather fat and needs more acidity for a higher score.
❢ On purchase ⓔ

CAVA(S) –

See under main name

CAVALLERI

Franciacorta, Italy

CAVALLERI 1993 BLANC DE BLANCS BRUT, FRANCIACORTA **72**

Full toasty aroma, with plenty of fruit on the palate, but needs more layers of flavour and finesse for a higher score.
❢ On purchase ⓔⓔ

CAVALLERI 1993 ROSÉ, FRANCIACORTA **70**

Fresh, fruity fizz in a sort of Latin Angas Brut *(see Yalumba)* style.
❢ On purchase ⓔⓔ

CAVE(S) DE –

See under main name

(DE) CAZANOVE

1 rue des Cotelles, 51204 Épernay
📞 (326) 59.57.40 📠 (326) 54.16.38

Always a good-value Champagne house, De Cazanove is trying to pro-duce higher quality *cuvées*. Current shipments have too much malolactic, but this will no doubt be improved.

CHARLES DE CAZANOVE NV BRUT AZUR **87**

The creamy-biscuity malolactic character is so dominant that it tastes odd in a blind tasting amid a sea of fresh, fruit-driven Champagnes, but this *cuvée* shows its true class and complexity at the table with food.
❢ Now–2001 ⓔⓔ 🍾102F

CHARLES DE CAZANOVE NV BRUT CLASSIQUE **85**

Fruit-driven style and really delicious, but with classic lean structure. No dominant malolactic characteristics, but it might develop some biscuitiness with age.
❢ On purchase ⓔⓔ

CHARLES DE CAZANOVE NV DEMI-SEC **82**

Simplistically sweet and clean now, but also one of the few *demi-sec* Champagnes that will repay ageing.
❢ Now–2000 ⓔⓔ

CHARLES DE CAZANOVE 1990 BRUT MILLÉSIME **85**

Similar creamy-malo character to the non-vintage Brut Azur, but this is richer and its more fruit-influenced style is taking longer to evolve. A safer bet than the Stradivarius prestige *cuvée*.
❢ Now–2005 ⓔⓔⓔ

CHARLES DE CAZANOVE 1990 STRADIVARIUS BRUT

This wine currently has a strange boiled-Chablis character – but "Strad" has had a good string of vintages since its inaugural 1985 vintage, so I am prepared to give this a year or two to settle down.
➤ Wait and see ⓔⓔⓔ ❦250F

CHARLES DE CAZANOVE 1990 BRUT AZUR

Rich in sweet, biscuity-ripe fruit.
❦ Now–2005 ⓔⓔⓔ ❦123F

H. LANVIN & FILS NV CUVÉE SUPÉRIEURE, BRUT

A secondary brand from the De Cazanove stable, this *cuvée* has simpler, easy-going fruit and a crisp finish.
❦ On purchase ⓔ

MAGENTA BRUT NV CHARLES DE CAZANOVE, CUVÉE SUPÉRIEURE

Another secondary brand from De Cazanove, it is technically the same level as Lanvin, but softer, like an easier going version of the Cuvée Classique.
❦ On purchase ⓔ

CELLAR BATTLE
See Gramona

CELLIER LE BRUN
See Brun

CHAMPAGNE –
See under main name

CHAMPALOU
Loire, France
Didier Champalou is ahead of the pack, but has some fine-tuning to do to reveal the true quality of this *cuvée*.

CHAMPALOU NV VOUVRAY BRUT

The finesse on the nose of this wine made it stand out from most Loire bubblies, but although the fruit is initially attractive and tangy in the mouth, it is let down by a hint of dry straw on the finish.
❦ On purchase ⓔ

(BODEGAS) CHANDON
Argentina
One of Moët & Chandon's oldest outposts. Most of the fizz is fresh, clean and amylic, with a slightly bitter finish, but Baron B. stands out, and there are rumours of new plantations of Chardonnay for improving future *cuvées*.

BARON B. NV EXTRA BRUT CHAMPAÑA

Just as fresh as below, but not amylic, with finer acidity and no bitter finish.
❦ On purchase ⓔ

BARON B. ROSÉ NV EXTRA BRUT CHAMPAÑA

Touch fatter than above and less elegant.
❦ On purchase ⓔ

(CAVA) CHANDON
Penedès, Spain
At one time this outpost of Moët & Chandon's sparkling wine empire seemed about as interesting as its Sekt factory, but it looks as if the quality has been improved.

CAVA CHANDON NV BRUT RESERVA

Much better acidity than this wine used to have, and above average quality for Cava, but still needs to find a more expressive character.
❦ On purchase ⓔ

CAVA CHANDON NV BRUT NATURE

The best Cava Chandon so far: clean, fresh, and good acidity for Cava, but definitely an early-drinking style.
❦ On purchase ⓔ

(DOMAINE) CHANDON AUSTRALIA

Victoria, Australia

This Domaine Chandon is under the auspices of Tony Jordan. Many New World wines are dominated by malolactic aromas, but only some of the base wines are put through this. Most are lovely when released, and can improve for up to 18 months. Sold as Green Point on export markets.

DOMAINE CHANDON 1995 BRUT **86**

The best vintage so far, this *cuvée* has a lovely understated richness, Pinot-led front and mid-palate, with a smooth Chardonnay finesse on the finish, and creamy-cushiony mousse of tiny bubbles. Stunning stuff!
❚ Now–2000 ⓔⓔ

DOMAINE CHANDON 1994 BRUT **80**

Firm and tight, with nice biscuity richness.
❚ Now–2000 ⓔⓔ

DOMAINE CHANDON 1994 ROSÉ BRUT **85**

A deliciously serious *rosé*, with lovely fruit and just beginning to develop a smooth vanilla finesse on the finish.
❚ Now–1999 ⓔⓔ

DOMAINE CHANDON 1993 BLANC DE BLANCS BRUT **85**

A lovely, elegant wine, with very fresh fruit for its age.
❚ Now–2000 ⓔⓔ

DOMAINE CHANDON NV CUVÉE RICHE **80**

A soft and sensuous, beautifully balanced dessert bubbly, Cuvée Riche is no longer the amylic horror it used to be.
❚ Now–2002 ⓔⓔ

(DOMAINE) CHANDON NEW ZEALAND

Marlborough, New Zealand
As Tony Jordan is Jane Hunter's consultant winemaker, it is little surprise that Hunter's has also been the testing ground for this *cuvée*.

DOMAINE CHANDON 1994 VINTAGE, MARLBOROUGH BRUT **75**

A very malty style *cuvée*. How it might develop is anyone's guess.
 Wait and see ⓔⓔ

(DOMAINE) CHANDON CALIFORNIA

Napa, California, USA
Moët & Chandon helped to kick-start the California sparkling wine industry in the 1970s. These wines have sometimes been inclined to rely too much on weight and character, and not enough on finesse and elegance although this may be changing, if the younger wines under the export label Shadow Creek are a sign of things to come. The Mount Veeder Chardonnay appellation has also begun to look interesting, especially when the malolactic is prevented. There is no doubting that winemaker Dawnine Dyer is every bit as talented as Tony Jordan in Australia – it is just that the problems they face are very different.

DOMAINE CHANDON NV RESERVE **73**

Full, spicy and quite deeply flavoured. Different than previous *cuvées*, which had a petrolly-terpene character.
❚ On purchase ⓔ

DOMAINE CHANDON NV ROSÉ BRUT **74**

An elegantly perfumed aroma with delicate red fruits on the palate and a smooth vanilla-style Chardonnay on the finish.
❚ On purchase ⓔ

DOMAINE CHANDON NV BLANC DE NOIRS **80**

Wonderfully fresh and fluffy fruit, with sherbetty finish.
❚ On purchase ⓔ

ÉTOILE **80**

Although Domaine Chandon's prestige *cuvée* was for years much too fat and toasty, more recent blends have been more compact and better focused.
❚ Now–1999 ⓔⓔ

CHANOINE

Avenue de Champagne, 51100 Reims
📞 (326) 36.61.60 📠 (326) 36.66.62

When relaunched in 1991, Chanoine
was meant to be a superior supermarket Champagne, but the wines were
so good and the bottles so beautifully
dressed with reproduction labels that
it became a brand in its own right.

CHANOINE NV BRUT

Fresh, easy and light, with a fine mousse
of tiny bubbles.
🍷 On purchase ££

CHANOINE 1990 BRUT

A rich, full and satisfying *cuvée*, with a
succulent finish.
🍷 On purchase ££

TSARINE NV BRUT, CHANOINE

New prestige *cuvée* in snazzy bottle with
a twisted fluting. A classy Champagne of
superb value and ageing potential.
🍷 Now–2005 ££

CHAPEL DOWN

Tenterden, England, UK

CHAPEL DOWN EPOCH 1993 BRUT

Deliciously fresh, peachy fruit underpinned by mouthwatering ripe acidity,
and with an excellent mousse.
🍷 On purchase £

CHAPEL DOWN EPOCH 1995 BRUT

Slightly less peachiness than the 1993, but
with an additional violet-vanilla finesse.
🍷 On purchase £

CHARBAUT

12 rue du Pont, 51160 Mareuil-sur-Aÿ
📞 (326) 52.80.59 📠 (326) 51.91.49
Guy Charbaut launched this grower
Champagne after selling the *négociant* house of Charbaut to Vranken.

GUY CHARBAUT 1990 BRUT

A characterful wine full of lemony
richness, rather than great finesse, but it
also promises to gain a toasty finesse as it
ages over the next few years.
🍷 Now–2002 £££

CHARLEMAGNE

4 rue de la Brèche d'Oger
51190 Le-Mesnil-sur-Oger
📞 (326) 57.52.98 📠 (326) 57.97.81

Top-class *blanc de blancs*.

GUY CHARLEMAGNE NV RÉSERVE BRUT, GRAND CRU

Flowery Chardonnay aromas, with delicious, classy fruit on the palate, and a long
finish, showing both complexity and finesse.
🍷 Now–2001 ££ 82F

CHARTOGNE-TAILLET

37-39 Grande Rue, 51220 Merfy
📞 (326) 03.10.17 📠 (326) 03.19.15

CHAMPAGNE CHARTOGNE-TAILLET NV BRUT, CUVÉE SAINTE-ANNE

Pure gold for lovers of toasty-rich,
creamy Champagne.
🍷 Now–2000 ££

CHÂTEAU DE BEAUREGARD

Loire, France

CHÂTEAU DE BEAUREGARD 1995 SAUMUR BRUT

Very fresh and very clean, with deliciously refreshing fruit and a lively finish.
🍷 On purchase £

CHÂTEAU DE BOURSAULT

Boursault 51480 prés Épernay
📞 (326) 58.42.21 📠 (326) 58.66.12

CHÂTEAU DE BOURSAULT NV BRUT

Although the least interesting wine in Boursault's range, the Non-Vintage Brut should be the excellent 1995-based *cuvée* by the time this guide is published, and that will be followed by the even better 1996-based blend.

❚ Now–1999 ⓔⓔ

CHÂTEAU DE BOURSAULT NV ROSÉ BRUT

Made by *saignée* method *(see p178)*, this is always Boursault's best *cuvée*, and actually benefits from two years ageing without losing its freshness. The current shipment has delicious, cherry-like fruit of Pinot Noir, which will deepen and take on a creamy richness.

❚ Now–2000 ⓔⓔ

CHÂTEAU DE BOURSAULT NV CUVÉE PRESTIGE BRUT

Boursault's recent addition to the range is a nice fruit-driven Champagne, but the first wine is 1992-based, and the 1994-based *cuvée* is a wine of much greater finesse. This could very well be a Champagne to watch.

❚ Now–1999 ⓔⓔ

CHÂTEAU DE L'HURBE

Bordeaux, France
This small château in St Laurent d'Arce has produced its own sparkling wine since 1996.

CHÂTEAU DE L'HURBE NV CRÉMANT DE BORDEAUX BRUT

Succulent fruit intermingles with toasty aromas on nose and palate.

❚ On purchase ⓔ

CHÂTEAU DE PASSAVANT

Loire, France

CHÂTEAU DE PASSAVANT NV CRÉMANT DE LOIRE BRUT

An invigorating fizz with lemony fruit.

❚ On purchase ⓔ

CHENEAU

See CIGRAVI

CHEURLIN

12 rue de la Gare
Gyé-sur-Seine 10250 Mussy-sur-Seine
☎ (25) 38.20.27

Of the Aube's ubiquitous Cheurlins, this one is the largest and most active in developing its export trade.

CHEURLIN & FILS NV GRANDE CUVÉE BRUT

Tangy fruit with ripe green-apples on the finish, and technically too much sulphur, but it is free, not fixed, and will go toasty.

➤ 1999–2000 ⓔⓔ 🥂78F

CHEURLIN & FILS NV PRESTIGE BRUT

Fatter and softer than the Grande Cuvée Brut, but just as much free sulphur waiting to go toasty!

➤ 1999–2000 ⓔⓔ 🥂88F

CHEURLIN & FILS 1991 BRUT ORIGINEL

Extraordinary Burgundian-like lemony-oak aromas. Obviously *barrique*-fermented, but far too much oak. Hopefully, future vintages will have more finesse.

➤ Wait and see ⓔⓔⓔ 🥂136F

CHILFORD HUNDRED

Cambridge, England, UK
Buy the 1994 while you can, because I have tasted the next vintage before it is disgorged and cannot see how it can become as good as the 1994.

CHILFORD HUNDRED 1994 ALURIC DE NORSEHIDE

Lovely old-gold colour, an appealing apple-blossom aroma and long, fruit-strewn flavour of ripe green apples and juicy Victoria plums, with just a touch of Muscat on the finish. An impressive wine.

❚ Now–1999 ⓔ

CHIARLO

Asti, Italy

Michele Chiarlo is now beginning to establish himself as one of Italy's premier sparkling wine producers.

MICHELE CHIARLO 1993 EXTRA BRUT

Complex biscuity aromas demonstrate that this is a serious, quality wine, but like so many Italian sparkling wines it lacks the correct acidity balance, thus misses out on length and finesse.
❚ On purchase ££

EOS, MICHELE CHIARLO 1993 EXTRA BRUT

This makes a fine, zesty fizz compared to most of the Italian competition. From the presentation alone this should be some avant garde restaurant's house wine.
❚ On purchase ££

CHIQUET

912 avenue du Général-Leclerc
Dizy, 51318 Épernay
☎ (326) 55.22.02 ⚏ (326) 51.83.81

Cousins to the Chiquet brothers who own Jacquesson.

GASTON CHIQUET NV BLANC DE BLANCS D'AŸ BRUT

This rare Aÿ *blanc de blancs* does not have the class or potential complexity of Aÿ Pinot Noir, but its succulent, creamy, juicy fruit is very moreish indeed.
❚ Now–2000 ££ ❦92F

GASTON CHIQUET NV TRADITION BRUT

A good, solid Champagne, which might not be special, but is recommended for its creamy-nutty-biscuity complexity.
❚ Now–2000 ££ ❦82F

GASTON CHIQUET 1989 BRUT

Noticeably deeper yellow colour than all other examples of this vintage, with a mature, full, malolactic complexity on nose and palate.
❚ Now–1999 £££ ❦110F

CIGRAVI

Penedès, Spain

Paul Cheneau is a French-owned Cava brand. CIGRAVI also produces Cava under the Masia Parera, Bell Duc and Giró Ribot labels.

BELL DUC 1995 CAVA BRUT

Sweet, toasty, fat and sassy.
❚ On purchase £

PAUL CHENEAU 1995 CAVA BRUT

Not as lush and elegant as the 1994, this vintage nevertheless has an easy-going fruity style that is as clean as a whistle, with good acidity and a soft finish.
❚ On purchase £

MASIA PARERA 1996 CAVA BRUT

When so many Cavas use Chardonnay, without having a Chardonnay character, it is ironic to find one that actually does taste of Chardonnay, yet contains none! Whatever is responsible does, however, give this *cuvée* a creamy feel in the mouth.
❚ Now–1999 £

CLICQUOT PONSARDIN

See Veuve Clicquot

CLOCKTOWER

See Thames Valley Vineyard

CLOUDY BAY

See Pelorus

CLOUET

8 rue Gambetta
Bouzy 51150 Tours-sur-Marne
☎ (326) 57.00.82

Small grower with a large range of often complex Champagnes.

ANDRÉ CLOUET NV SILVER BRUT, GRAND CRU

Rich, Pinot-dominated, oxidative style.
On purchase ££

ANDRÉ CLOUET NV GRANDE RÉSERVE, BRUT GRAND CRU **85**

Very much like the Silver Brut, just a tad smoother on the finish.
On purchase ££

CLOVER HILL
See Taltarni

COCKATOO RIDGE
South Australia, Australia
A joint venture between Geoff Merrill, the "flying-moustache" of Mount Hurtle fame, and Yalumba.

COCKATOO RIDGE NV BRUT **75**

Fat and fresh, with a touch of vanilla on the finish, this is quite a serious wine for its low price point.
On purchase £

CODORNÍU
Penedès, Spain
Despite its ancient origins, Codorníu is the most innovative firm in the Cava industry today,

CODORNÍU CUVÉE RAVENTÓS NV CAVA BRUT **70**

Clean, elegant and fruity, with a creamy-citrussy finish.
On purchase £

ANNA DE CODORNÍU CHARDONNAY 1995 CAVA BRUT

There used to be a Codorníu Chardonnay and an Anna de Codorníu, and they have been effectively merged as from the 1995 vintage, but it has not been a smooth transition. This has the makings of a fine wine, but should still be in Codorníu's cellars.
 Wait and see £

RAIMAT CHARDONNAY NV CAVA BRUT **75**

Rich and fruity, with good acidity, but usually more rustic than a properly aged Anna de Codorníu.
On purchase £

RAIMAT CAVA NV GRAN BRUT **87**

Subtle barrel-fermented aromas pervade the pineapple and other tropical fruits that fill the mouth, and promise to go lightly toasty. The acidity is excellent and the wine promises further interesting development. Great value for money.
Now–2000 £

CODORNÍU NAPA
Napa Valley, California, USA
A high-tech facility (though all you can see is the tip of a bunker protruding from the hillside) that has come to California to do battle with Freixenet, its Catalonian adversary, which set up Gloria Ferrer in 1982.

CODORNÍU NAPA NV BRUT **79**

Pale coloured, with a firm mousse of tiny bubbles, and some malolactic complexity creeping through the lush creamy freshness on the nose. The tangy-rich fruit needs very little time to develop some biscuity complexity.
 1999 £

CODORNÍU NAPA VINTAGE 1992 CARNEROS CUVÉE **79**

The aromas are young and relatively undeveloped for a California fizz of this age, yet the fruit is soft and supported by an even soft mousse of minuscule bubbles, so it should not be long before the nose catches up with the palate.
 1999 £

COLIO
Ontario, Canada
Founded by a group of Italian businessmen who wanted to import Italian wines, but found it easier to build a winery and make their own.

**CHARDONNAY LILY 1995
COLIO ESTATE VINEYARDS,
VIN MOUSSEUX**

If you like a fairly sweet fizz, this *cuve close* will be preferable to more expensive Canadian *méthode champenoise*. Creamy-flowery aroma, with moreish sweet fruit, although the mousse can be a bit explosive.
On purchase ©

COLLET

34 rue Jeanson, 51160 Aÿ-Champagne
☎ (326) 55.15.88 ℻ (326) 54.02.40
A low-profile cooperative in the great *grand cru* of Aÿ-Champagne.

**RAOUL COLLET NV
CARTE NOIRE BRUT**

Lightly structured and flowery-peppery with some biscuitiness on the finish.
On purchase ©©

**RAOUL COLLET NV
CARTE PERLE BRUT, 1ᴱᴿ CRU**

More intensity of fruit and a more serious quality than Carte Noire, with a certain potential for development.
Now–1999 ©©

**RAOUL COLLET 1990
CARTE D'OR BRUT**

Firm, lean, biscuity style that needs food to show at its best.
Now–2000 ©©©

COMTE –

See under main name

COMTESSE DE DIE

Rhone, France
Deliciously sweet pure Muscat wines.

**COMTESSE DE DIE TRADITION
1996 CLAIRETTE DE DIE, BRUT** ⑧⓪

Deliciously fresh, off-sweet richness of Muscat fruit – like Asti for grown ups.
On purchase ©

CONTRATTO

Asti, Italy

**CONTRATTO 1990
RISERVA GIUSEPPE
CONTRATTO, SPUMANTE**

Fresh, peppery fruit.
On purchase ©©

**CONTRATTO DE MIRANDA
1995 ASTI**

Bottle-fermented Asti! Everything about this wine is a class apart even from other good Asti, from the colour to the richness, sweetness, balance and finesse.
On purchase ©©

CORBANS

*Auckland/Gisborne/Napier/
Blenheim, New Zealand*
Many excellent upmarket wines.

**CORBANS VERDE NV
METHODE CHAMPENOISE**

Perfectly acceptable in a firm, fizzy style, but not exactly special.
On purchase ©©

**CORBANS AMADEUS 1993
CLASSIC RESERVE BRUT**

Not as impressive as previous vintages, but it could be in a developmental phase.
Wait and see ©©

(LES) CORDELIERS

Bordeaux, France
The oldest, most famous sparkling Bordeaux producer, with showcase cellars beneath the ruined cloisters of Cordeliers in St Emilion, but a surprising number of *cuvées* failed this year.

**LES CORDELIERS 1892-1992 NV
CRÉMANT DE BORDEAUX BRUT**

This special celebration *cuvée* has plenty of rich, clean fruit, but needs more acidity and finesse for a higher score.
On purchase ©

COURBET
See Marne et Champagne

COVIDES
Penedès, Spain
A large Spanish wine cooperative formed in 1964, COVIDES has three wineries and 800 members.

DUC DE FOIX NV CAVA BRUT　75

Fatter than most Cavas, with more fruit and a better mouth-fill and acidity.
 On purchase ⓔ

XENIUS NV CAVA BRUT　70

This light-bodied *cuvée* shows some elegance and ripeness, but is essentially for those who prefer a sweeter-styled *brut*.
On purchase ⓔ

CRAIGMOOR
New South Wales, Australia
This Mudgee-based winery is part of the Orlando group.

CRAIGMOOR VINTAGE CHARDONNAY 1994 BRUT　72

Big, malty-rich *cuvée*.
On purchase ⓔ

CRANSWICK
New South Wales, Australia
Mostly inexpensive fruity fizz, such as Barramundi and Aldridge, but also a serious Sparkling Shiraz.

ALDRIDGE ESTATE NV BRUT　70

Light-bodied, gentle fruit pepped-up by a firm mousse to provide some elegance.
On purchase ⓔ

BARRAMUNDI NV BRUT　71

This cheap fizz has developed a sweet, creamy, toffee-like complexity.
 On purchase ⓔ

THE CRANSWICK ESTATE NV SPARKLING SHIRAZ　80

Out of its class for Cranswick, which makes no pretensions over its inexpensive, commercial style of wine, this is a quality sparkling Shiraz with a lovely, ripeness of blackcurrant-raspberry fruit. Drier than most, with no oak at all.
On purchase ⓔ

THE CRANSWICK ESTATE NV PINOT CHARDONNAY BRUT　74

The very creamy, almost oaky, smoothness underlying the zesty-lemony flavour of this fizz is quite impressive for the price.
On purchase ⓔ

CRISTALINO
See Jaume Serra

CROS
Burgundy, France

BERNARD ET ODILE CROS 1993 CRÉMANT DE BOURGOGNE BRUT　70

Fresh lemon fruit with a firm mousse.
On purchase ⓔⓔ

CROSER
See Petaluma

DAMPIERRE
5 Grande rue, 51140 Chenay
☎ (326) 03.11.13　FAX (326) 03.18.05
The wonderfully eccentric Comte Audoin de Dampierre is offering 2,000 magnums of an excellent 1990.

COMTE AUDOIN DE DAMPIERRE NV BLANC DE BLANCS, BRUT　82

Creamy, rich and flavoursome, with some elegance. Good value, but lacking finesse.
Now–1999 ⓔⓔ 🍇133F

COMTE AUDOIN DE DAMPIERRE NV CUVÉE DES AMBASSADEURS, BRUT

Rich, smooth and full of biscuity fruit.
❦ Now–1999 ©© ♚128F

COMTE AUDOIN DE DAMPIERRE 1990 BRUT ROSÉ OEIL DE PEDRIX

Delicious strawberry-cherry fruit. To be consumed as fresh as possible.
❦ On purchase ©©© ♚140F

COMTE A. DE DAMPIERRE 1990 BLANC DE BLANCS, GRAND CRU, BRUT ⑧⑧

A delicately rich, finely tuned *cuvée* of slow-building complexity, bottled in magnum, and sealed by waxed-cord agraffe, an 18th-century method.
▶ 2000–2002 ©©©

DARWIN'S PATH
See Manquehue

D'-, DE –
See under main part of name

DEIDESHEIM
Pfalz, Germany

RIESLING SEKT 1990 DEIDESHEIMER PARADIESGARTEN SEKT EXTRA BRUT ⑦④

Fresh, peachy, pure Riesling fruit, with a nice juicy finish. Bottle-fermented.
❦ On purchase ©©

DEIS
Mosel-Saar-Ruwer, Germany
Matthias Deis has been producing hand-riddled Sekt by the *méthode champenois* since 1985.

WEINGUT MATTHIAS DEIS 1993 RIESLING SEKT TROCKEN

Fine, fresh Riesling with vanilla on the finish. Bottle-fermented.
❦ On purchase ©©

DELALEU
Loire, France
This has been a consistently successful sparkling wine producer over the last five years or so.

VOUVRAY, CUVÉE CLÉMENT NV BRUT, PASCAL DELALEU

Very fresh with delicate fruit lifted by a fine mousse of tiny bubbles.
❦ On purchase ©

DELAMOTTE
7 rue de la Brèche d'Oger,.51190
Le Mesnil-sur-Oger
☎ (326) 57.51.65 ⓕ (326) 57.79.29
The sister company to Salon, which is next door, Delamotte's wines are always rich, ripe and good value.

DELAMOTTE NV BRUT

Fine aromas, with elegant fruit on the palate, and a touch of pepperiness, which will disappear with more bottle-age.
❦ Now–2000 ©© ♚105F

DELAMOTTE 1990 BLANC DE BLANCS

A number of the 1990s had a creamy, exotic-fruit character, but this was one of the creamiest and most exotic.
❦ Now–2002 ©©© ♚150F

DELAROY
See Boizel

DELATITE
Victoria, Australia

DELATITE DEMELZA NV BRUT

Ignore the awful label and you will
discover that this *cuvée* has a nice
creamy-richness of fruit. Apparently, it
is a blend of Pinot Noir and Chardonnay
from 1994 and 1995, and the label will
be revamped if exported!
On purchase ⓔ

DELBECK

39 rue du Général Sarrail, 51100 Reims
📞 (326) 77.58.00 📠 (326) 77.58.01
An old Champagne brand which has
been bought and sold so often that it
has yet to establish a style.

DELBECK NV BRUT HÉRITAGE

Firm, well-structured, high-acid fruit
made without malolactic fermentation.
This non-vintage *brut* could do with
longer post-disgorgement ageing prior to
shipment or a higher dosage, however it
is still early days.
1999–2001 ⓔⓔ 🍾113F

DELBECK NV ROSÉ HÉRITAGE BRUT 86

A far more mature wine than the above,
with the mellow, strawberry richness of
Bouzy Pinot Noir dominating.
Now–2000 ⓔⓔ 🍾138F

DELBECK NV CRAMANT 87

Pure creamy-walnutty richness.
Now–2005 ⓔⓔⓔ 🍾145F

DELBECK NV BOUZY 88

Apricot aroma with ripe Pinot Noir red
fruits on the palate, and a typically Bouzy
touch of fatness on the finish.
Now–2000 ⓔⓔⓔ 🍾145F

DELBECK NV ORIGINE 90

A 1995-based *cuvée* in magnums only – a
youthful, intensely flavoured Champagne.
2000–2010 ⓔⓔⓔ

DELBECK VINTAGE 1990 BRUT 88

The 1990 vintage is a wine with young,
developmental, ethereal-minerally fruit,
and very fine acidity.
2000–2002 ⓔⓔⓔ 🍾138F

DELIANCE
Burgundy, France

The two highest-scoring Crémant de
Bourgogne tasted this year came
from this producer, which under blind
conditions speaks volumes. Made
from Côte Chalonnaise grapes.

RUBAN MAUVE, CRÉMANT DE BOURGOGNE NV BRUT, DELIANCE PÈRE ET FILS 88

Beautiful, fluffy fruit, with sherbetty
freshness and great acidity.
Now–2000 ⓔ

RUBAN VERT, CRÉMANT DE BOURGOGNE NV BRUT, DELIANCE PÈRE ET FILS 88

Lovely Burgundian Chardonnay fruit of
some class and finesse. Well selected,
skilfully made, with the potential to age.
Now–2001 ⓔ

DEMOISELLE
See Vranken

DÉTHUNE

2 rue du Moulin, 51150 Ambonnay
📞 (326) 57.01.88 📠 (326) 57.09.31
Usually a rich, ripe, Pinot-driven style.

PAUL DÉTHUNE 1990 BRUT 89

Tremendously rich and fruity in a easy-
drinking style, yet does not lack finesse.
Now–2000 ⓔⓔⓔ

DEUTZ

16 rue Jeanson, 51160 Aÿ-Champagne
📞 (326) 55.15.11 📠 (326) 58.76.13
Deutz went through an uneven patch
in the late 1980s, but everything
came right in 1990. The profitability
of this house suffered from under-
funding until Louis Roederer
acquired the firm in 1993.

DEUTZ NV BRUT CLASSIC

Fresh, expressive fruit, with a touch of pepper, which should go minerally-biscuity. Should be aged.
1999–2001 ££ ⚑142F

DEUTZ 1990 BRUT

As with many Deutz Champagnes, there is some pepperiness to the fruit, but the acidity is excellent. Will become complex.
1999–2002 £££ ⚑177F

DEUTZ 1989 BLANC DE BLANCS BRUT

Still tight and firm, especially for a 1989, with plenty of extract for development.
1999–2003 £££ ⚑240F

CUVÉE WILLIAM DEUTZ 1990 MILLÉSIMÉ BRUT

A flavour-packed wine with such bitter-ness from undeveloped extract that it promises to be complex when mature.
2000–2010 £££ ⚑382F

DEUTZ MARLBOROUGH

See Montana

DEVAUX

Domaine de Villeneuve, 10110 Bar-sur-Seine
☎ (25) 38.30.65 ℻ (25) 29.73.21
The Aube region's fastest-improving, most go-ahead and innovative cooperative, run by Claude Thibault.

VEUVE A. DEVAUX NV GRANDE RÉSERVE, BRUT

This *cuvée* was strangely almondy in 1997, but the current shipment is more classic, with some biscuit character.
❚ Now–1999 ££ ⚑99F

VEUVE A. DEVAUX NV CUVÉE ROSÉE, BRUT

Mature rooty-Pinot aromas, with hints of toastiness on the nose, and rich, toasty Chardonnay fruit on the palate. Rosée is not a mis-spelling; Devaux says that the extra "e" is intentional.
❚ Now–1999 ££

VEUVE A. DEVAUX NV BLANC DE NOIRS, BRUT

This is one pure Pinot *cuvée* that will definitely go toasty, rather than biscuity.
❚ Now–1999 ££

OEIL DE PERDRIX TRADITION NV BRUT, VEUVE A. DEVAUX

Very pale peach colour, with light and delightful fruit. Elegant and tangy.
❚ Now–1999 ££

VVE. A. DEVAUX 1990 MILLÉSIME BRUT

With heaps of super creamy-biscuit fruit, this pure Chardonnay *cuvée* knocks the spots off the 1990 Distinction.
❚ Now–2002 £££

VVE. A. DEVAUX 1990 CUVÉE DISTINCTION, BRUT

Fresh, fruity style with a hint of biscuiti-ness building in the middle, and an after-taste reminiscent of apple purée.
❚ Now–2000 £££ ⚑150F

VEUVE A. DEVAUX 1988 CUVÉE DISTINCTION BRUT

Lovely salmon colour with classy, creamy, slow-developing red-fruit aromas.
❚ Now–2001 £££

NICOLE D'AURIGNY 1992 BRUT

The depth and structure promise good development.
❚ Now–1999 £££

DIE

See Comtesse de Die

DIETRICH

Alsace, France

CLAUDE DIETRICH 1994 CRÉMANT D'ALSACE BRUT

Classy aromas are not reflected on the palate, which is okay, but workmanlike. It will be interesting to see how this particular *cuvée* develops.
❚ Now–1999 ££

DOMAINE CARNEROS

See Carneros

DOMAINE CHANDON

See Chandon

DOMAINE DE BRIZÉ

Loire, France

DOMAINE DE BRIZÉ NV CRÉMANT DE LOIRE BRUT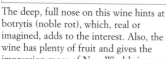

The deep, full nose on this wine hints at botrytis (noble rot), which, real or imagined, adds to the interest. Also, the wine has plenty of fruit and gives the impression more of New World ripeness than the Old World, let alone the Loire. A serious effort.
❦ On purchase ⓔ

DOMAINE DE LA GLORIETTE

Loire, France

DOMAINE DE LA GLORIETTE NV CUVÉE PRESTIGE, CRÉMANT DE LOIRE BRUT ⑦⑤

This wine had similar botrytis-like hints on the bouquet to those of Domaine de Brizé, but without any of the "New World" fruit on the palate, although it is still very fruity.
❦ On purchase ⓔ

DOMAINE DE LA PALEINE

Loire, France

DOMAINE DE LA PALEINE NV SAUMUR BRUT ⑦⓪

A very fresh, easy-going and clean wine for the Saumur appellation.
❦ On purchase ⓔ

DOMAINE DE NERLEUX

Loire, France

Better-known for Saumur-Champigny.

DOMAINE DE NERLEUX NV CRÉMANT DE LOIRE BRUT ⑦⓪

I much preferred the tangy, peppery fruit in this wine to Domaine de Nerleux's equally peppery, but dull Saumur.
❦ On purchase ⓔ

DOMAINE DES VARINELLES

Loire, France
This producer used to produce good Saumur-Champigny and Rosé de Loire, and now sparkling wines.

DAHEUILLER, DOMAINE DES VARINELLES NV CRÉMANT DE LOIRE BRUT ⑦⓪

This decent, zesty fizz might only just qualify, but that makes it superior to the vast majority of Loire bubblies I tasted.
❦ On purchase ⓔ

DOMAINE DU BOUXHOF

Alsace, France

DOMAINE DU BOUXHOF NV CRÉMANT D'ALSACE BRUT ⑦②

Lots of pineapple sprightly fruitiness gives this wine a real richness, but it has the acidity to support it.
❦ On purchase ⓔ

DOMAINE STE. MICHELLE

See Ste. Michelle

DOMAINE SYLVAIN GAUDRON

Loire, France

VOUVRAY BLANC DE BLANCS NV BRUT, DOMAINE SYLVAIN GAUDRON

Soft, easy and elegant sparkler with gentle fruit and a smooth mousse of small bubbles.
On purchase ⓔ

VOUVRAY PÉTILLANT NV DEMI-SEC, DOMAINE SYLVAIN GAUDRON

Fresh, creamy fruit.
On purchase ⓔ

DOM PÉRIGNON
See Moët & Chandon

DOM RUINART
See Ruinart

DON PEREJÓN
Spain
The white *cuvée* would have been hard pushed to score 10 points out of 100, but the *rosé* scraped in.

DON PEREJÓN NV MENCÍA ROSÉ BRUT

Although not a Cava, this is made by the *método tradicional* and its accessible fruit made it more enjoyable than many Cavas.
On purchase ⓔ

DOPFF AU MOULIN
Alsace, France
Pierre-Etienne Dopff puts a personal face on the Moët & Chandon of Alsace.

DOPFF AU MOULIN, CUVÉE BARTHOLDI 1993 CRÉMANT D'ALSACE BRUT

A richly flavoured wine that has consistently aged well since its inception. This vintage will peak in five or six years.
Now–1999 ⓔⓔ

DOPFF AU MOULIN, CUVÉE JULIEN NV CRÉMANT D'ALSACE BRUT

There is a good weight of fruit for a correctly lean structure here.
Now–1999 ⓔ

DOQUET-JEANMAIRE
44 Chemin Moulin Cense Bizet
☎ (326) 52.16.50 🖷 (326) 59.36.71

DOQUET-JEANMAIRE NV BLANC DE BLANCS, CARTE OR BRUT

Sprightly fruitiness on nose, with extremely rich fruit on the palate.
On purchase ⓔⓔ 🍷71F

DOQUET-JEANMAIRE NV BLANC DE BLANCS, RÉSERVE, DEMI-SEC ⊖

The first bottle had very little fizz, the second only a bit more, and both were deep yellow, with a mature sweet flavour and coconutty complexity that had nothing to do with oak, and everything to do with age. Curious, but not disliked.
On purchase ⓔⓔ 🍷85F

DOQUET-JEANMAIRE 1989 BLANC DE BLANCS BRUT ⓼⓪

Very soft and creamy, and needs to lengthen on the palate, but does not have the balance to age. Scrapes in on current enjoyment only.
On purchase ⓔⓔⓔ 🍷90F

DOWN ST. MARY
Crediton, England, UK
Simon Pratt is determined to produce the best English sparkling wine of which his vineyard is capable.

DOWN ST. MARY BUBBLY 1994 DRY

The 1992 was too oxidative, but this is far more skilfully made, with a fruit-driven style that promises to go toasty rather than oxidative after a year or so.
Now–1999 ⓔ

DRAPPIER

Grande rue, 10200 Urville
☎ (25) 27.40.15 ℻ (25) 27.41.19

Ultra-fruity Champagnes that quickly attain a lovely biscuity complexity.

DRAPPIER NV CARTE D'OR BRUT 88

Succulently fruity when first released, this goes deliciously biscuity within a year.
🍷 Now–1999 ££ 🥂80F

DRAPPIER NV ROSÉ BRUT 88

Rich, creamy-fruity that is already developing biscuity bottle-aromas.
🍷 Now–1999 ££

DRAPPIER NV SIGNATURE BRUT 89

Extremely rich and fruity, this will go very toasty after another year in bottle.
🍷 Now–2000 ££ 🥂90F

DRAPPIER 1990 CARTE D'OR BRUT 88

Incredibly fruity when first launched, this now has a great depth of intense fruit infused with biscuity complexity.
🍷 Now–1999 £££

DRAPPIER 1989 GRANDE SENDRÉE 90

Rich, sweet and pure, with complex after-aromas and great finesse, this is a single-vineyard Champagne from 70-year-old vines grown on soil with ash in it.
🍷 Now–2000 £££ 🥂120F

DRAPPIER 1995 CUVÉE DE L'AN 2000 88

The quality was evident although it is not commercially disgorged until May 1999. Capable of great finesse.
➤ 2000–2002 £££

DUC DE FOIX

See COVIDES

DUMANGIN

3 rue de Rilly, 51500 Chigny-les-Roses
☎ (326) 03.46.34 ℻ (326) 03.45.61

J. DUMANGIN FILS NV CARTE D'OR, DEMI-SEC, 1ᴱᴿ CRU 84

Fresh fruity aromas followed by soft, mellow sweetness.
🍷 On purchase ££ 🥂78F

J. DUMANGIN FILS 1992 BRUT, 1ᴱᴿ CRU 84

Firm, but more fruit-driven than biscuity.
🍷 Now–1999 £££ 🥂110F

J. DUMANGIN FILS 1993 CUVÉE 2000 ⊖

Under blind conditions I noted the biscuitiness building and gave this wine 83 points. However, this is not yet a fully commercial product, so I will reserve judgement.
➤ Wait and see £££ 🥂125F

J. DUMANGIN FILS 1991 BRUT MILLÉSIMÉ, 1ᴱᴿ CRU 84

Full-flavoured style with mellow-ripeness.
🍷 Now–1999 £££ 🥂110F

DUMONT

11 rue Gambetta, 51500 Rilly-la-Montagne
☎ (326) 03.40.67 ℻ (326) 03.44.82
A respected grower from the same village as Vilmart.

DANIEL DUMONT NV PREMIER CRU GRANDE RÉSERVE BRUT 85

This has grown richer, and fuller in bottle.
➤ On purchase ££ 🥂73F

DANIEL DUMONT NV GRANDE RÉSERVE ROSÉ BRUT 82

Deepish salmon-peach colour, with sprightly fruit on the nose. Little finesse, but bags of fruit in a big, rich, soupy way.
🍷 On purchase ££ 🥂73F

DANIEL DUMONT 1988 CUVÉE D'EXCELLENCE, BRUT 86

Creamy-biscuity richness.
🍷 Now–1999 £££ 🥂97F

DURBACH

Baden, Germany

WINZERGENOSSENSCHAFT DURBACH 1994 DURBACHER KOCHBERG ROSÉ SEKT BRUT

An old gold colour with hues of a setting sun. Gorgeously rich Pinot fruit on the palate, gently cushioned by an impeccable mousse of tiny pinhead bubbles.
❚ On purchase ⓔⓔ

DUVAL-LEROY

69 avenue de Bammental, F-51130 Vertus
☎ (326) 52.10.75 ☏ (326) 57.54.01
This house has always produced elegant Champagne of good value, and the quality improved in the 1990s.

FLEUR DE CHAMPAGNE NV DUVAL-LEROY

Very fresh, fragrant style of Chardonnay-dominated Champagne.
❚ On purchase ⓔⓔ

FLEUR DE CHAMPAGNE BLANC DE NOIRS NV DUVAL-LEROY

Made from Pinot Noir and Meunier, yet relatively more full-bodied than the *rosé*, which is just Pinot Noir. Fuller and more intense than other Duval-Leroy.
❚ On purchase ⓔⓔ

FLEUR DE CHAMPAGNE SAIGNÉE ROSÉ NV DUVAL-LEROY

A pure Pinot Noir *cuvée,* this delicious, easy-drinking *rosé* is teeming with beautiful, elegant, juicy ripe fruit.
❚ On purchase ⓔⓔ

FLEUR DE CHAMPAGNE BLANC DE BLANCS NV DUVAL-LEROY

Very fresh, floral aromas with light, fluffy fruit and a juicy-sweet finish.
❚ On purchase ⓔⓔⓔ

FLEUR DE CHAMPAGNE BLANC DE BLANCS 1995 DUVAL-LEROY

Its fresh, lime-blossom aromas and fluffy-citrussy fruit are so inviting that for this wine to be released any time after the legal minimum January 1999 would not be too soon. And the 1996 has such beautifully ripe acidity that I cannot wait for 2000.
❚ Now–2005 ⓔⓔⓔ

FLEUR DE CHAMPAGNE 1995 DUVAL-LEROY

Similar comments to the Blanc de Blancs 1995, but with sweeter, creamier fruit.
❚ Now–2005 ⓔⓔⓔ

FLEUR DE CHAMPAGNE 1990 DUVAL-LEROY

Wonderful richness of cream for such light body and elegant structure, with a lovely sweet-vanilla finish.
❚ Now–2005 ⓔⓔⓔ

EDWARDS & CHAFFEY
See Seaview

EHRHART
Alsace, France

ANDRÉ EHRHART NV CRÉMANT D'ALSACE BRUT, ROTENBERG

Some biscuity complexity with sweet, malty fruit.
❚ Now–2000 ⓔ

ELSTREE
See Highfield

EMRICH
Nahe, Germany

CHRISTIAN UND RICHARD EMRICH 1995 KREUZNACHER BLAUER SPÄTBURGUNDER SEKT EXTRA SEKT TROCKEN

An off-dry *rosé* with soft, elegant cherry fruit and fine acidity. Bottle-fermented.
❚ On purchase ⓔⓔ

ENDRIZZI
Trentino, Italy

ENDRIZZI NV COLLEZIONE MASETTO BRUT

Satisfying clean richness of fruit, a firm mousse and very small bubbles.
▮ On purchase ⓔ

MICHEL FAHRER NV CRÉMANT D'ALSACE BRUT

Very fresh fruit, but would benefit from a more individually expressive style.
▮ On purchase ⓔ

ENGEL

Alsace, France
A family enterprise with vineyards at the foot of Haut-Koenigsbourg.

ENGEL TRADITION NV CRÉMANT D'ALSACE BRUT

Touch of Chablis-like character, with firm fruit, structure and acidity. Could develop.
▮ Now–1999 ⓔ

FAUSTINO MÁRTINEZ

Rioja, Spain
One of a small number of Rioja wineries producing Cava. The firm's Reserva and Gran Reserva still red wines are also very good.

FAUSTINO MARTINEZ NV CAVA EXTRA SECO

Fresh and simple tropical fruit flavour.
▮ On purchase ⓔ

FACCOLI

Italy
My first encounter with Faccoli, and an extremely happy one it was too. One of Franciacorta's top producers.

FACCOLI NV BRUT ROSÉ, FRANCIACORTA

Old gold colour, with mature, toasty aroma, but very fresh apricot fruit on the palate.
▮ On purchase ⓔ

FACCOLI NV EXTRA BRUT, FRANCIACORTA

Rich toasty aromas and superior acidity balance for an Italian sparkling wine.
▮ On purchase ⓔ

FACCOLI NV BRUT, FRANCIACORTA

Seriously fine, mature aromas of toast and coffee follow perfectly onto the palate. A Champagne-lover's Italian fizz.
▮ On purchase ⓔ

(DE) FAVERI

Veneto, Italy
Only six Prosecco survived the test, two of which were from this producer, including the highest scorer.

DE FAVERI, PROSECCO DI VALDOBBIADENE NV VINO SPUMANTE BRUT

Similar to, but a lighter version of, the De Faveri in the prestige bottle below.
▮ On purchase ⓔ

DE FAVERI, PROSECCO DI VALDOBBIADENE NV VINO SPUMANTE BRUT

Same name as above, but in a prestige-shaped bottle. Very fresh, Mâcon-style fruit on nose and palate, with the freshness and elegance following right through to the aftertaste.
▮ On purchase ⓔ

FAHRER

Alsace, France
This grower has a certain reputation for Rouge de St-Hippolyte, but only just passes muster on his *crémant*.

FAZI-BATTAGLIA

Italy
This producer's makes the excellent Verdicchio di Castelli di Jesi Le Moie, a still wine, as well as this *spumante*, which just scraped in.

FAZI-BATTAGLIA NV VINO SPUMANTE BRUT

Ripe fruit overlaid with wet straw.
On purchase £

FERRARI

Trentino, Italy

To maintain the motoring theme, Ferrari is acknowledged by many as the "Rolls Royce" of Italian fizz,

FERRARI NV BRUT, TRENTO

A firm, rich flavour of some complexity, although it still has room to develop.
Now–2000 £

FERRER

See Gloria Ferrer

FEUILLATTE

CD 40a Chouilly, 51206 Épernay
☎ (326) 54.50.60 📠 (326) 55.33.04

This Champagne brand has improved over the last 10 years, but the performance is still patchy for a cooperative that has so many good vineyards at its disposal.

NICOLAS FEUILLATTE 1992 BLANC DE BLANCS BRUT, PREMIER CRU

A rich, clean and flavoursome *cuvée* that promises to develop some complexity. It is nice to see Nicolas Feuillatte succeed in a relatively modest vintage.
Now–1999 £££ 🍾109F

NICOLAS FEUILLATTE 1988 CUVÉE SPÉCIALE BRUT, 1ᴇʀ CRU

This biscuity *cuvée* is very mature for a 1988, showing its age particularly on the finish. This is one of two prestige *cuvées*, the other being Palmes d'Or, and only the first vintage of the latter (1985 Palmes d'Or) has lived up to the expectation of a luxury Champagne.
On purchase £££ 🍾130F

FIRMATO

Trentino, Italy

FIRMATO NV BRUT, TRENTO

Rich, smooth fruit, firm mousse and a tasty finish.
On purchase £

FITZ

Pfalz, Germany

The oldest Sekt-producing house in the Pfalz, dating from 1837.

FITZ NV RIESLING SEKT EXTRA BRUT

This is an elegant pure Riesling with a hint of peaches. Made by *cuve close*.
On purchase ££

FLUTEAU

5 Rue de la Nation, 10250 Gyé-sur-Seine
☎ (325) 38.20.02 📠 (325) 38.24.84

This Aubois house run by Thierry and Jennifer Fluteau is the smallest in Champagne, even smaller than Salon.

G. FLUTEAU NV BLANCHE BRUT

Rich and fruity, with good weight, with a gentle mousse of medium-small bubbles.
On purchase ££

G. FLUTEAU 1993 BLANCHE BRUT

Richer and fruitier, with tinier bubbles in the mousse than the above.
Now–2000 ££

FOIX

See Covides

FORGET-BRIMONT

11 route de Louvois, 51500 Craon de Ludes
☎ (326) 61.10.45 📠 (326) 61.11.58

FORGET-BRIMONT NV CARTE BLANCHE, EXTRA BRUT

Lacks a bit of finesse on the nose, but is really quite rich and ripe on the palate.
❚ Now–1999 ⓔⓔ ❦82F

FOURNY
5 rue du Mesnil, 51130 Vertus
☎ (326) 52.16.30 ⅎ (326) 52.2013

VVE FOURNY NV BLANC DE BLANCS, BRUT PREMIER CRU

Lovely fresh and fluffy sherbetty fruit.
❚ On purchase ⓔⓔ ❦80F

FRATI
See Cà dei Frati

FREIXENET
Penedès, Spain
The Freixenet group includes Castellblanch, Segura Viudas, Conde Caralt and Canals Nubiola, Gloria Ferrer in California and an operation in Mexico, plus the Champagne house of Henri Abelé, but it is most famous for its black bottle Cava.

FREIXENET MONASTRELL-XARELLO NV CAVA BRUT

Now on the third or fourth release of this ground-breaking *cuvée* (the first commercially available white Cava to include black grapes), this wine shows a hint of black grape colour, some creamy-richness and a flowery perfume on the finish.
❚ On purchase ⓔ

FREIXENET 1991 CAVA BRUT NATURE

The non-dosage, vintage version of Cordon Negro was fine in 1997 when the 1991 was on the shelf – one of the best vintages of this *cuvée* since the 1975 – and it will still serve you well. (Not so the 1994 Brut Nature vintage.)
❚ On purchase ⓔ

GAILLARD-GIROT
43 rue Victor Hugo, 51530 Mardeuil
☎ (326) 51.64.59 ⅎ (326) 51.70.59

GAILLARD-GIROT NV BRUT

Rich, fruity and tasty, with creamy-biscuity finesse building on the finish.
❚ Now–1999 ⓔⓔ ❦66F

GALLIMARD
18-20 rue du Magny, 10340 Les Riceys
☎ (325) 29.32.44 ⅎ (325) 38.55.20
Jean and Didier Gallimard have recently received a fair bit of well-deserved attention in the French press for their sparkling wines.

GALLIMARD NV CUVÉE DE RÉSERVE BRUT

Has a fine, flowery finesse and an incredibly long finish.
❚ Now–1999 ⓔⓔ ❦70F

GALLIMARD 1992 CUVÉE PRESTIGE BRUT

Very rich and biscuity.
❚ Now–2000 ⓔⓔⓔ ❦80F

GALLO
California, USA
It is almost too much to comprehend, but E&J Gallo has a total production under numerous brands equal to one-and-a-half times the entire output of Australia. The latest sparkler only just scrapes in, but this is the sort of producer that could, with investment and the right consultant, produce a world class sparkling wine. We will have to see whether Indigo Hills is as ambitious as Gallo gets or the blue-print for something more serious.

INDIGO HILLS

An easy-drinking fizz in a clean, fresh and fruity style that is a tad too sweet, but probably just right for the mass market.
❚ On purchase ⓔ

GARDET

13 rue Georges Legros
51500 Chigny-les-Roses
☎ (326) 03.42.03 📠 (326) 03.43.95

A small house with a good reputation among British traditionalists. The wines can sometimes be too heavy and oxidative, but when there is enough fruit, these elements come together to make *cuvées* of stunning richness and potential complexity.

GARDET 1988 BRUT

Very fruity with none of the oxidative aromas that can detract from some Gardet *cuvées*. Could do with more finesse, but there is an interesting peppery character that promises to mellow, and a certain richness.
➤ 1999–2002 €€€ ⚘113F

CUVÉE CHARLES GARDET 1995 BRUT 85

An advance sample shows fine balance and potential, providing it is not left on its lees longer than three years.
➤ 2000–2005 €€€

GATINOIS

7 rue Marcel Mailly, 51160 Aÿ
☎ (326) 55.14.26 📠 (326) 52.75.99

Pierre Cheval sells part of his production to Bollinger, but increasingly makes more of his own Champagne.

GATINOIS NV TRADITION 85

This is an easy-to-drink *cuvée*. However, it does need 18–24 months to smooth down the raw elements of the floral aromas that pervade this young, soft, elegant Champagne.
➤ 2000 €€

GATINOIS NV RÉSERVE 87

This is the Tradition with an extra year or two yeast-contact, and the raw-floral notes have disappeared to be replaced by fine autolytic aromas, consequently this is ready to drink but also offers more serious, age-worthy potential.
❚ Now–2003 €€

GATINOIS 1991 BRUT

I was not convinced by this vintage, but the 1985 is full of delicious, honeyed fruit, so I will reserve my opinion for now, hence the lack of an overall score.
➤ Wait and see €€€

GATINOIS 1992 BRUT

Similar feelings to the 1991.
➤ Wait and see €€€

GAUCHER

10200 Arconville
☎ (325) 27.87.31 📠 (325) 27.85.84
This Aube producer is currently on as good a form as I can remember.

BERNARD GAUCHER NV CARTE D'OR BRUT 86

A full, strong Pinot style that builds in the mouth. This *cuvée's* high extract is supported by a fine structure, making it a good food wine, but there is already some complexity and the finish is beginning to mellow out.
❚ Now–1999 €€

GAUDRON

See Domaine Sylvain Gaudron

GAUTHIER

See Marne et Champagne

GENET

22 rue des Partelaines, 51530 Chouilly
☎ (326) 55.40.51 📠 (326) 59.16.92
An inconsistent producer in my experience.

MICHEL GENET NV BLANC DE BLANCS BRUT, GRAND CRU 80

Fresh and rich, but rather too almondy for a classic *blanc de blancs*.
❚ On purchase €€

GEOFFROY

150 rue du Bois-des-Jots
Cumières 51480 Damery
☎ (326) 55.32.31 ℻ (326) 54.66.50

The Geoffroys are quality-conscious,
in both the vineyard and winery,
harvesting grapes in sweeps,
using oak foudres and preventing
the malolactic.

RENÉ GEOFFROY NV CUVÉE PRESTIGE, BRUT

Softer and smoother than the Cuvée de
Réserve, with some finesse.
🍷 On purchase £€ 🥂108F

RENÉ GEOFFROY NV CUVÉE DE RÉSERVE BRUT, PREMIER CRU

Fine flavours and good acidity, with more
finesse than the current Cuvée Sélectionnée.
🍷 Now–1999 £€ 🥂75F

RENÉ GEOFFROY 1993 CUVÉE SÉLECTION BRUT

A fresh and zesty *cuvée* that is drinking
well, but will age gracefully.
🍷 Now–2001 £€

GERMAIN

38 rue de Reims, 51500 Rilly-la-Montagne
☎ (326) 03.40.19 ℻ (326) 03.43.11

The basic non-vintage is boringly
amylic, although some of the top
cuvées can be excellent value.

HENRI GERMAIN 1990 BRUT 88

Very exotic, rich and fulsome fruit. Huge
fun when tasted, but will probably go
through an awkward developmental stage
before emerging in a more classic, complex
style. A second sample via the importer
had a creamy-toffee malolactic richness.
🍷 Now–2002 £€€

HENRI GERMAIN NV BRUT RESERVE 86

I was glad to find no amylic aroma in the
latest *cuvée,* which is fresh and fruity,
with some mellow-vanilla on the finish.
The best non-vintage Germain in memory.
🍷 Now–1999 £€

GERMANIER

See SAVISA

GIANNI

Asti, Italy

GIANNI NV ASTI

Sweet, fresh, rich and piquant, this wine
had the most muscatty fruit of all the Asti
tasted this year.
🍷 On purchase £

GIERSBERGER

Alsace, France

GIERSBERGER NV CRÉMANT D'ALSACE BRUT

Oxidative complexity with sweet fruit on
the palate.
🍷 On purchase £

GIESEN

Christchurch, New Zealand

This is almost as good as Giesen's
wonderful still Pinot Noir.

VOYAGE, SPECIAL CUVÉE BRUT NV GIESEN WINE ESTATE

Beautifully bright Pinot fruit. A stunner.
🍷 Now–1999 £

GIMONNET

1 rue de la République, 51530 Cuis
☎ (326) 59.78.70 ℻ (326) 59.79.84

All Gimonnet vineyards are planted
exclusively with Chardonnay, hence
every wine is a *blanc de blancs*,
which is a rare phenomenon in
Champagne, even among growers
on the Côte des Blancs. Quality can
be exceptionally high and prices
very reasonable.

**PIERRE GIMONNET & FILS
NV BLANC DE BLANCS
BRUT, PREMIER CRU**

Clean, rich flavour. Should develop well.
❗ Now–2000 ££ 🍾87F

**PIERRE GIMONNET & FILS
NV OENOPHILE, BLANC
DE BLANCS MAXI-BRUT**

Patience!
➡ 1999 ££ 🍾113F

**PIERRE GIMONNET & FILS
1993 GASTRONOME, BLANC
DE BLANCS BRUT**

Huge mouthful of flavour with an
extremely persistent finish.
➡ 1999–2003 £££ 🍾96F

**PIERRE GIMONNET & FILS
1992 GRAND CRU -
CHARDONNAY BRUT**

Rich and fruity, but too young to drink yet.
➡ 2000–2002 £££ 🍾115F

**PIERRE GIMONNET & FILS
1990 FLEURON,
BLANC DE BLANCS BRUT**

A classy combination of succulent fruit,
richness and finesse.
❗ Now–2003 £££ 🍾108F

**PIERRE GIMONNET & FILS
1989 BLANC DE BLANCS BRUT**

A big, flavour-packed wine that needs
either food or time.
❗ Now–2005 £££ 🍾127F

GISSELBRECHT

Alsace, France
The Auxerrois *crémant* failed muster
this year, while the *rosé* scraped in.

**W. GISSELBRECHT BRUT
ROSÉ NV CRÉMANT D'ALSACE**

Soft, pure Pinot fruit.
❗ On purchase £

GLORIETTE

See Domaine de la Gloriette

GLORIA FERRER

Sonoma, California, USA

The Spanish Cava house Freixenet
founded this in California in 1982,
and it is named after the wife of José
Ferrer, the president of Freixenet.

**GORIA FERRER SONOMA BRUT
NV FREIXENET SONOMA CAVES**

Light and creamy with fat, sassy fruit and
a sherbetty finish.
❗ On purchase £

**GLORIA FERRER BLANC
DE NOIRS BRUT NV
FREIXENET SONOMA CAVES**

A few years ago, this *cuvée* had raw
fermentation odours, but the current
shipment is deliciously fresh and juicy.
❗ On purchase £

GOERG

4 Place du Mont Chenil, 51130 Vertus
☎ (326) 52.15.31 📠 (326) 52.23.96
A superior cooperative Champagne
that is usually good for vintage *cuvées*,
but I was not able to recommend the
1992 submitted for tasting.

**PAUL GOERG NV BLANC
DE BLANCS BRUT**

Rich flavours supported by a structure
that will be better after a little bottle-age.
➡ 1999–2001 ££ 🍾75F

GOLAN HEIGHTS WINERY

Israel
This winery in the Golan Heights is
renowned for its still wines, but it still
has a lot of fine-tuning to do to its
sparkling wine *cuvées*.

**YARDEN BLANC DE BLANCS NV
GOLAN HEIGHTS WINERY BRUT**

Shipments of this wine seem to vary. A
lightly rich malo style with elegant,
mellow fruit on the finish.
❗ On purchase £

(MICHEL) GONET

196 avenue Jean-Jaurès, 51190 Avize
☏ (326) 57.50.56 **FAX** (326) 57.91.98

An inconsistent grower who hits as many lows as highs.

MICHEL GONET NV BLANC DE BLANCS BRUT GRAND CRU

Fruity, with nice finesse on finish.
▌Now–1999 **££** 🍾90F

MICHEL GONET 1989 BLANC DE BLANCS BRUT GRAND CRU 87

A bit of a contradiction, this, with its fresh, delicately perfumed aromas sitting on an unexpectedly firm structure, as if there were some Pinot Noir in the blend.
▌1998–2001 **£££** 🍾100F

(PHILIPPE) GONET

1 rue de la Brèche d'Oger
51190 Le-Mesnil-sur-Oger
☏ (326) 57.51.07 **FAX** (326) 57.51.03

Philippe is Michel's cousin (above).

PHILIPPE GONET 1988 BLANC DE BLANCS BRUT 85

Creamy-nutty style with low dosage.
 1999–2000 **£££** 🍾140F

GOSSET

69 rue Jules Blondeau
51160 Aÿ-Champagne
☏ (326) 55.14.18 **FAX** (326) 51.55.88

I queried the quality of Gosset recently, but I am now sure that the quality is as good as it has ever been.

GOSSET BRUT EXCELLENCE 83

Fresh, sweet, easy-drinking fruit.
▌Now–1999 **££** 🍾129F

GOSSET NV GRANDE RÉSERVE BRUT 94

A lovely depth of flavour, plenty of finesse and great potential complexity in a smooth, non-oxidative biscuity style.
▌Now–1999 **£££** 🍾218F

GOSSET GRANDE MILLÉSIME 1989 BRUT

Maturing relatively quickly on the nose for Gosset, but there is a strand of freshness running through the richness on the palate, hinting that it might well go through another stage of development.
▌Now–2002 **£££** 🍾284F

GOSSET GRANDE MILLÉSIME 1985 BRUT

The depth of flavour in this wine is incredible and it gets deeper and more sustained each time I taste it. Although it already has the rich, biscuity complexity and finesse that Gosset drinkers expect, it will be even greater in five years.
▌Now–2015 **£££**

GOSSET CELEBRIS 1990 BRUT 91

New prestige *cuvée* with a significantly higher proportion of Chardonnay. Almost too delicious to be true, but it has a classic structure and will develop well.
▌Now–2010 **££££**

GOSSET CELEBRIS 1988 BRUT 91

Great promise, but needs lots more post-disgorgement ageing.
 2003–2018 **££££** 🍾390F

GOSSET GRAND ROSÉ 1990 BRUT

This exotically creamy-floral *cuvée* seems atypical for Gosset, but it is superb nonetheless and is still very young.
▌Now–2002 **££** 🍾296F

GOSSET GRAND ROSÉ 1988 BRUT

Refined and strongly perfumed in its youth, this is now taking on the smooth, biscuity finesse expected from Gosset.
▌Now–2002 **££**

GOUTORBE

9 rue Jeanson, 51160 Aÿ-Champagne
☏ (326) 55.21.70 **FAX** (326) 54.85.11

Henri Goutorbe has produced some excellent Champagnes in the past, but nothing to touch the quality and complexity of the 1990 vintage now on the market.

HENRI GOUTORBE NV CUVÉE TRADITIONNELLE BRUT **84**

Fine, perfumed and elegant.
❚ Now–2001 ⓔⓔ ⏳75F

GOUTORBE NV BRUT, CUVÉE PRESTIGE **85**

Rich citrus-like fruit.
❚ Now–2000 ⓔⓔ ⏳84F

HENRI GOUTORBE 1990 BRUT, GRAND CRU **91**

Blockbusting combination of succulence and complexity, with a touch of vanilla on the finish.
❚ Now–2005 ⓔⓔⓔ ⏳116F

GRAEGER

Rheinhessen, Germany

GRAEGER PRIVAT RESERVE 1995 SPÄTBURGUNDER SEKT BRUT **74**

The intensity of Pinot Noir fruit in this wine is so satisfying and mellow it is almost gamey. Bottle-fermented.
❚ On purchase ⓔⓔ

GRANDIER

See Manquehue

GRANT BURGE

South Australia, Australia
Owner-winemaker Grant Burge originally founded Krondorf (now part of Mildara Blass). He has a solid foundation of good vineyards and in just ten years has quickly built up a reputation for the richness and consistency of his eponymous brand.

GRANT BURGE NV METHODE TRADITIONELLE BRUT **74**

I did not like the green-malic Pinot Chardonnay *cuvée* tasted a couple of months earlier, but this is softer with a touch of vanilla finesse on the finish.
❚ On purchase ⓔ

GRAMONA

Penedès, Spain

This small family-owned firm has its own vineyards, and regularly produces some of the best Cavas available.

III LUSTROS 1991 CAVA BRUT **70**

Creamy-cedary fruit and good underlying acidity enable this *cuvée* to scrape in. Last year it had lovely lemony-toasty fruit that would have warranted a score of 80 points, but, unfortunately, terpene aromas have developed over the last 12 months.
❚ On purchase ⓔ

CELLAR BATTLE 1989 CAVA BRUT **77**

Terpenes have also appeared on the nose of this vintage since I tasted it one year ago (80 points then). This has leached away some of the finesse, but it is still packed with creamy-peachy-vanilla fruit on the palate, and a sweet vanilla finish.
❚ On purchase ⓔ

GRATIEN

30 rue Maurice Cerveaux, 51201 Épernay
☎ (326) 54.38.20 ℻ (41) 51.03.55
This is one of my favourite producers, but I was surprised by the small selection submitted for the organized tastings (especially compared to the large number of Loire *cuvées* from its sister company Gratien & Meyer).

ALFRED GRATIEN NV BRUT RÉSERVE **88**

Alfred Gratien's Brut Réserve is a full, firm, classic-structured *cuvée* that shows rich, spicy fruit of excellent finesse. This wine is capable of considerable longevity and ultimate complexity, which is a tribute to the much-maligned Meunier grape, since it accounts for more than 45 per cent of this blend.
❚ Now–2002 ⓔⓔ

ALFRED GRATIEN 1989 BRUT **90**

Astonishing acidity underscores an intensity of fruit that promises to become very complex in a few years.
 2000–2010 ⓔⓔⓔ

GRATIEN & MEYER

Loire, France

One of the top fizz producers in the Loire, this was founded in 1864 at the same time as Alfred Gratien.

GRATIEN & MEYER NV CUVÉE ROYALE, CRÉMANT DE LOIRE BRUT

Very rich, fresh, fruity aroma. I much preferred this to Gratien & Meyer's Saumur Brut, although the "same" wine under the own-label of The Wine Society (UK) was distinctly better.
❙ On purchase ⓔ

GRATIEN & MEYER NV HARMONIE DRY, SAUMUR

The freshest *sec* on the nose, and as rich and sweet as a *demi-sec* on the palate, with nice juicy fruit that I preferred to Gratien & Meyer's Demi-Sec.
❙ Now–2000 ⓔ

GRATIEN & MEYER NV CUVÉE FLAMME, SAUMUR BRUT

Apricots and custard on the nose, with elegant apricot fruit and a twist of tangerine on the palate. An expressive Loire sparkling wine that shows some potential for complexity, it is the best Loire fizz I have tasted in recent memory.
❙ Now–2000 ⓔ

GRATIEN & MEYER NV BRUT ROSÉ, CUVÉE FLAMME, SAUMUR

A well-structured *rosé* capable of some improvement in bottle.
❙ Now–2000 ⓔ

GRATIEN & MEYER, CARDINAL NV NOIR DE NOIRS, VIN ROUGE MOUSSEUX, DEMI-SEC

A dark, deep feast of tannic, black fruit flavours, with a long, very sweet finish.
❙ On purchase ⓔ

GRATIEN & MEYER COLLECTION 1989 BLANC DE BLANC, SAUMUR BRUT

Mature, creamy-fruit aroma and flavour. This is a serious Saumur that some Loire devotees would probably rate higher.
❙ On purchase ⓔⓔ

GREEN POINT

See Chandon Australia

GRENELLE

Loire, France

LOUIS DE GRENELLE NV SAUMUR ROSÉ SEC

Fresh and sweetish, with very clean, easy-drinking fruit.
❙ Now–1999 ⓔ

LOUIS DE GRENELLE NV SAUMUR BRUT

Tight, lemony fruit of some specificity. Expressive.
❙ Now–2000 ⓔ

GRÉSILLE

Loire, France

ANNE DE LA GRÉSILLE NV CRÉMANT DE LOIRE BRUT

A slight oxidative complexity adds a dimension of interest to the clean, lean fruit in this wine. Good length.
❙ On purchase ⓔ

GRUSS

Alsace, France

A few wines from this Eguisheim grower, including two good *crémants*.

GRUSS BRUT PRESTIGE NV CRÉMANT D'ALSACE

Lovely, fat and sassy fruit and a nice cushiony mousse, but it would have scored even higher with more acidity.
❙ On purchase ⓔ

JOSEPH GRUSS & FILS NV CRÉMANT D'ALSACE BRUT

Very fruity aroma, sherbetty fruit, cushiony mousse, and a fresh, breezy finish.
❙ On purchase ⓔ

HAGNAU

Baden, Germany

WINZERVEREIN HAGNAU 1995 HAGNAUER BURGSTALL KERNER SEKT EXTRA TROCKEN

I'm not overly fond of the Kerner grape, but this *cuvée* is a good example of how fresh, flowery, off-dry fizz should be. Bottle-fermented.

❙ On purchase ⓔⓔ

HAMBACHER SCHLOSS

Pfalz, Germany
This cooperative has 150 members who produce 50,000 cases of Sekt each year by the transfer method.

HAMBACHER SCHLOSS 1993 HAMBACHER REBSTÖCKEL DORNFELDER SEKT TROCKEN

Very winey style. A curiosity.

❙ On purchase ⓔⓔ

HANDLEY

Mendocino, California, USA
Méthode champenoise specialist in the top-performing Anderson Valley.

HANDLEY 1992 BLANC DE BLANCS

Even when a vintage has lacked acidity, the soft, creamy-lemony Chardonnay fruit in the Blanc de Blancs makes it stand out.

❙ Now–1999 ⓔⓔ

HANDLEY 1992 BRUT

Good acidity and a soft mousse of tiny bubbles add a crisp dimension to the creamy-vanilla richness in this *cuvée*.

❙ Now–1999 ⓔⓔ

HARDY'S

South Australia, Australia
Hardy's Nottage Hill is a real winner.

HARDY'S NV BRUT

Malo-dominated nose and palate here, with deep, malty richness of fruit, and a good balance.

❙ On purchase ⓔ

SIR JAMES NV SPARKLING SHIRAZ

Soft spicy red fruits put this sparkling Shiraz in a different class to the 1993 white Sir James Hardy Brut.

❙ On purchase ⓔ

NOTTAGE HILL SPARKLING CHARDONNAY 1996 BRUT

A fresh, fluffy, gently rich and creamy fizz that hits the spot. Not great quality, but certainly a satisfying wine that offers great value for money.

❙ On purchase ⓔ

OMNI NV BRUT

A more individual character than most at this price point, with a reasonable structure of firm, creamy fruit.

❙ On purchase ⓔ

YARRA BURN CHARDONNAY PINOT NOIR 1993 BRUT

This zesty-lemony *cuvée* is a very fresh sparkling wine, with its five years of age only just beginning to mellow the sherbetty fruit on the finish.

❙ On purchase ⓔⓔ

LEASINGHAM CLASSIC CLARE 1991 SPARKLING SHIRAZ

Classic cedary-oaky sparkling red Shiraz.

❙ On purchase ⓔ

HARTENBERGER

Alsace, France
Normally one of the best Crémant d'Alsace producers, particularly for Pinot Gris, but the current *cuvées* are somewhat below par.

HARTENBERGER, BLANC DE BLANCS NV CRÉMANT D'ALSACE BRUT

Rich and ripe, with more than enough fat for mouthfill and a rather sweet finish. Needs more acidity for a higher score.

❙ On purchase ⓔ

HASELGROVE

South Australia, Australia

Established in 1980 by Nick Haselgrove, who laid down a *solera* for his increasingly popular Sparkling Garnet as recently as 1991. The notes below were based on SG3 (1995-based) and SG4 (1996-based), both of which were uncannily similar in style and quality, I am glad it is such a young *solera* because old *soleras* have too many drawbacks for sparkling wine in terms of terpenes and coarse oxidative characteristics.

HASELGROVE NV McCLAREN VALE SPARKLING GARNET

Full of tangy, bilberry and cranberry fruit, this lavishly flavoured fizz is marked by its fresh, billowy mousse.
❚ On purchase Ⓔ

HAUTE BOURGOGNE

Burgundy, France
This cooperative started producing Crémant de Bourgogne in 1994.

LES VIGNERONS DE HAUTE BOURGOGNE NV DEMI-SEC, CRÉMANT DE BOURGOGNE

Some creamy-biscuity malolactic complexity on the nose, with rich, sweet, caramel fruit on the palate, and a touch of vanilla on the finish.
❚ Now–2000 Ⓔ

HAUTES-CÔTES

Burgundy, France
Grapes grown in the Hautes-Côtes de Nuits and Hautes-Côtes de Beaune.

CRÉMANT DE BOURGOGNE NV BRUT, LES CAVES DES HAUTES-CÔTES

Some biscuity maturity on the nose, with good acidity underpinning light, elegant fruit on the palate.
❚ Now–1999 Ⓔ

CRÉMANT DE BOURGOGNE BLANC DE BLANCS NV BRUT, LES CAVES DES HAUTES-CÔTES

Creamy-malo-biscuity aromas, good length of flavour, plenty of ripe acidity.
❚ Now–1999 Ⓔ

HEEMSKERK

See Jansz and Rebecca Vineyard

(CHARLES) HEIDSIECK

4 Blvd. Henry Vasnier, 51100 Reims
☎ (326) 84.43.50 ⊠ (326) 84.43.99
This is the home of Daniel Thibault, the maestro of master blenders who built up a stock of reserve wines to create the top-performing Brut Réserve. This has now been relaunched in three versions based on the date of bottling, which is confusing even for wine critics. The quality is as brilliant as ever, but I hope that fractionalizing the Brut Réserve image does not divide its loyal customers. Meanwhile, look out for a release of mature Champagne "Charlie" vintages.

CHARLES HEIDSIECK NV BRUT RÉSERVE, MIS EN CAVE 1995

This was a pre-commercial *cuvée* I tasted, and it was still in sweet young-fruit mode, with none of the creamy-vanilla finesse for which Brut Réserve is famous.
❚ Now–2003 ⒺⒺ

CHARLES HEIDSIECK NV BRUT RÉSERVE, MIS EN CAVE 1994

Extraordinary finesse for such a rich and full wine, this has the finest bead (tiny bubbles) of the Mis en Cave *cuvées*, with the most cushiony mousse and smoothest palate. Beautifully balanced dosage.
❚ Now–2002 ⒺⒺ 🍷130F

CHARLES HEIDSIECK NV BRUT RÉSERVE, MIS EN CAVE 1993

Soft and mellow, this is the easiest Mis en Cave to drink, but the 1994 offers more interest on the palate.
❚ Now–2001 ⒺⒺ 🍷145F

CHARLES HEIDSIECK NV BRUT RÉSERVE, MIS EN CAVE 1992

You would not think that this was the oldest of the three *cuvées* originally launched. Still quite tight when tasted, it will loosen up by Christmas 1999.
➤ 1999–2003 ££ ❦160F

CHARLES HEIDSIECK 1990 BRUT 93

Rich and creamy, but still building, this vintage was a change of style for Charles Heidsieck, with more emphasis on Chardonnay fruit, going for intensity and elegance, rather than Pinot weight.
❘ Now–2010 £££ ❦180F

CHARLES HEIDSIECK 1989 BRUT 90

Extraordinarily successful for the vintage, this was the bridge in style between the old Charles Heidsieck vintages as last expressed by the 1985, and the new direction of 1989.
➤ 1999–2004 £££

CHARLES HEIDSIECK 1990 CUVÉE DES MILLÉNAIRES 92

The creamy-rich fruit in this *cuvée* has the slow-building capacity for which Millénaires has quickly become noted, and promises an exceptional balance of finesse and complexity in years to come.
❘ Now–2005 £££

CHARLES HEIDSIECK 1985 CUVÉE DES MILLÉNAIRES 92

The second vintage of this *cuvée* is even more intensely flavoured than the first, and has taken just as long to reveal its true mellow-biscuity richness.
❘ Now–2005 £££ ❦250F

(PIPER-)HEIDSIECK

51 Boulevard Henri Vasnier, 51100 Reims
☎ (326) 84.41.94 ⚊ (326) 84.43.49
Marilyn Monroe used to claim that a glass of Piper each morning spread a little warmth throughout her body! The house has been part of Remy-Cointreau since 1990, prior to which it had built its reputation as a non-malolactic Champagne, but, through the advice of Daniel Thibault, all *cuvées* now undergo the malo.

PIPER-HEIDSIECK NV BRUT 85

The real jump in Piper's quality came with the 1992-based blend, two years after Thibault started making it. The non-vintage is lighter than Charles Heidsieck's Brut Réserve, with a more straightforward plumpness and bright southern ripeness in the fruit, but underneath there is a minerally finesse, and if allowed to age it curiously develops a Charles-like creamy-vanilla richness. Lay down a few bottles.
❘ Now–2000 ££ ❦110F

PIPER-HEIDSIECK 1989 BRUT 84

There was no such thing as a straight Piper vintage until this *cuvée* was launched in 1997. It is not special, though, and you will have to wait for the excellent 1990 before you get to taste a Thibault-made Piper vintage.
❘ Now–2000 £££ ❦160F

PIPER-HEIDSIECK 1989 BRUT SAUVAGE

Ever since this *cuvée* went from non-vintage to vintage, the fruit has appeared to be more low-dosage than the non-dosage that its label suggests. The 1989 has been in something of a time warp since 1996 when it has had a lovely toasty-richness of fruit, with a long, mellow-flavoured finish.
❘ Now–2000 £££

HEIDSIECK MONOPOLE

17 avenue de Champagne
51205 Épernay Cedex
☎ (326) 59.50.50 ⚊ (326) 51.87.07
Belgian-born entrepreneur Paul Vranken purchased Heidsieck & Co Monopole from Mumm and put the stock in Charbaut's old cellars.

HEIDSIECK & CO MONOPOLE NV BRUT 82

Light, fresh and easy.
❘ On purchase ££

HEIDSIECK & CO MONOPOLE 1989 BRUT 84

Creamy-malo fruit supported by high acidity.
❘ Now–2004 ££

HEIM

Pfalz, Germany

The Heim'sche Privat-Sektkellerei has been making the unusual sparkling wine below since 1989.

MARTIN HEIM 1994 GEWÜRZTRAMINER TROCKEN SEKT

This was one of only two German fizzy Gewürztraminers I tasted, and it was far better balanced than I imagined such a product could be, with the sort of clean, truly pungent spicy fruit that most producers of still Gewürztraminer outside of Alsace can only dream about.

❚ On purchase ⓔⓔ

HEIM IMPERIAL

See Westhalten

HEITZMANN

Alsace, France

A capable producer of Pinot Gris and Vendange Tardive, and this *crémant* is also surprisingly good.

LÉON HEITZMANN NV CRÉMANT D'ALSACE BRUT

Despite the straw-like aroma, there is a nice, fat, fruity flavour, a hint of spice and good acidity.

❚ On purchase ⓔ

HENRIET-BAZIN

9 rue Dom Pérignon, 51380 Villers-Marmery
☎ (326) 97.96.81 ℻ (326) 97.97.30

D. HENRIET-BAZIN 1990 CARTE D'OR, BRUT 1ᴱᴿ CRU

One for the buttery-malo brigade, this wine has so much butterscotch fruit that it has lost all hope of finesse, but some drinkers go for this style.

❚ On purchase ⓔⓔⓔ

M.N. HENRIET 1989 CUVÉE PRESTIGE BLANC DE BLANCS, BRUT 1ᴱᴿ CRU

Sprightly fruitiness on the nose, with a very rich finish.

❚ On purchase ⓔⓔⓔ

HENRIOT

3 Place des Droits de l'Homme
51100 Reims
☎ (326) 89.53.0 ℻ (326) 89.53.10
Look to Henriot for good bottle-age and unrelenting high quality from the former head of Veuve Clicquot.

HENRIOT NV SOUVERAIN BRUT

Creamy-peppery-biscuity aromas, with long, lush, creamy fruit on the palate. This Champagne is one of the best that Henriot has ever produced.

❚ Now–2000 ⓔⓔ 🥂105F

HENRIOT NV BLANC DE BLANCS BRUT

A very rich *cuvée* that is just beginning to develop some creaminess.

❚ Now–2000 ⓔⓔ 🥂112F

HENRIOT 1989 BRUT MILLÉSIMÉ

Toasty aroma with peppery fruit on the palate, and very good acidity.

❚ Now–2001 ⓔⓔⓔ 🥂130F

HENRIOT 1988 BRUT MILLÉSIMÉ

Exclusively for those who love to be reminded of farmyard fruit when drinking a sparkling wine, which counts me out.

❚ On purchase ⓔⓔⓔ 🥂130F

HENRIOT 1988 ROSÉ MILLÉSIMÉ BRUT

A mature fruitiness, truly dry, but gentle and soft, with peppery undertones.

❚ Now–2000 ⓔⓔⓔ 🥂140F

HENRIOT 1985 CUVÉE DES ENCHANTELEURS BRUT 87

The slow-building toasty complexity of this Champagne and its high acidity make it a must with food.

❚ Now–2000 ⓔⓔⓔ 🥂190F

HÉRARD

31 Grande Rue, 10250 Neuville-sur-Seine
☎ (325) 38.20.14

I have always found this Aube producer reliable and good value, especially for bright and sunny, fruit-driven *blanc de noirs*.

PAUL HÉRARD NV BLANC DE NOIRS BRUT

Ultra-fruity aromas with strawberry-like fruit on the palate.
❚ On purchase ££

PAUL HÉRARD NV BLANC DE NOIRS, DEMI-SEC

An ultra-fruity aroma followed by a *demi-sec* flavour that tastes sweeter and more complete than others, perhaps because the acidity was initially very high and thus could carry substantially more dosage, although there is nothing green about the finish.
❚ Now–2000 ££

HERTZ

Alsace, France

PRINCE ALBERT NV CRÉMANT D'ALSACE BRUT, ALBERT HERTZ

A curiosity, this! Tastes like sparkling Muscat to me, but whatever it actually is, it needs some sweetness, and would be an absolute stunner in a rich *demi-sec* style.
❚ On purchase £

HIDDEN SPRING

Horam, England, UK
Martyn Doubleday and Chris Cammel won the English Sparkling Wine Trophy in 1997 for their first fizz.

HIDDEN SPRING VINEYARD NV PINOT NOIR BRUT

Pale salmon colour, with some cherry-Pinot. May develop well over the next couple of years.
❚ Now–2000 £

HIESTAND

Rheinhessen, Germany
Erich Hiestand has made Sekt since 1990 by the *méthode champenoise*.

WEINGUT HIESTAND 1992 GUNTERSBLUMER EISERNE HAND PINOT BLANC SEKT BRUT

Crisp, clean and very pale with a gentle, slow-rising bead. A fine food wine in a tall Rhine bottle. Bottle-fermented.
❚ On purchase ££

HIGHFIELD

Marlborough, New Zealand
This Anglo-Japanese-Kiwi-owned estate initially turned to Champagne Drappier, but now makes its Elstree sparkling wine independently.

ELSTREE 1993 MARLBOROUGH

As rich as it has been in the past, but more malty in style than the creamy-vanilla character it used to have.
❚ On purchase ££

HILL

Penedès, Spain
The origins of this old Cava firm go back to Mr Hill, an Englishman who established a vineyard at Moja.

CAVAS HILL 1995 RESERVA ORO SECO

Much better than the 1994, this vintage has some flowery finesse on the nose, but the lightweight fruit lacks mouthfill, despite the higher dosage.
❚ On purchase £

HILL OF HOPE

New South Wales, Australia
From the former Saxenvale winery, this changed name in 1996 when it was bought by pharmacist Michael Hope.

HILL OF HOPE 1996 BLANC DE NOIR BRUT

Although I liked the ripe, sweet, succulence on the finish of this wine, I am concerned by the maturity of its fruit and deep yellow colour.
▬► Wait and see ⓔ

HOCHRIEGL
See Kattus

HOEN
See Baron de Hoen

HOLLICK
Coonawarra, Australia

HOLLICK 1994 SPARKLING MERLOT, COONAWARRA

Huge fruity-oak flavour with rich, floral aromas and cherry, plum and blackberry fruit. Drier than other Oz fizzy reds.
❦ Now–2001 ⓔⓔ

HORNBERG
See Burg Hornberg

HOUËT & TESSIER
Loire, France

HOUËT & TESSIER NV SAUMUR BRUT

Just scrapes through on fruit and length.
❦ On purchase ⓔ

HUGUET
Penedès, Spain
Some of the best Cava available.

HUGUET 1993 CAVA BRUT NATURE

Very tight and young, but promising.
▬► 1999–2000 ⓔ

HUGUET 1993 CAVA BRUT CLASSIC

Wonderful, sweetish fruit.
▬► 1999–2000 ⓔ

HUNAWIHR
Alsace, France

CALIXTE NV CRÉMANT D'ALSACE BRUT

Fresh, finely balanced, elegant style.
❦ On purchase ⓔ

HURBE
See Château de L'Hurbe

HUNTER
Sonoma, California, USA
Pinot Noir was not in demand in the early 1980s, but Robert Hunter's vineyard was full of the stuff. He had no idea what to do with it until his friend Dan Duckhorn suggested he make sparkling wine.

ROBERT HUNTER 1993 BRUT DE NOIRS

Always a richly flavoured *cuvée* with plenty of complexity, yet still quite young.
❦ Now–1999 ⓔⓔ

HUNTER'S
Marlborough, New Zealand
Jane Hunter owns one of New Zealand's best wineries, and her services to wine were rewarded a few years ago with an OBE. Her vintage Brut is starting to show promise, and the new export Mirru Mirru is excellent.

HUNTER'S MIRRU MIRRU NV BRUT

It was lip-smacking good when first released, but quickly tightened up and
became almost unpleasantly sharp. A few
months more, and Mirru Mirru had
developed great depth of flavour, classic
structure and evolved into a serious wine.
❗ On purchase or wait six months ⓔⓔ

INDIGO HILLS
See Gallo

IRON HORSE
Sonoma, California, USA
Iron Horse is one of those rare New
World sparkling wines that can not
only take plenty of post-disgorgement
ageing, but positively needs it. The fruit
structure here has always been
superb for *méthode champenoise*.

IRON HORSE 1993 BRUT
Deep, beautifully intense fruit. A class act.
❗ Now–2000 ⓔⓔ

IRON HORSE 1993 BLANC DE BLANCS
Fat and weighty with creamy-complexity.
❗ Now–2000 ⓔⓔ

IRON HORSE 1993 ROSÉ
A wickedly deep strawberry colour, with
fruit so brash that it slaps you in the face!
❗ On purchase ⓔⓔ

J WINE COMPANY
Sonoma, California, USA
It was not until the elegant 1991 hit
the shelves that the "J" brand was
established as a world-class fizz.

"J" 1993 BRUT
Since the 1991 vintage this *cuvée* has
been lovely to drink when the fruit is
young and elegant. Great finesse.
❗ On purchase ⓔⓔ

JACKSON ESTATE
Marlborough, New Zealand
This was originally intended to be a
specialist sparkling wine brand, but
the owners have made still wines too.

JACKSON ESTATE 1993 MARLBOROUGH
Not as good as the inaugural 1992
vintage (82 points). It should benefit
from additional bottle-age, gradually
acquiring a creamy-toasty complexity.
❗ Now–1999 ⓔⓔ

JACQUART
6 rue de Mars, 51066 Reims
☎ (326) 07.20.20 ⊠ (326) 57.78.14
An ambitious cooperative brand that
grew in quality in the 1990s. It uses
the initials NM (for "house") in its mat-
riucation number instead of CM (for
"cooperative") because a new company was formed in which the members simply became shareholders.

JACQUART NV BRUT TRADITION
A fresh, clean, youthful nose belies the
creamy-biscuity richness on the palate.
❗ Now–1999 ⓔⓔ 🍾121F

JACQUART NV BRUT MOSAÏQUE
Sweeter, riper and fatter than the Brut
Tradition, but not as biscuity, and more
fruit-driven than creamy.
❗ Now–2000 ⓔⓔ 🍾127F

JACQUART 1990 BRUT
This was brilliant in 1997, with massive
fruit and potential, but started developing complexity in 1998, and this has not
made it shine as well as it used to or will
be. Preferably leave until the Millennium.
▬▶ 2000–2005 ⓔⓔⓔ

JACQUART 1992 CUVÉE MOSAÏQUE, BLANC DE BLANCS
A creamy-malo aroma adds some complexity to the richness of fruit on the
palate. But will it go the same way as the
1990 vintage (an early demise)?
❗ Now–2000 ⓔⓔⓔ 🍾163F

JACQUART 1990 CUVÉE MOSAÏQUE, BLANC DE BLANCS (80)

This vintage appeared to die quickly in 1997, but it showed such great early promise that I'll give it a couple of years before issuing a death certificate.
Now–2000 £££ 163F

JACQUART CUVÉE MOSAÏQUE 1990 BRUT ROSÉ (80)

Soft fruit, starting to mellow, but should develop nicely over the next few years.
Now–2002 £££ 163F

JACQUESSON

68 rue du Colonel Fabien, 51200 Dizy
(326) 55.68.11 FAX (326) 51.06.25

Quality-conscious house on par with Billecart-Salmon, but with more emphasis on complexity, less on elegance.

JACQUESSON & FILS NV PERFECTION BRUT (85)

Very fresh, fine and delicious in an easy-drinking style.
Now–1999 £££ 119F

JACQUESSON & FILS NV PERFECTION ROSÉ (87)

Succulent, creamy-soft, red fruits served on a pin-cushion mousse.
Now–1999 £££ 134F

JACQUESSON & FILS 1990 BLANC DE BLANCS (91)

This was extravagantly fruity when first released, then went through a strange phase before emerging as a beautiful, creamy-walnutty *cuvée* that has fine acidity to ensure future evolution.
Now–2005 £££ 160F

JACQUESSON & FILS 1990 SIGNATURE BRUT (93)

Champagnes like this humble the taster because it was coarse, oxidative and not very attractive when tasted prior to commercial disgorgement. Now, however, it has beautifully pure fruit of great concentration and such high acidity that it needs time to show its full potential. A great *vin de garde rosé* like this is a rare beast indeed.
Now–2005 £££

JACQUESSON & FILS 1989 SIGNATURE BRUT (90)

Superb walnutty complexity, with huge promise for future development, and excellent high acidity for a 1989 vintage.
Now–2008 £££ 233F

JACQUESSON & FILS 1988 SIGNATURE BRUT (91)

This went through a strangely coarse period a couple of years ago, but had previously shown its great potential, and has developed beautifully over the last year. It has a huge amount of fruit with complex bottle-aromas only just beginning to emerge, but will eventually be suffused with toasty finesse.
Now–2005 £££

JACQUESSON & FILS 1990 SIGNATURE ROSÉ BRUT (91)

This went through a strangely oxidative stage a few years ago, but is back on track as one of the most delicious, delicately succulent *rosé* Champagnes available.
Now–2005 £££ 257F

JACQUESSON & FILS 1985 DÉGORGEMENT TARDIF (BOTTLE) (–)

An intensely flavoured Champagne, though there was a touch too much sulphur when it was first released as a late-disgorged vintage. Since this fault might not appear in a future shipment, I will reserve judgement until next year.
Wait and see ££££ 300F

JACQUESSON & FILS 1985 DÉGORGEMENT TARDIF (MAGNUM) (95)

The magnum is a totally different wine: a *blanc de blancs* as opposed to the traditional blend of three Champagne grapes in the 75cl bottle. It actually indicates *blanc de blancs* on the magnum label, whereas there is no such mention on the ordinary bottle-size, although the labels in both cases are very intricate (beautiful 19th-century replicas). What is not on the magnum's label, however, is that this *blanc de blancs* is also a mono-*cru*, made exclusively from Avize grapes. It is not classic, but it is rather wonderful in a fat, creamy, exotic fashion.
Now–2010 ££££ 700F

JACQUINET-DUMEZ

26 rue de Reims, 51370 Les Mesneux
☎ (326) 36.25.25 ℻ (326) 36.58.92

JACQUINET-DUMEZ 1992 CUVÉE L'EXCELLENCE BRUT

Rich lean fruit of an impressive depth, with lots of finesse.
❦ Now–2000 ©©© ⚇100F

(SIR) JAMES

See Hardy's

JANSZ

Tasmania, Australia
Formerly majority-owned by Louis Roederer and, dare I say, significantly better after it was sold to the Heemskerk Group in 1994. However, the Jansz brand has recently been sold again, to Samuel Smith & Son of Yalumba fame.

JANSZ TASMANIA 1993 BRUT CUVÉE 90

Lovely creamy-biscuit complexity, classic lean structure, yet juicy fruit acidity.
❦ Now–2003 ©©

JANSZ TASMANIA 1992 BRUT CUVÉE 74

Not in the same class as Janz 1993; it has a toffee aftertaste and lacks finesse.
❦ On purchase ©©

JECHTINGEN

Baden, Germany

WINZERGENOSSENSCHAFT JECHTINGEN 1994 PINOT SEKT BRUT 74

Good full, fruity style, with expansive feel to the Pinot Blanc character, and a soft, cushiony mousse. Bottle-fermented.
❦ On purchase ©©

JONGEGEZELLEN

See Twee Jongegezellen

JORDAN

See J Wine Company

JOURDAN

Paarl, South Africa
Highly regarded fizz from the Cabriere Estate, which is owned by Achim von Arnim, who used to be the winemaker at Boschendal.

PIERRE JOURDAN NV BRUT 70

Just scrapes in on the fresh and fruity ticket, but needs layering with more flavours and a touch of finesse to make the grade of a top estate fizz.
❦ On purchase ©

PIERRE JOURDAN NV BLANC DE BLANCS, CLOS CABRIÈRE BRU 74

The extraordinary mint-caramel character of this wine is almost certainly derived in part from malolactic and/or oak, but exactly where the mint comes from is anybody's guess. Certainly it's a first in sparkling wine, giving this wine some novelty value, and the higher acidity gives it the edge over most other Pierre Jourdan *cuvées*.
❦ On purchase ©

PIERRE JOURDAN NV BRUT SAUVAGE, CLOS CABRIÈRE 72

Too much creamy-caramel malolactic dominates the nose and detracts from the potential finesse of the wine. It has a very rich, soft, fat, caramel and vanilla flavour but needs more acidity. A fascinating concoction.
❦ On purchase ©

PIERRE JOURDAN NV CUVÉE BELLE ROSÉ 74

A golden colour with barely any hint of pink, but plenty of soft, succulent fruit.
❦ On purchase ©

KAAPSE VONKEL

see Simonsig

KALIFELZ

Mosel-Saar-Ruwer, Germany

KALIFELZ RIESLING 1995 RIESLING SEKT EXTRA BRUT ⑦⑦

Satisfying peachy fruit with a fresh floweriness on the finish. Bottle-fermented.
❘ On purchase ££

KARTHÈUSERHOF

Mosel-Saar-Ruwer, Germany

KARTHÈUSERHOF 1995 TYRELL RIESLING SEKT BRUT ⑦⑦

Fresh, fruit-driven style. Bottle-fermented.
❘ On purchase ££

KASSNER-SIMON

Pfalz, Germany

KASSNER-SIMON 1994 RIESLING SEKT EXTRA BRUT ⑧⑩

Elegant flowery fruit. Bottle-fermented.
❘ On purchase ££

KASSNER-SIMON 1994 RIESLING SEKT EXTRA SEKT TROCKEN ⑦⑦

Let down by a touch of sulphur on the nose, but there was so much richness of fruit that it deserved recommendation.
❘ On purchase ££

KATNOOK

South Australia, Australia

KATNOOK NV BRUT ⊖

Too much malolactic, but there is promise underneath.
▬► Wait and see ££

KATTUS

Austria

HOCHRIEGL EXTRA TROCKEN ⑦⓪

Fresh, appley Sekt style.
❘ On purchase £

KIRSTEN

Mosel-Saar-Ruwer, Germany

WEINGUT KIRSTEN 1992 WEISSER BURGUNDER SEKT BRUT ⑦⑦

Very flowery aroma with soft, elegant fruit on the palate.
❘ On purchase ££

WEINGUT KIRSTEN 1993 RIESLING SEKT BRUT ⑧⓪

Some classy, ripe-peachy Riesling fruit.
❘ On purchase ££

KLOSTERMÜHLE

Nahe, Germany

KLOSTERMÜHLE 1995 MONFORT PINOT NOIR SEKT BRUT ⑦⑥

A very clean and well-focused *rosé* with red-fruit pastilles on the nose and crisp acidity on the palate. Bottle-fermented.
❘ On purchase ££

KNYPHAUSEN

Rheingau, Germany
Just 250 cases of Sekt annually, made from Spätlese grapes. The 1990 was one of the three best Sekt wines tasted this year, and the greatest Riesling Sekt of the tasting.

BARON ZU KNYPHAUSEN 1993 RIESLING SEKT EXTRA BRUT ⑦⑦

A seriously glugable pure Riesling Sekt that is just beginning to develop petrolly bottle-aromas.
❘ On purchase £

BARON ZU KNYPHAUSEN 1990 RIESLING SEKT EXTRA BRUT

Class and elegance were the first two words to come to mind as soon as I tasted this fine, petrolly Riesling Sekt with its lovely peachy-ripeness of fruit on the finish. Like most German so-called *extra bruts*, it is dry, but not especially dry.
❚ On purchase ⓔⓔ

KOEHLY

Alsace, France

Koehly is a brilliant producer of varietal wines, and the richness and ripeness of his style comes through especially in this *crémant*.

KOEHLY, CRÉMANT ST-URBAIN ROSÉ NV CRÉMANT D'ALSACE

Attractive aroma of creamy cherries, soft and easy on the palate, with fat fruit dominating the finish.
❚ On purchase ⓔ

KÖWERICH

Mosel-Saar-Ruwer, Germany

The Köwerichs include Beethoven's mother in their family line, thus when they started making Sekt in 1989, they named the *cuvée* below after the great composer. (Perhaps this was in the hope that one day someone might describe the wine as "music to their ears", but, like Beethoven, I will remain deaf to that!).

WEINGUT GESCHWISTER KÖWERICH 1994 LUDWIG VAN BEETHOVEN RIESLING SEKT BRUT

The first bottle I tried was unfortunately corked, but the back-up sample was very ripe, round and perfumed. Bottle-fermented.
❚ On purchase ⓔⓔ

KRIPTA

See Torelló

KRISTONE

Santa Maria, California, USA

Kendall-Jackson's prestige sparkling wine is the pet-project of "Mad Harry" Harold Osborne, who was Schramsberg's first winemaker and more recently a consultant for Pelorus.

KRISTONE BLANC DE BLANCS 1992 CALIFORNIA CHAMPAGNE

Like a classy oaked California Chardonnay on the nose, with no aromas that hint it might be sparkling. This is not as blowzy as the 1991, but still very toasty and too oaky on the palate. Too rich for the balance, it needs a bucketful of acid!
❚ On purchase ⓔⓔⓔ

KRISTONE BLANC DE BLANCS 1991 CALIFORNIA CHAMPAGNE

Much better than I imagined, especially on the nose, which was so toasty and blowzy when first released, but has developed an amazing cappuccino aroma. I would love to taste this side-by-side with Billecart-Salmon's Blanc de Blancs 1973, which is cappuccino right down to the sprinkling of chocolate powder. Kristone gets its toast from the barrel before it's even bottled.
❚ On purchase ⓔⓔⓔ

KRISTONE BLANC DE NOIRS 1992 CALIFORNIA CHAMPAGNE

Like the 1991, this is an authentic *blanc de noirs*, which is to say white not pink. Also like the 1991, this is fruit-driven rather than *barrique*-dominated, thus has far more elegance, soft, creamy fruit and better acidity.
❚ On purchase ⓔⓔⓔ

KRISTONE BRUT ROSÉ 1992 CALIFORNIA CHAMPAGNE

Toasty nose, very rich, ripe and sweet red-fruit flavours, particularly strawberry. Needs more acidity.
❚ On purchase ⓔⓔⓔ

KRONE BOREALIS

See Twee Jongegezellen

KRUG

5 rue Coquebert, 51100 Reims
☎ (326) 84.44.20 ⚏ (326) 84.44.49

Krug is Krug is Krug. It is purchased by a relatively small number of Krugist aficionados around the world, and the price steadily increases at auction.

KRUG NV GRANDE CUVÉE   ⓸

The aromas on this prestige *cuvée* are the epitome of finesse, even when with age it develops huge, lemony-oak aromas and the palate becomes so succulently rich and so fruity that but for the classic lean structure would seem fat and exotic. Buy Grande Cuvée by the magnum and keep it perfectly cellared for five years, and you will be assured of the most fabulous supply of exquisite Champagne.
❚ Now–2008 ⓔⓔⓔⓔ

KRUG NV ROSÉ   ⊖

I have to reserve opinion about the current *cuvée* because it was overly mature. Normally this very pale *rosé* is fine and refined, with an exquisitely clean summer-fruit flavour of exceptional length for such a light balance. I have always considered this to be a great *rosé* that improves with an extra year or two in bottle, but some critics have damned it for being too young and austere, so it is possible that Krug could have reacted to this by issuing a more mature *cuvée*. On the other hand, it could be a duff bottle!
❚ Now–2008 ⓔⓔⓔⓔ

KRUG VINTAGE 1989   ⓸

Released prior to the 1988, this *cuvée* already has an opulent creamy-walnutty fruit, with a silkiness on the palate and softness of acidity on the finish. A gorgeous mouthful now, it still has plenty of development ahead.
❚ Now–2009 ⓔⓔⓔⓔ

KRUG VINTAGE 1988   ⓺

Not released at the time of writing, the 1989 was launched in preference because of the blistering ripe-acidity in this wine. In time this will prove to be one of Krug's greatest vintages, although rumour has it that the 1990 is even better!
❚ Now–2008 ⓔⓔⓔⓔ

KRUG VINTAGE 1985   ⓼

When first released, the complexity and class of the 1985 stood out, but it has since clammed up, and will take a few years to emerge in Krug's typically honeyed-rich, mellow and even more complex second life.
▬ 2002–2015 ⓔⓔⓔⓔ

KRUG CLOS DU MESNIL 1989   ⓺

I put my hands up: tasted blind I thought this was the 1988, with its alpine-fresh, fluffy, lemon-pie fruit. Pure delight now, it will be fascinating to see how the 1989 develops beside the 1988. This might well be the surprise winner at Krug tastings in the future because most of the money will be on the 1988 Clos du Mesnil coming out on top in the long run, whereas the Krugs themselves will probably back the Vintage over Clos du Mesnil. And should someone slip in a magnum of 1988-based Grande Cuvée, we might all end up with egg on our faces!
❚ Now–2009 ⓔⓔⓔⓔ

KRUG CLOS DU MESNIL 1988   ⓸

Even lighter, fluffier lemon-pie fruit than the above, but this has the distinctive vanilla and cream aromas of new oak.
❚ Now–2009 ⓔⓔⓔⓔ

KWV

Paarl
A huge national cooperative that officially controlled the South African wine industry until privatized in 1995.

LABORIE BRUT 1993 CAP CLASSIQUE   ⑧②

Classic biscuity fruit supported by high acidity for length, and satisfying mid-palate mouthfill.
❚ On purchase ⓔ

LABORIE BRUT 1992 CAP CLASSIQUE   ⑦③

Nice toasty aromas intermingling with malolactic creaminess, and although there is a soft violety-vanilla smoothness on the finish, it lacks mid-palate mouthfill, depriving the wine of a higher score.
❚ On purchase ⓔ

LABORIE

See KWV

LACRIMA

See Lavernoya

LAFITTE

See Vranken-Lafitte

LAISEMENT

Loire, France

This producer is well-known for his excellent Vouvray Moelleux, and I have enjoyed the sparkling Vouvray before, but it did not pass this year, whereas the Touraine *cuvée* did well.

TOURAINE ROSÉ NV BRUT, JEAN-PIERRE LAISEMENT

Not great in a classic sense, but so rich and succulent that it is definitely yummy.
❙ On purchase ₤

LAMIABLE

8 rue de Condé 51150 Tours-sur-Marne
☎ (326) 58.92.69 ⨳ (326) 58.94.96

LAMIABLE NV JLP BRUT, GRAND CRU 82

Very sweet and undemanding style.
❙ On purchase ₤₤

LANCELOT-PIENNE

1 allée de la Forât, 51530 Cramant
☎ (326) 57.55.74 ⨳ (326) 57.53.02

Albert Lancelot's family have been growers in Champagne for about 120 years. I preferred his basic Blanc de Blancs to the classic Brut Sélection.

A. LANCELOT-PIENNE NV BLANC DE BLANCS BRUT

Fresh, zingy-zippy sherbetty fruit with a mouthwatering crisp finish.
❙ Now–1999 ₤₤ ♚76F

LANG

Rheingau, Germany

Hans Lang wastes nothing; after bottling his best wines, including 2,500 cases of Sekt, he not only distils the leftovers for Weinbrand (brandy), but the skins and pips for Testerbrand (grappa), and even the yeast for Hefebrand (yeast-brandy).

JOHANN MAXIMILIAN 1993 RIESLING SEKT EXTRA BRUT, HANS LANG

Fresh sherbetty pure Riesling fruit, quite fluffy, with a satisfying almondy complexity on the finish.

CHARDONNAY & WEISSBURGUNDER 1992 HANS LANG

Just scrapes in for those sparkling wine drinkers who like butterscotch aromas. Those with a more classic bent might prefer to see Hans Lang use a malolactic culture that produces much less diacetyl, but this is a curiosity nonetheless. Bottle-fermented.
❙ On purchase ₤₤

LANGENBACH

Rheinhessen, Germany

This large commercial bottler is best known for its Crown of Crowns Liebfraumilch, but also produces a passable sparkling Chardonnay.

LANGENBACH NV CHARDONNAY EXTRA BRUT

Although not Deutscher Sekt, this sparkling Chardonnay, which was made in Germany from grapes of no fixed abode, has good varietal fruit, and a fresh elegant style.
❙ On purchase ₤

LANGLOIS

Loire, France

Owned by Champagne Bollinger, Langlois-Château places emphasis on blending a wide selection of wines from a diversity of *terroirs*,

LANGLOIS NV CRÉMANT DE LOIRE BRUT

Firm, assertive flavour set against a soft mousse backdrop, and an intense finish. I much preferred it to Quadrille de Langlois-Château, which should be the Bollinger of the Loire, yet sadly is not.
❦ Now–1999 ⓔ

LANGLOIS ROSÉ NV CRÉMANT DE LOIRE BRUT

The *rosé* is made in typical Bollinger food-wine fashion. A serious wine with firm fruit.
❦ Now–1999 ⓔ

LANGLOIS RÉSERVE 1993 CRÉMANT DE LOIRE BRUT

Lovely biscuity aromas illustrate the sort of bottle-aged complexity expected from a mature sparkling wine, but it does not quite follow through on the palate. But it shows that some winemakers in the Loire are serious about increasing quality.
❦ On purchase ⓔ

LANSON

12 Boulevard Lundy, 51100 Reims
📞 (326) 78.50.50 📠 (326) 78.50.99
Shortly after the purchase of this famous and popular *grande marque* by Marne et Champagne, the Champagne market plummeted, and rumour has it that it will take the owner 390 years to repay the loan.

LANSON NV BLACK LABEL BRUT

I would not touch Lanson Black Label with a barge-pole! Not, that is, until it had undergone at least two years in my cellar, preferably five, after which I would serve it blind to Masters of Wine, asking them to name the house and vintage year.
◀ 2000–2003 ⓔⓔ

LANSON NV BRUT ROSÉ

Pale-salmon colour suggests age, but beautifully fresh, with a long, elegant fruit flavour. Has finesse, and works with or without food.
❦ Now–1999 ⓔⓔ

LANSON NV DEMI-SEC

Very strong flavour with plenty of sweetness that currently lacks harmony, but promises to develop with bottle-age.
◀ 1999–2000 ⓔⓔ

LANSON 1993 GOLD LABEL, BRUT

Promises to be a relatively quick developing vintage in Lanson terms. Nice already and will improve, but not top stuff.
◀ 1999–2002 ⓔⓔⓔ

LANSON 1990 GOLD LABEL, BRUT

Very soft and easy for Lanson when launched, this vintage now has a nice toastiness, but has developed slower than I had initially imagined.
❦ Now–2005 ⓔⓔⓔ

BLANC DE BLANCS DE LANSON 1990 BRUT

Mature, forward and well-developed, but with expansive fruit underneath.
❦ Now–2000 ⓔⓔⓔ

NOBLE CUVÉE DE LANSON 1988 BRUT

Still miles away from showing its full potential, this wine can be useful with food now – in fact it needs food – but true Champagne lovers will lay this down until well into the next millennium.
◀ 2000–2012 ⓔⓔⓔⓔ

BARON EDOUARD MASSÉ NV BRUT

Once itself a *grande marque*, but little more than the *sous marque* of Lanson these days, this *cuvée* is very fruity, with fine aromas that will soon go toasty.
❦ Now–2000 ⓔⓔ

LANVIN

See Cazanove

LARMANDIER

30 rue du Général Koenig, 51130 Vertus
☎ (326) 52.12.41 ℻ (326) 52.19.38

Of the several Larmandiers on the Côtes des Blancs. Guy Larmandier can be relied on to produce clean, precise, elegantly fruity Champagne.

GUY LARMANDIER NV CRAMANT GRAND CRU, BLANC DE BLANCS, BRUT

Floral-fruity aromas, with clear, precise flavours on palate, and clean, well-focused fruit on finish.
❦ Now–1999 ⒺⒺ

GUY LARMANDIER NV BRUT PREMIER CRU

Lemon-blossom aroma, with a flowery finesse to the fruit on the palate, and a citrussy finish.
❦ Now–2000 ⒺⒺ

LARMANDIER-BERNIER

43 rue du 28 août, 51130 Vertus
☎ (326) 52.13.24 ℻ (326) 52.21.00

LARMANDIER-BERNIER NV BLANC DE BLANCS BRUT, 1ᴱᴿ CRU

Very rich, but not in the same class as the Vieilles Vignes Cramant or the Grand Cru 1990.
❦ Now–1999 ⒺⒺ 🍾89F

LARMANDIER-BERNIER, VIEILLES VIGNES DE CRAMANT NV BLANC DE BLANCS, EXTRA BRUT ⑨⓪

Luscious, crisp, creamy fruit – this is wonderfully fresh and just beginning to develop creamy-walnutty richness.
❦ Now–2002 ⒺⒺⒺ

LARMANDIER-BERNIER 1990 GRAND CRU BLANC DE BLANCS BRUT ⑧⑨

Not quite as rich as the Vieilles Vignes, but certainly not lacking in richness. More slow-building biscuity than creamy-walnutty, but equally high finesse.
❦ Now–2002 ⒺⒺⒺ

LARMANDIER-BERNIER 1992 GRAND CRU BLANC DE BLANCS BRUT

Plenty of grip and intensity, but it is almost stern and not ready for drinking.
▬ 2000–2002 ⒺⒺⒺ

LATEYRON

Bordeaux, France
The second-oldest producer of sparkling Bordeaux wine, having been established in 1897.

PAULIAN NV CRÉMANT DE BORDEAUX BRUT, LATEYRON

Lime is commonly found in top quality Australian Semillon, but it is unusual to have such a distinctive lime aroma and flavour in a Bordeaux wine. Intriguing.
❦ On purchase Ⓔ

LAUFFEN

Württemberg, Germany

WINZERGENOSSENSCHAFT LAUFFEN-AM-NECKAR 1995 LAUFFENER KATZENBEISSER SCHWARZRIESLING SEKT BRUT

Bit of a mouthful for a pure Meunier *blanc de noirs*, but this fine, fresh *cuve close* also offers quite a mouthful of tangy fruit, and scored higher than any of the bottle-fermented Sekt of the same style.
❦ On purchase ⒺⒺ

LAURENT-PERRIER

Domaine de Tours-sur-Marne
51150 Tours-sur-Marne
☎ (326) 58.91.22 ℻ (326) 58.77.29

Laurent-Perrier is back on top after a period when this firm's finances were overstretched with holdings in Bordeaux, Burgundy and beyond. The group will now concentrate on Champagne, including the tiny but great house of Salon, Delamotte, De Castellane, Joseph Perrier and Lemoine.

LAURENT-PERRIER NV BRUT L.P. ⑧⑤

Much bigger and more forceful than Brut
L.P., with rich citrus-toasty overtones.
The only characteristic reminiscent of the
L.P. style is its hint of undeveloped
peppery-fruit. A good non-vintage
Champagne, but regular L.P. consumers
will be confused, to say the least.
❙ Now–2001 ⓔⓔ ⚲139F

LAURENT-PERRIER NV CUVÉE ROSÉ BRUT

Unlike most non-vintage *rosés*, this
salmon gold-coloured wine always repays
keeping a year or two.
❙ Now–2000 ⓔⓔⓔ ⚲197F

LAURENT-PERRIER NV CUVÉE ULTRA BRUT ⑧⑤

The most distinctive of the non-dosage
cuvées on the nose, with a tart-toastiness
on the palate. Needs food.
❙ On purchase ⓔⓔⓔ ⚲173F

LAURENT-PERRIER 1990 VINTAGE BRUT ⑨①

Apart from a small number of off bottles
circulating in the UK in early to mid-
1997, this has always promised to be one
of the best 1990s, and the sample tasted
for this guide fulfilled that potential. A
beautiful wine full of delicious fruit that
still has a long way to go.
❙ Now–2005 ⓔⓔⓔ ⚲173F

LAURENT-PERRIER GRAND SIÈCLE "LA CUVÉE" ⑨⑧

The original Grand Siècle and still my
favourite, this is always a blend of three
different vintage years and half-and-half
Chardonnay and Pinot Noir. The *cuvée* at
the time of publication is 1990/1988/1985
and as these three exceptional vintages
suggest, the wine is one of the greatest
cuvées in a long line of extraordinarily
great Champagnes. It has fine, crisp fruit
with a hint of violets, and biscuity aromas
starting to build, and is a Champagne of
great finesse and length. I have tasted
every blend of "La Cuvée" (the first was
a sumptuous blend of 1955/1953/1952),
and they all age as gracefully, which
brings me to my *bête noir* – why doesn't
Laurent-Perrier indicate the component
years on the back label as Cattier does?
❙ Now–2010 ⓔⓔⓔⓔ

LAURENT-PERRIER GRAND SIÈCLE 1990 EXCEPTIONELLEMENT MILLÉSIMÉ ⑨⑧

I have always preferred the classic "La
Cuvée" to the vintaged version of Grand
Siècle, which commenced with the 1982
sold in the USA. The 1985 and 1988 were
both superb, but not quite in the same
class as "La Cuvée" when it is of a com-
parable age. However, although I have
my preferences, they are by no means
prejudices, and the sublime depth of fruit
and finesse in this wine is incontestable.
The magnums will be even more
spectacular in 10 or 20 years.
❙ Now–2020 ⓔⓔⓔⓔ ⚲368F

LAURENT-PERRIER GRAND SIÈCLE 1988 ALEXANDRA ROSÉ ⑨②

Firmer than the 1985 or 1982 Alexandra
Rosé, the 1988 is not as immediately
accessible as either of those two vintages,
but its rich fruit is softening, and the
balance makes for finesse.
❙ Now–2020 ⓔⓔⓔⓔ ⚲440F

LAURENT-PERRIER GRAND SIÈCLE 1985 ALEXANDRA ROSÉ ⑨⑤

Exquisite fruit and finesse.
❙ Now–2010 ⓔⓔⓔⓔ

LAVERNOYA

Penedès, Spain
An old-established firm, Cavas
Lavernoya was founded in 1890,

LACRIMA BACCUS RESERVA 1995 CAVA BRUT ⑦⓪

This spicy concoction is better than the
almonds and aldehydes in the 1993.
❙ On purchase ⓔ

LACRIMA BACCUS RESERVA 1995 CAVA SEMI SECO ⑦⑦

This *cuvée* has some real richness and
depth of fruit, with excellent acidity.
❙ On purchase ⓔ

LE, LES –

See under main name

LECLERC BRIANT

67 rue Chaude Ruelle, 51204 Épernay
☎ (326) 54.45.33 ☒ (326) 54.49.59

The launch of three single-vineyard Champagnes (Les Chèvres Pierreuses, Les Crayères, and Les Clos des Champions) was a bold initiative, flawed by the non-vintage status of these *cuvées*. If this has made it difficult for critics to plot the progress of each wine, it has made it virtually impossible for customers to know how old the wines are and whether or not to lay them down. However, the Lot number reveals the year of bottling: the system starts with 43 for 1991, then jumps 10 digits per year – 53 for 1992, 63 for 1993 etc. In most cases, the wines are from a single vintage in the year prior to the bottling year. I urge readers to wait for the 1995s (L83) and the super 1996s (L93) before judging these *cuvées*.

LECLERC BRIANT 1988 DIVINE BRUT 87

If you can bring yourself to buy such a gaudy bottle, you will be rewarded with a fruity Champagne that promises some complexity in the future.
🍸 Now–2000 ⓔⓔⓔ 🥂157F

LECLERC BRIANT, LE CLOS DES CHAMPION NV LES AUTHENTIQUES COLLECTION BRUT 80

Very fruity, but lacks the finesse shown by the first release of this *cuvée*.
🍸 On purchase ⓔⓔ 🥂103F

LECLERC BRIANT, LES CHÈVRES PIERREUSES NV LES AUTHENTIQUES COLLECTION BRUT 80

This is *cuvée* L43CH, which is like a mature Mâcon with bubbles, but it should have been consumed a few years ago.
🍸 On purchase ⓔⓔ 🥂103F

LEASINGHAM

See Hardy's

LENOBLE

34 rue Paul-Douce, 51480 Damery
☎ (326) 58.42.60 ☒ (326) 58.65.57

A.R. LENOBLE NV RÉSERVE BRUT 85

Very ripe and fruity.
🍸 On purchase ⓔⓔ 🥂85F

A.R. LENOBLE 1990 BRUT 86

Creamy-rich, easy, gluggy fruit.
🍸 On purchase ⓔⓔⓔ

LE PHANTOM

See Saxenburg

LÉPITRE

4 rue de l'Eglise
51390 Coulommes-la-Montagne
☎ (326) 49.78.20 ☒ (326) 49.27.26

JEAN-CLAUDE LÉPITRE 1989 BRUT PRESTIGE 82

Oxidative, creamy-biscuity aroma with a whiff of clean, free sulphur, which will eventually go toasty. Requires more finesse for a higher score.
🍸 On purchase ⓔⓔⓔ 🥂70F

LEPRINCE

See Beaumont des Crayères

LÉTÉ-VAUTRAIN

11 rue Semars, 02400 Château-Thierry
☎ (323) 83.05.38 ☒ (323) 69.98.29

LÉTÉ-VAUTRAIN NV TRADITIONNEL BRUT 83

Has a flowery aroma, and there is a rather off-putting explosive foaminess to the mousse, but it is also very rich and fruity, with a creamy finish.
🍸 Now–1999 ⓔⓔ 🥂67F

LÉTÉ-VAUTRAIN NV GRANDE RÉSERVE BRUT

Light, creamy-malo style.
⟨ On purchase ⓔⓔ 🍇76F

LEVASSEUR
Loire, France

CLAUDE LEVASSEUR NV BRUT, MONTLOUIS

More correct than special, with more of a sugary sensation than any true ripeness of fruit. This wine just scrapes in, but I have had some truly excellent Montlouis Pétillant in the past.
⟨ On purchase ⓔ

CAPE LEVANT
See SAVISA

LILBERT

223 rue du Moutier51200 Cramant
📞 (326) 57.50.16 📠 (326) 58.93.86

A consistent producer of firm *blanc de blancs* that show finesse and age gracefully, particularly the vintage *cuvées*, although the fruity non-vintage is definitely for drinking now.

LILBERT-FILS NV BLANC DE BLANCS BRUT, GRAND CRU ⑧⑥

Sprightly fruitiness, with a pure, clean, fresh, precise, fruit-driven palate.
⟨ On purchase ⓔⓔ 🍇80F

LINDAUER
See Montana

LOCRET-LACHAUD

40 rue Saint-Vincent, 51160 Hautvillers
📞 (326) 59.40.20 📠 (326) 59.40.92

DE L'ABBATIALE NV BRUT, 1ᴱᴿ CRU

Made by Locret-Lachaud, the De L'Abbatiale Premier Cru *cuvée* has good acidity, and is building some creaminess for the nose and palate, but it is let down by the mousse, which could have finer, more cushiony, bubbles.
━━ 1999–2000 ⓔⓔ 🍇115F

LORENT
See Beaumont des Crayères

LORENTZ
Alsace, France
Lorentz is one of Alsace's best-known producers, located in the beautiful village of Bergheim.

LORENTZ NV CRÉMANT D'ALSACE BRUT

The terpene aromas in this *cuvée* suggest there is Riesling in the blend, although there is no mention of Riesling on the label of the bottle. Good acidity.
⟨ On purchase ⓔ

LUBIANA
Tasmania, Australia
A family-owned wine company established in 1990 by Steve "Stefano" Lubiana and Monique Lubiana, whose first sparkling wine was made as recently as 1993.

STEFANO LUBIANA NV BRUT ⑦⑦

Stefano Lubiana's basic Brut has complex, malty aromas on the nose, with rich, tangy fruit on the palate.
⟨ On purchase ⓔ

STEFANO LUBIANA 1995 BRUT ⑦②

This young, deliciously sherbety fizz is currently spoilt by amylic aromas, although these might drop out after a while in bottle.
━━ 1999–2000 ⓔ

LUGNY

Burgundy, France

This well-known cooperative has been producing sparkling Burgundy since 1975.

CRÉMANT DE BOURGOGNE NV BRUT ROSÉ, CAVE DE LUGNY

The sample I tasted appeared to be very recently disgorged, so I will forgive it having a slight whiff of free sulphur, which should disappear before this guide is published and will eventually end up as part of the wine's toasty complexity. Lots of lovely red fruits on the palate, with a hint of vanilla on the finish.

❦ On purchase ⓔ

LUSTROS

See Gramona

MAILLY

28 rue de la Liberation
51500 Mailly-Champagne
📞 (326) 49.41.10 ☎ (326) 49.42.27

This mono-*cru* cooperative produced Champagnes of exceptional value and character throughout the 1970s and much of the 1980s, but there has been a certain lack of finesse in some of the *cuvées* on the market during the 1990s. Mailly is, however, back on form, pruducing its best Champagnes in over ten years.

MAILLY NV BRUT RESERVE, GRAND CRU

There is a fine flowery-Pinot aroma with really rich fruit underneath, but this *cuvée* is best drunk young.

❦ On purchase ⓔⓔ

MAILLY NV BLANC DE NOIRS, GRAND CRU, BRUT

Full, flowery-Pinot aroma of some finesse, followed by rich fruit, with some biscuitiness building.

❦ Now–2000 ⓔⓔ ☙131F

MAILLY 1990 BRUT, GRAND CRU

A whiff of sulphur, but it is clean and free, and will turn toasty after a year or so. On the other hand, there is a strangely undeveloped character about this wine, and it compels me to withhold judgement for at least another year.

▶ Wait and see ⓔⓔⓔ

MAILLY CHAMPAGNE NV CUVÉE DES ECHANSONS, 100% GRAND CRU BRUT

Very full Pinot aroma, with big, intense fruit on the palate, yet it shows some elegance as well.

❦ Now–2000 ⓔⓔⓔ

MANDOIS

66 rue du Gal-de-Gaulle, 51200 Pierry
📞 (326) 54.03.18 ☎ (326) 51.53.66

HENRI MANDOIS NV CUVÉE DE RÉSERVE BRUT

Soft, fresh, elegant, this is definitely a fruit-driven style of Champagne made for early and easy drinking.

❦ Now–1999 ⓔⓔ ☙76F

HENRI MANDOIS NV BRUT ROSÉ, PREMIER CRU

Bright, cherry fruit aromas, with ripe, elegant fruit on the palate.

❦ Now–1999 ⓔⓔ

HENRI MANDOIS 1993 CHARDONNAY BRUT, PREMIER CRU

Succulent fruit, with a surprisingly intense finish, suggesting this has more potential ageing capacity than Mandois *cuvées* normally offer.

❦ Now–2001 ⓔⓔⓔ ☙86F

MANQUEHUE

Chile

Viña Manquehue makes both *méthode champenoise* and *cuve close* wines. Grandier is called Darwin's Path on some export markets, and wines are also sold under the Rabat label.

GRANDIER 1996 VIÑA MANQUEHUE BRUT

This surprised me by the lovely succulent fruit on the nose, but it needs a lighter hand on the palate to inject more freshness and elegance.

🍸 On purchase ⓔ

MANSARD

14 rue Chaude Ruelle, 51200 Épernay
📞 (326) 54.18.55

Quite how this obscure producer has recently managed to grow into a house half as big again as Bollinger is perplexing, but there are some interesting *cuvées* here, including at least one of exceptionally fine quality.

MANSARD NV BRUT

Light structure, ultra-fruity aroma and flavour, with fresh finish.

🍸 On purchase ⓔ

MANSARD NV PREMIER CRU BRUT

Just as fruity as the basic non-vintage, but with a more serious quality about it.

🍸 Now–1999 ⓔⓔ

TRADITION DE MANSARD 1993 GRANDE CUVÉE BRUT

Fresh and firm with good fruit structure. A different style than all the rest.

🍸 Now–1999 ⓔⓔⓔ

MANSARD 1990 BLANC DE BLANCS, GRAND CRU

An odd-looking, discordant label on the bottle, but the wine inside certainly does not lack harmony, with its lovely, mellow-toasty aromas and succulent, sweet, toasty-fruit on the palate.

🍸 Now–2000 ⓔ

MARIENBERG

New South Wales, Australia
This winery was established in 1966 by Australia's first woman winemaker, Ursula Pridham, who retired in 1990. The new winemaker is Grant Burge.

MARIENBERG PINOT NOIR CHARDONNAY NV BRUT

Fine, firm fruit showing some biscuity complexity, yet still age-worthy.

🍸 On purchase ⓔ

MARGAINE

3 avenue de Champagne
51380 Villers-Marmery
📞 (326) 97.92.13 📠 (326) 97.97.45

Basic *cuvées* are often too amylic, but the Cuvée Club is a good find.

A. MARGAINE 1989 CUVÉE CLUB BLANC DE BLANCS

Very rich fruit, yet lean structure, with excellent acidity.

🍸 Now–2003 ⓔⓔⓔ

MARIE STUART

8 Place de la République, 51059 Reims
📞 (326) 77.50.50 📠 (326) 77.50.59

Recently acquired by Alain Thienot, who has his own eponymous brand.

MARIE STUART NV CUVÉE DE LA REINE BRUT

A real treat, this is light, fresh and elegant, yet complex, with clean fruit and lovely slow-building biscuitiness.

🍸 Now–2000 ⓔⓔⓔ 🍾133F

MARIE STUART 1991 BRUT

A classless depth of crisp fruit with a mellow finish.

🍸 Now–1999 ⓔⓔⓔ 🍾100F

MARINGER-THEES

Mosel-Saar-Ruwer, Germany

MARINGER-THEES 1988 TRITTENHEIMER ALTRÄCHEN RIESLING SEKT BRUT

Quite sweet for a so-called *brut*, but the rich and concentrated fruit is very fresh for a ten-year-old Sekt.

🍸 On purchase ⓔⓔ

MARLBOROUGH

See Montana

MARNE ET CHAMPAGNE

22 rue Maurice-Cerveaux, 51205 Épernay
 (326) 78.50.50 FAX (326) 54.55.77

In addition to Lanson and Besserat de Bellefon, which operate as individual houses (although Besserat de Bellefon *cuvées* are all made here), Marne et Champagne markets in excess of 200 labels. A number of bargain wines have won Vincent Malberbe the Sparkling Winemaker of the Year award at *Wine* magazine's International Wine Challenge.

MARC ANTOINE NV CARTE NOIRE BRUT

Amylic, but scrapes in because of its easy-drinking fruit.
On purchase £

CHARLES COURBET NV SPECIALE CUVÉE, BRUT

In pure quality terms this should not even scrape in, because it is too amylic, too fat and too soft, but it has its use for those who insist on serving Champagne even though they usually find it too acidic.
On purchase ££

GAUTHIER NV BRUT GRANDE RESERVE

Fresh, light and fruity. Nothing amylic.
Now–1999 ££

GAUTHIER 1988 BRUT

The toasty Chablis-like fruit would make a very good own-label Champagne for a merchant who likes to offer a more mature product at the bottom of the range, yet this will also improve with further age.
Now–2000 ££

MARNIQUET

8 rue des Crayères, 51480 Venteuil
 (326) 58.48.99

JEAN-PIERRE MARNIQUET NV BRUT

Not a classic by any means, this *cuvée* has a Muscat-like exotic twist to the fruit that until now I would have thought must be alien to Champagne, but it is an enjoyable sparkling wine within its own right.
On purchase ££

MARQUÉS DE MONISTROL

Penedès, Spain
Owned by Martini & Rossi, this Cava firm was established in 1882 and now owns 400 hectares of vineyards.

MARQUÉS DE MONISTROL GRAN COUPAGE NV CAVA SEMI SECO RESERVA 78

Very sweet, even for *semi-seco (demi-sec)*, which is why it beats its competitors hands down. Drinkers of this style want and expect a seriously sweet sparkler, but despite its high degree of sweetness this *cuvée* is light and elegant.
On purchase £

MARTINEZ

See Faustino Martinez

MASACHS

Penedès, Spain
Josep Masachs is a family-owned Cava firm that owns more than 40 hectares of vineyards, and started sparkling wine production in 1940.

LOUIS DE VERNIER BLANC DE BLANCS NV CAVA BRUT 76

Fresh and clean, in an uncomplicated fruit-driven style.
On purchase £

CAROLINA DE MASACHS NV BRUT NATURE RESERVA 76

This one is light, elegant and fruity, with good acidity.
On purchase

MASCARÓ

Penedès, Spain

Don Narcisi Mascaró Marcé was born into a family of well-established distillers, but set up this winery in 1945 in order to produce exclusively sparkling wines.

MASCARÓ NV CAVA BRUT NATURE **70**

Mascaró's Brut Nature is a richly flavoured sparkling wine of good depth and nice acidity, without any of the coarseness that blights many Cavas.
❦ On purchase Ⓔ

MASIA PARERA

See Cigravi

MASOTTINA

Italy

One of only six Prosecco recommended in this guide, and I preferred it to the two non-Prosecco submitted,

MASOTTINA NV PROSECCO DI CONEGLIANO E VALDOBBIADENE, EXTRA DRY **70**

Fresh, light, amylic-style fruit, but with more elegance than most.
❦ On purchase Ⓔ

MASSÉ

See Lanson

MATHIEU

Les Riceys, 10340 Avirey-Lingey
☎ (25) 29.32.58 ℻ (25) 29.11.57

This small, immaculately equipped producer makes the most elegant Champagnes of any grower in the Aube region of Champagne.

SERGE MATHIEU NV CUVÉE TRADITION, BLANC DE NOIRS BRUT **84**

Soft, easy fruit with a touch of elegance.
❦ On purchase ⒺⒺ 🍷75F

SERGE MATHIEU NV SELECT, TÊTE DE CUVÉE BRUT **87**

An object lesson for anyone who does not think that the Aube can produce finesse.
❦ Now–1999 ⒺⒺ 🍷99F

SERGE MATHIEU NV CUVÉE PRESTIGE BRUT **85**

Elegantly rich fruit.
❦ On purchase ⒺⒺ 🍷81F

MATUA VALLEY

Waimauku, New Zealand

This superbly equipped winery is renowned for expressive wines of excellent focus and purity of fruit.

MATUA VALLEY NINETEEN NINETY TWO BRUT **82**

Rich, yet fluffy fruit, with a fine balance that somehow reveals the serious quality of the wine.
❦ Now–1999 ⒺⒺ

MAXIM'S

See Castellane

MERCIER

68/70 avenue de Champagne
51200 Épernay
☎ (326) 51.22.00 ℻ (326) 54.84.23

Although seen by many as a down-market brand compared to Moët & Chandon, it is Mercier that is the brand-leader in France, and it always has been. The style is generally fuller, riper and less elegant than that of Moët, although some of the vintages can be dark horses, while the Cuvée du Fondateurs offers extraordinary quality for the price.

MERCIER NV BRUT

What this *cuvée* lacks in finesse it more than makes up for in frank, unashamed Aube fruit ripeness.

On purchase ⓔⓔ ⌇89F

EUGÈNE MERCIER NV CUVÉE DU FONDATEUR BRUT

Fat and rich, and what it lacks in finesse, it more than makes up for with flavour and value for money. It works especially well at the table.

Now–1999 ⓔⓔ ⌇105F

MERCIER 1993 VENDANGE BRUT

There is an attractive light richness here in what appears to be a quick-developing vintage *brut*.

Now–1999 ⓔⓔⓔ ⌇115F

MERCKLÉ

Alsace, France

I have been disappointed with M. Mercklé's *crémant* in the past, even when it has won a gold medal at Dijon, but I take off my hat to him for this impressive *cuvée*.

ANDRÉ MERCKLÉ NV CRÉMANT D'ALSACE BRU

Good fruity acidity gives a tangy-pineapple finish, which should go toasty with a year or two bottle-age.

Now–1999 ⓔ

(DE) MERIC

17 Rue Gambetta, 51160 Aÿ-Champagne
☎ (326) 55.20.72 🖷 (326) 54.84.12

This small house is owned by Christian Besserat, whose family founded Besserat de Bellefon.

DE MERIC NV CATHÉRINE DE MEDICI

This prestige *cuvée* is a very special Champagne that is best enjoyed with food and rewards true Champagne aficionados with sublime finesse and seductively mellow bottle-aromas.

Now–2002 ⓔⓔⓔ ⌇119F

(LE) MESNIL

Union des Propriétaires Récoltants
51390 Le Mesnil-sur-Oger
☎ (326) 57.53.23

Only an occasional glitch mars the exceptional potential in quality of this cooperative.

LE MESNIL NV BLANC DE BLANCS, BRUT

Smooth and rich, with fine acidity.

Now–1999 ⓔⓔ

LE MESNIL 1990 RÉSERVE SÉLECTION, BLANC DE BLANCS BRUT

Excellent crisp, rich, fullness of fruit with mellowing toasty aromas and finesse.

Now–2002 ⓔⓔⓔ

MESTRES

Penedès, Spain

The methods are traditional, and the style very much the sort of thing that lovers of well-matured Cavas adore.

MESTRES COQUET NV CAVA BRUT NATURE

Fresh, light and slightly amylic.

On purchase ⓔ

LOS CUPAGES DES MESTRES NV CAVA BRUT NATURE

Firmer, tighter and capable of some ageing.

Now–1999 ⓔⓔ

MESTRES CLOS NOSTRE SENYOR 1990 CAVA BRUT NATURE

Honeyed terpenes.

On purchase ⓔⓔ

MESTRES CLOS DAMIANA 1987 CAVA BRUT NATURE

Honeyed, with a toffee richness.

On purchase ⓔⓔ

MESTRES RESERVA 1986 MAS VIA BRUT

A ripe-mature sweetness with honeyed aromas.

On purchase ⓔⓔ

MEURGIS

Burgundy, France

MEURGIS, CUVÉE BLANC DE NOIRS 1995 CRÉMANT DE BOURGOGNE

A light, early-drinking wine with a perfumed Pinot aroma and some elegance.
On purchase ©©

MEURGIS, CUVÉE BLANC DE NOIRS 1994 CRÉMANT DE BOURGOGNE **70**

Not an outstanding wine by any means, but there is nothing wrong with it, and it just scrapes through because of its exceptionally fine mousse.
On purchase ©©

MEYER FONNÉ

Alsace, France
My first encounter of this producer, who started making *crémant* as recently as 1992.

MEYER FONNÉ NV CRÉMANT D'ALSACE BRUT EXTRA **72**

Fresh, fizzy Chablis style.
On purchase ©

MIGNON & PIERREL

24 Rue Henri Dunant, 51200 Épernay
(326) 51.93.39 FAX (326) 51.69.40
"Roll up, roll up! Get your floral-patterned, shrunk-wrapped Champagne bottles here!"

MIGNON & PIERREL NV BRUT, PREMIER CRU **85**

If you can bring yourself to buy the extravagantly decorated bottle, then you will be rewarded by a *cuvée* of light but satisfying richness, with some serious, creamy biscuitiness. This applies to the wine in the bottle with a blue floral pattern: beware the green!
Now–1999 ©© 120F

MILAN

6 route d'Avize, 51190 Oger
(326) 57.50.09 FAX (326) 57.78.47
Traditional producers who use oak barrels for some of their *cuvées*, although not for the one below.

JEAN MILAN NV BRUT SPÉCIAL, GRAND CRU **87**

Fresh, with fine aromas and lean fruit.
Now–1999 ©© 81F

MILLS REEF

Bay of Plenty, New Zealand
A typical boutique-style winery that has quickly developed a reputation for the consistency of its oaky fizz.

MILLS REEF CHARISMA NV METHODE TRADITIONELLE, HAWKES BAY **75**

Heaped with rich coconutty fruit, this *cuvée* is always far too oaky for my liking, but I recognise the quality of fruit and the excellent level of ripe acidity.
On purchase ©©

MOËT & CHANDON

20 avenue de Champagne, 51200 Épernay
(326) 51.20.00 FAX (326) 51.20.37
Moët is the largest and most popular Champagne house, and surely the only way it can expand further is to attract those who have been put off by its high-volume operation. Even wine snobs acknowledge the quality of Cuvée Dom Pérignon, and the new *rosé* and Brut Premier Cru should also attract quality-seeking customers.

MOËT & CHANDON NV BRUT IMPÉRIAL **85**

If judged for drinking on purchase, the world's greatest-selling non-vintage *cuvée* might just scrape in with 80 points, but if kept for 12 months, it picks up toasty aromas and a nice mellowed elegance.
1999–2000 ©© 125F

MOËT & CHANDON NV BRUT PREMIER CRU

This relatively new *cuvée* is restricted to the French market. Interestingly, Moët has not gone for anything bigger or richer, just an extra dimension of finesse.
On purchase ⓔⓔⓔ 🍷140F

MOËT & CHANDON NV BRUT ROSÉ

Wonderfully fresh, delicately floral fruit aromas, elegant and long. I love the mellowed richness of the vintage *rosé*, but the extra finesse in this new non-vintage *cuvée* makes it significantly superior.
Now–1999 ⓔⓔ

MOËT & CHANDON 1992 BRUT IMPÉRIAL ROSÉ

Apricot-gold colour, perfumed Pinot aromas, and a mellow fruit flavour.
Now–1999 ⓔⓔⓔ 🍷155F

MOËT & CHANDON 1992 BRUT IMPÉRIAL

Not a top Moët vintage, but going toasty and is at least as good as a well-matured non-vintage Brut Impérial.
Now–1999 ⓔⓔⓔ 🍷55F

CUVÉE DOM PÉRIGNON 1990 BRUT

The toasty bottle-aromas have evolved quicker than the extract on the palate, which promises further development, but you might have a more recently disgorged bottle, which will be pure, creamy-fruit. Indisputably a great wine, but its disgorgement should have been left to 2000.
▬▶ 2000–2015 ⓔⓔⓔⓔ 🍷420F

CUVÉE DOM PÉRIGNON 1988 BRUT

Floral-toasty aromas and firm, pineapple-fruit. Very linear, with a heightened perception of acidity on the finish.
▬▶ 1999–2015 ⓔⓔⓔⓔ

CUVÉE DOM PÉRIGNON 1985 BRUT

Fruit-driven aromas with toastiness peeping through very tightly focused fruit on the palate. There is a huge concentration on the finish that promises to go biscuity, with some Christmas cake complexity.
▬▶ 1999–2015 ⓔⓔⓔⓔ

MÖLLER

Pfalz, Germany

SEKTKELLEREI MÖLLER 1995 CHARDONNAY SEKT

An apricot and custard concoction that just scrapes in for its curiosity value. Bottle-fermented.
On purchase ⓔⓔ

MONISTROL

See Marqués de Monistrol

MONMOUSSEAU

Loire, France

MONMOUSSEAU, CUVÉE J.M. 1992 BLANC DE BLANCS BRUT, TOURAINE

Clean, fresh, ripe and fruity for a Touraine sparkling wine of this age.
Now–1999 ⓔ

PRINTEMPS GRAND VIN PÉTILLANT NV VOUVRAY, MONMOUSSEAU

For those who prefer a less sweet style of *demi-sec,* this fresh-flavoured fizz has quite intense fruit.
On purchase ⓔ

MONTANA

Marlborough, New Zealand
New Zealand's largest wine producer, with an excellent new Blanc de Blancs.

LINDAUER NV BRUT

This high-volume transfer-method fizz is normally fresh and fluffy, with lemon-meringue fruit, but the current shipment is fuller, fatter and richer, with a certain complexity and not lacking in finesse. Is this a deliberate change in style or simply an effect of age on a quick-moving *cuvée*?
On purchase ⓔ

LINDAUER NV SPECIAL RESERVE BRUT

Exquisite finesse for such mouthfilling fruit. Soft fruits, sweetish vanilla smoothness on finish.
 On purchase ⓔ

DEUTZ MARLBOROUGH NV BRUT ⑦⑧

Refreshing, fruity style with a serious edge when young, this wine usually develops a toasty, high-acid Chablis character with bottle-age.
Now–1999 ⓔ

DEUTZ MARLBOROUGH 1991 BLANC DE BLANCS ⑧②

Were you to play yardsticks, then 1991 would be a seriously mature Cava, and most Cavas of this age would be well past their best. In fact, this *cuvée* is so young that it needs more time. Will turn into creamy-rich nectar in the future.
➤ 1999–2004 ⓔⓔ

MONTAUDON

6 rue Ponsardin, 51100 Reims
☎ (326) 47.53.30 ℻ (326) 47.88.82
Established by Auguste-Louis Montaudon, the winemaker at Bouvet-Ladubay. The non-vintage and vintage have always been okay, but not special, but this *cuvée* was better.

MONTAUDON NV CHARDONNAY PREMIER CRU BRUT ⑧⑤

Starting to go very toasty, so what it lacks in finesse is compensated for drinkers who like their Champagnes to come complete with a continental breakfast.
Now–1999 ⓔⓔ 🍾100F

MONTE ROSSA

Franciacorta, Italy

MONTE ROSSA NV FRANCIACORTA BRUT ⑦⓪

Very fruity, everyday drinking style.
On purchase ⓔ

MONTE ROSSA NV FRANCIACORTA BRUT SATÈN ⑦⑤

Some creamy-malo finesse showing through slow-building toasty aromas, with toast, coffee and a twist of lemon on the palate.
On purchase ⓔ

MONTE ROSSA 1992 FRANCIACORTA BRUT ⑦②

A distinctive fresh pepperiness on the nose, and soft, sweet fruit on the palate, this wine would have received a higher score but for a hollow touch on its finish.
On purchase ⓔⓔ

MONT MARÇAL

Penedès, Spain

MONT MARÇAL CAVA NV GRAN RESERVA BRUT ⑦⓪

Creamy-malolactic aromas dominating rich, mellow fruit, but it lacks the finesse necessary for a higher score.
➤ 1999–2000 ⓔ

MONT MARÇAL CAVA 1993 BRUT NATURE ⑦⑧

Young and firm, with plenty of promise and a delightful cushiony mousse.
➤ 1999–2000 ⓔ

MÔRESON

Paarl, South Africa

SOLEIL DU MATIN BRUT NV CAP CLASSIQUE ⊖

Fresh and obviously young, the flavour is quite long for such a light-bodied wine, but otherwise unexceptional. It would normally score 70 points, but I am in uncharted water here, and it could develop far more favourably.
➤ Wait and see ⓔ

MORIANO

Trentino, Italy

MORIANO BRUT NV TRENTO

The fruit is good, if a little oaky, but the structure could be leaner.
❙ Now–2000 ⓔ

MORRIS

Victoria, Australia

Established in 1897, and now part of the French-owned Orlando group, Morris is actually famous for its fortified wines, but has also been producing sparkling wine since 1989. Although this winery belongs to one of Australia's four largest groups, the original owners are still involved, with the *cuvée* below having been made by David Morris.

MORRIS SHIRAZ-DURIFF NV BRUT

Very creamy-oaky style of red fizz. Confusingly, in California the Duriff (more commonly spelt Durif) is called the Petite-Sirah, which writers go to pains explaining is not related to the true Syrah or Shiraz, yet in recent years many of the so-called Petite-Sirah have been identified as authentic Syrah!
❙ On purchase ⓔ

MORTON

Bay of Plenty, New Zealand

This white-wine specialist produces one of New Zealand's finest and potentially complex sparkling wines, but there is a high incidence of bad corks.

MORTON ESTATE NV SPARKLING BRUT, METHODE TRADITIONELLE ⊖

One sample at the tasting had sweet, ripe fruit that was spoilt by green-apple on the finish, the other was more complex, less fruit-driven.
❙ Now–1999 ⓔⓔ

MOULIN

See Dopff au Moulin

MOUNTADAM

South Australia, Australia

The Mountadam vineyard in the Eden Valley belongs to Adam Wynn, who was one of the founders of the legendary Wynns Coonawarra Estate, which now belongs to Southcorp. Wynn makes his sparkling wines with a pale *rosé* hue because he believes that all the best non-*rosé* Champagnes are not decolourised and are thus "usually pink" (whereas in reality the best Champagne producers actually take a pride in making the palest possible *cuvée* without resorting to artificial means).

MOUNTADAM 1992 BRUT

With so much toffee-malo and creamy-coconut character dominating the wine, any finesse that was once present has unfortunately been lost, but I cannot help admiring the richness of this *cuvée* and the obvious high quality of the raw materials used.
❙ On purchase ⓔ

MOUNTADAM 1991 BRUT

Like the 1992, this is too heavily malo-dominated, but should appeal to anyone who likes Devon toffees.
❙ On purchase ⓔ

MOUNTAIN DOME

Washington, USA

Dr Michael Manz has worked hard to produce a classic sparkling wine, and this year the *rosé* was best.

MOUNTAIN DOME NV BRUT ROSÉ

A succulent melange of strawberry-dominated red-fruits. This lovely *rosé* is very soft, fresh and fruity with an excellent mousse of tiny bubbles.
❙ On purchase ⓔⓔ

MOUNTAIN DOME NV BRUT

Rich coconutty fizz with a label depicting "little people".
❙ On purchase ⓔⓔ

MOUTARD

Buxeuil, 10110 Bar-sur-Seine
C (25) 38.50.73 **FAX** (25) 38.57.72

The full name of the house is Moutard-Diligent – the brand is simply called Moutard, although there is a second label called François Diligent. Most Moutard *cuvées* are pure Chardonnay.

MOUTARD NV ROSÉ BRUT **85**

Salmon-pink, with nice Pinot Noir aromas, this *cuvée* is rich, flavoursome and crisp, with a firm mousse.
 Now–1999 ⓔⓔ 🍾70F

MOUTARD NV CUVÉE PRESTIGE BRUT **82**

Some biscuity complexity, but let down by a touch of coarseness, which robs the wine of any finesse, and a touch of green fruit on the finish.
 On purchase ⓔⓔ 🍾91F

MOUTARD NV VIEILLES VIGNES, CÉPAGE ARBANE ⊖

Not recommended, but included as a curiosity because it's made from Arbane, an ancient and almost extinct variety that is still technically permissible in Champagne. Apparently, local producers can pick out its distinctive floral aroma even if it represents less than one per cent of a blend – and this one is a pure example!
 Wait and see ⓔⓔ 🍾109F

MOUTARD NV RÉSERVE BRUT **84**

A sprightly nose, with soft, billowy fruit on the palate.
 On purchase ⓔⓔ 🍾68F

MOUTARD 1983 BRUT MILLÉSIME ⊖

Liquorice-fruit intensity, with a spicy-dry finish. Worth keeping an eye on.
 Wait and see ⓔⓔⓔ 🍾101F

MOUTARD NV CUVÉE SANS DOSAGE, EXTRA BRUT **80**

The pungent nose suggests this wine is over the hill, but upon tasting there is a lot of undeveloped extract, which goes well with food, particularly game dishes. It might have been better if disgorged two years ago and given a full *brut* dosage!
➤ On purchase ⓔⓔ 🍾91F

MOUTARDIER

51210 Le Breuil
C (326) 59.21.09 **FAX** (326) 59.21.25

Run by Englishman Jonathan Saxby. Le Breuil is one of the best sites for Meunier, and the Carte d'Or, Rosé Brut and Millésime are made exclusively from this grape. These are not Moutardier's best, but I still hope that one day Saxby will make the world's greatest pure Meunier *cuvée*.

JEAN MOUTARDIER NV CARTE D'OR BRUT **85**

An initial whiff of sulphur, but it was clean, free sulphur, and disappeared after a good swirl of the glass. Fresh, light and fruity palate, with a hint of vanilla.
 Now–1999 ⓔⓔ 🍾75F

JEAN MOUTARDIER NV SÉLECTION BRUT **86**

Still the most complete Champagne in the Moutardier range, this is on par with the Centenaire *cuvée*.
 Now–1999 ⓔⓔ 🍾87F

JEAN MOUTARDIER NV LA CENTENAIRE BRUT **86**

A richly flavoured *cuvée* with some malo-dominated complexity, and plenty of clean fruit.
 Now–1999 ⓔⓔ 🍾95F

JEAN MOUTARDIER NV ROSÉ BRUT **80**

Apricot-peach colour, with a fresh, easy-drinking fruity style.
 Now ⓔⓔ 🍾85F

JEAN MOUTARDIER 1990 MILLÉSIME BRUT ⊖

This vintage was very good when I tasted it for *Decanter* magazine in 1997, but the sample submitted more recently was not at all special. Judgement reserved.
 Wait and see ⓔⓔⓔ 🍾82F

MOUZON-LEROUX

16 rue Basse des Carrières, 51380 Verzy
C (326) 97.96.68 **FAX** (326) 97.97.67

PH. MOUZON-LEROUX NV BRUT ROSÉ, 1ER CRU

Although this distinctly pink-looking *rosé* has an amylic aroma, it is richly flavoured, has a long, crisp finish, and will age well.

❘ Now–2000 ££ ✹82F

PH. MOUZON-LEROUX NV GRANDE RÉSERVE BRUT, 1ER CRU

Biscuity, but rustic in character, with a rather disjointed balance.

❘ On purchase ££ ✹72F

PH. MOUZON-LEROUX NV CUVÉE PRESTIGE BRUT, 1ER CRU

Richer than the Grande Réserve, with better balance, and it could even develop a touch of finesse.

❘ Now–1999 ££ ✹92F

MULLER

Alsace, France

CHARLES MULLER ROSÉ NV CRÉMANT D'ALSACE BRUT

Very soft fruit, hinting of cherries and strawberries, with a smooth mousse of tiny bubbles.

❘ On purchase £

MUMM

29 rue du Champ-de-Mars, 51053 Reims
☎ (326) 49.59.69 ⊠ (326) 40.46.13

While Pierre-Yves Harang produced some of the cleanest Mumm wines for a long time from the 1995 harvest, it is the 1996s that indicate a return to the light, pure, fluffy style for which Mumm used to be renowned. The 1995-based non-vintage *cuvées* should be on the shelf for the Millennium.

MUMM CORDON ROUGE NV BRUT

This shipment has a light, biscuity-malo aroma with a really quite dry flavour. This is Mumm Cordon Rouge on the up, and there should be better *cuvées* to come.

❘ On purchase ££ ✹110F

MUMM CORDON ROUGE 1989 BRUT MILLÉSIMÉ

The hint of malolactic on the nose does not show through on the palate, which is dominated by sprightly fruit.

❘ On purchase £££ ✹128F

MUMM DE CRAMANT NV BLANC DE BLANCS BRUT

This *cuvée* (originally called Crémant de Cramant) would benefit from less, rather than more, time on yeast, about 15–18 months. This would result in an even lighter, fresher and fluffier style.

❘ On purchase ££ ✹213F

MUMM CHAMPAÑA

Chile

A relatively recent venture, but the best *cuvée* lacks the finesse of the current shipment of Torres Chilean fizz, and does not even stack up against Moët & Chandon's Baron B. made in neighbouring Argentina.

CUVÉE MUMM CHAMPAÑA NV BRUT

With a sweet and slightly amylic aroma, and a better balance of fruit and acidity than either the Nature or Demi-Sec, this just scrapes in.

❘ On purchase £

MUMM NAPA

Napa, California, USA

This high-tech operation produced better sparkling wine than Mumm's authentic Champagne in the late 1980s and early 1990s.

MUMM CUVÉE NAPA NV BRUT PRESTIGE

The basic non-vintage Mumm Cuvée Napa Brut Prestige (known as Cuvée Napa by Mumm Brut on export markets) can sometimes be a bit young, but seems to have settled down over the last year or two, and is back to its simple, fresh, light and easy fruity self.

❘ On purchase £

MUMM CUVÉE NAPA 1991 DVX

A single-vineyard sparkler from the Devaux vineyard in Carneros, this has retained an impressive purity of fruit for several years now. Long, rich and tangy.
❧ Now–1999 £ £

MUMM NAPA NV BLANC DE BLANCS

This is not only the finest quality, but also consistently the greatest value *cuvée* in the whole Mumm Napa range, with lovely, creamy fruit. There is a delicious intensity that comes in part from its 30 per cent Pinot Gris content, the balance being Chardonnay, of course.
❧ Now–2000 £

MUMM NAPA 1991 WINERY LAKE

Although it is more intense than any other wine in the Mumm Napa range, Winery Lake does not travel particularly well. Hence, if you have enjoyed it on an export market, you will really love it in California, while Americans may be disappointed to try it elsewhere.
❧ Now–1999 £ £

MUMM NAPA NV BLANC DE NOIRS

Labelled Rosé on export markets, this soft, easy, ready-drinking *cuvée* has a more traditional style than Mumm Napa's Sparkling Pinot Noir.
❧ On purchase £

MUMM NAPA SPARKLING PINOT NOIR

Take a trip on the wild side with this deep-cerise coloured fizz. A single-vineyard *cuvée* from the Devaux vineyard in Carneros, this is a true love or hate wine, with a wonderful aroma of wild strawberries, and outrageously perfumed Pinot fruit on the palate. It has got to be the ultimate picnic wine.
❧ On purchase £

MUMM SOUTH AFRICA

Tulbagh, South Africa
Made in conjunction with Nicky Krone at Twee Jongegezellen.

MUMM CAP CLASSIQUE NV

Fresh, zesty fruit that is long and elegant, with a lovely soft mousse of tiny bubbles. Knowing Krone's past record, this will develop some mellow complexity, but it is too easy to drink now even to bother.
❧ On purchase £

MURÉ

Alsace, France
A great estate, especially for Vendange Tardive, but it has struggled to equal the excellence of the pure Riesling sparkling wine it produced in 1982.

RENÉ MURÉ NV CRÉMANT D'ALSACE BRUT

Fresh, elegant, fruity style, with a very fine mousse. In a classy Krug-like bottle.
❧ On purchase £

NAUTILUS

Marlborough, New Zealand
Nautilus is owned by the Australian Yalumba group,

NAUTILUS ESTATE NV CUVÉE BRUT MARLBOROUGH

An overtly fruity style that is not exactly complex, but easy and delicious to drink.
❧ On purchase £ £

NEDERBURG

Stellenbosch, South Africa
Owned by Stellenbosch Wine Farmers who named this brand after an estate that was renamed Johann Graue in 1972 to honour SWF's first winemaker.

NEDERBURG BLANQUETTE 1993 CAP CLASSIQUE DE CHARDONNAY

A soft, easy-drinking fizz that had not developed any post-disgorgement aromas when tasted, but scraped through on the fluffy freshness of its fruit.
❧ On purchase £

NEIPPERG

Württemberg, Germany

The Counts of Neipperg have grown vines around their castle for more than 700 years, and made a very positive start with Sekt in 1992.

GRAF VON NEIPPERG 1992 NEIPPERGER SCHLOSSBERG SCHWARZRIESLING SEKT TROCKEN

Just as French ampelographers have decided that Meunier is not part of the Pinot family, so the Germans make a pure Meunier that tastes more like Pinot Noir than Pinot Noir! Bottle-fermented.
❙ On purchase ⓔⓔ

NERLEUX

See Domaine de Nerleux

NEUMEYER

Alsace, France

Although I have had a few wines from this producer in Molsheim, none was particularly special, so I was pleasantly surprised to see Neumeyer's name on this _cuvée_ when the covers came off.

GÉRARD NEUMEYER, CUVÉE MILLÉSIMÉE 1993 CRÉMANT D'ALSACE BRUT

This has a creamy-malo nose, followed by creamy-rich fruit on the palate, and very good acidity.
❙ Now–2000 ⓔⓔ

NORDHEIM

Württemberg, Germany

This cooperative has 250 members producing some 1,500 cases of Sekt each year. The quality ranges from a chemical-tasting Pinot Blanc to the fourth-best Sekt I tasted this year.

WEINGÄRTNERGENOSSENSCHAFT NORDHEIM 1995 PINOT NOIR SEKT EXTRA BRUT

Really quite sweet for an _extra brut_, but this pure Pinot Noir Sekt has lovely fruit, all cherries and strawberries, with a perfumed aftertaste. Bottle-fermented.
❙ On purchase ⓔⓔ

NORMANS

South Australia, Australia

An underrated producer of still wines, Normans also shows excellent potential for sparkling wines. The basic Brut Cuvée is a blend of Semillon, Chenin Blanc and Trebbiano.

NORMANS CONQUEST NV BRUT

A nice melange of fruit buoyed up by a lovely cushiony mousse, this is almost a _blanc de noirs_ made primarily from Pinot Noir and Grenache, but with five per cent of Riesling, which makes for an unusual, but very successful blend.
❙ On purchase ⓔ

NORMANS NV BRUT PINOT NOIR

This is serious stuff, with such a good balance that it has plenty of real Pinot flavour despite the lightweight body, supported by a lovely fluffy mousse.
❙ Now–1999 ⓔ

NORTHBROOK SPRINGS

Bishop's Waltham, England, UK

NORTHBROOK SPRINGS 1993 BRUT

This _cuvée_ has some flowery finesse on the nose, with rich fruit, correct structure and a firm mousse of small bubbles. It would be interesting to age this one further, both on and off the yeast.
❙ Now–1999 ⓔ

NOSTALGIE

See Beaumont des Crayères

NOTTAGE HILL

See Hardy's

NYETIMBER

West Chiltington, England, UK
The first vintage of Nyetimber was
such a success that it was chosen
for the Queen's Golden Anniversary,

NYETIMBER 1992 PREMIÈRE CUVÉE BLANC DE BLANCS

This is one of a rare breed of sparkling
wine that needs at least three years on its
yeast and, rarer still, a further two years
after disgorgement to slowly develop a
mellow, biscuity complexity. At £15 it is
the second-most expensive English fizz,
but it is far and away the best value for
money. The 1993 Chardonnay-Pinot
blend is even better, and I have great
hopes for 1994.
➤ 1999–2002 ££

NYETIMBER 1993 PREMIÈRE CUVÉE BLANC DE BLANCS

Not quite the creamy quality of the first
vintage, this has a more "English" herbaceous character, but this is uncharted
waters and I will follow its development.
❚ Now–2000 ££

NYETIMBER 1993 ⑧⑦

This blend of Chardonnay and Pinot
Noir has shown exceptional finesse.
If anyone still needs convincing about
Nyetimber after its debut vintage, this is
the *cuvée* that will do it.
➤ 1999–2004 ££

OAK VILLAGE

South Africa
The primary label of an export-only
organisation called Vinfruco, which is
funded by South Africa's largest fruit
exporter. Behind the rather commercial name and presentation of
Oak Village lurks a serious-quality,
brilliant-value sparkling wine.

OAK VILLAGE CUVÉE BRUT NV CAP CLASSIQUE

I was so surprised by the classic quality
and creamy-walnutty richness of this
cuvée that I had to repeat the tasting.
❚ Now–1999 £

OASIS

Virginia, USA
One of the more consistent
producers in the State of Virginia.

OASIS BRUT NV VIRGINIA SPARKLING WINE ⑦④

The creamy-caramel nose on the Oasis
Brut suggests that the malolactic has been
too heavy-handed, and the wine certainly
could do with more finesse, but it is a
drinkable *cuvée*, eminently drinkable in
fact. This is very much in the fizzy Devon-
toffee mode, but with a little bit more
experience of producing sparkling wine,
Oasis could be a classy little number.
❚ On purchase £

ODE PANOS

See Spyopoulos

OMNI

See Hardy's

ORLANDO

South Australia, Australia
This French-owned group produces a
quarter of Australia's wine production
through a number of wineries and
brands, including Craigmoor, Morris
and Wyndham Estate.

ORLANDO CARRINGTON FINE CHAMPAGNE NV BRUT

A firm and flavourful wine with some
creamy fruit on nose and palate.
❚ On purchase £

ORLANDO CARRINGTON ROSÉ NV BRUT

Inexpensive fruity fizz for unthinking, everyday drinking when first released, this *cuvée* quickly picks up a touch of biscuity complexity for those who prefer a more serious style.
On purchase ⓔ

ORLANDO CARRINGTON 1996 BRUT

Fresh, easy, vanilla-fruit.
On purchase ⓔ

ORLANDO TRILOGY NV BRUT 78

Elegant fruit aromas follow through onto the palate with plenty of ripe acidity.
On purchase ⓔ

ORTENBERG

See Schloss Ortenberg

OUDINOT

12 rue Godat-Roger, 51207 Épernay
☎ (326) 54.60.31 ℻ (326) 54.78.52
From the same stable as Beaumet (see entry) and Jeanmaire (none submitted), and most of the wines are exactly the same *cuvées*.

OUDINOT NV CUVÉE ROSÉ, BRUT 80

Although this pink-coloured *cuvée* has an amylic nose, it also has such easy-going, fresh floral fruit that many casual drinkers of Champagne will enjoy it.
On purchase ⓔⓔ

OUDINOT NV CUVÉE BRUT 80

More amylic than the Marks & Spencer (UK) own-label shipment, but it has easy-going fruit and a soft mousse.
On purchase ⓔⓔ

OUDINOT 1990 CUVÉE BRUT 82

Fresh and flowery, without being amylic, and with very youthful fruit. A good buy for those who want a fruit-driven *cuvée* that does not threaten to turn toasty too quickly in the cellar.
Now–1999 ⓔⓔⓔ

OUDINOT

Loire, France

VEUVE OUDINOT NV TOURAINE BRUT

Fresh and rich with bright flavours underpinned by high acidity to produce a wine for ready drinking in a lively style.
On purchase ⓔ

PAILLARD

avenue du Champagne, 51100 Reims
☎ (326) 36.20.22 ℻ (326) 36.57.72
The consistency of its elegant Champagnes is likely to make this house the patrimoine of the Paillard family for many generations to come.

BRUNO PAILLARD NV BRUT PREMIÈRE CUVÉE 87

Fresh, elegant and satisfying, with a lovely minerally finesse, this is one of the most consistent non-vintage Champagnes on the market.
Now–1999 ⓔⓔ 🍾125F

BRUNO PAILLARD NV BRUT ROSÉ PREMIÈRE CUVÉE 87

A *rosé* of great charm and elegance, with delicate red-fruits on the palate and a lovely softness and freshness on the finish.
Now–1999 ⓔⓔ 🍾145F

BRUNO PAILLARD NV BRUT CHARDONNAY RÉSERVE PRIVÉE 87

Wonderfully ripe, creamy Chardonnay that is obviously mature, yet with all the freshness that recent disgorgement brings.
Now–2002 ⓔⓔ 🍾160F

BRUNO PAILLARD 1989 BRUT 91

This has evolved brilliantly, with oodles of creamy digestive-biscuit richness, and a wonderfully lush, creamy-smooth finish.
Now–2009 ⓔⓔⓔ 🍾170F

PALEINE

See Domaine de la Paleine

PALMER

67 rue Jacquart, 51100 Reims
 (326) 07.35.07 (326) 07.45.24

If you judge a cooperative by its reputation with the *négoce* (Champagne houses), which do business with cooperatives every day, then Palmer is one of the very best.

PALMER 1989 BRUT   **89**

The best vintage Palmer has produced in a long time; rich, expansive, perfumed fruit with amazing freshness for the year.
❙ Now–2005 ⓔⓔⓔ 🍾140F

BRUT NV AMAZONE DE PALMER   **90**

This prestige *cuvée* has deep, penetrating flavour that develops slowly, and is one of the best integrated examples of Chardonnay and Pinot fruit.
❙ Now–2005 ⓔⓔⓔ 🍾180F

PANNIER

23 rue Roger Catillon,
02400 Château-Thierry
 (23) 69.13.10 (23) 69.18.18

This Aisne cooperative has greatly improved as the proportion of grapes gathered from the Marne has gradually increased in recent years. Pannier has two prestige *cuvées* – Louis Eugène, which is non-vintage and expressive of the house style; and Egérie, which is vintaged and expressive or even an exaggeration of the year in question.

PANNIER NV BRUT TRADITION/SÉLECTION   **85**

Not recommendable until 1994, Pannier's basic non-vintage has consistently improved since then, and is now really quite rich and satisfying for such a light-structured *cuvée*, with some elegant flowery-finesse on the finish.
❙ On purchase ⓔⓔ 🍾110F

PANNIER NV BRUT ROSÉ   **86**

Currently on very good form with attractive cherry Pinot fruit.
❙ On purchase ⓔⓔ 🍾120F

PANNIER NV LOUIS EUGÈNE   **89**

Delicate richness of fruit with fine acidity and slow-building biscuitiness on the finish.
❙ Now–2002 ⓔⓔⓔ 🍾150F

PANNIER NV LOUIS EUGÈNE ROSÉ   **89**

Excellent balance of red-fruit richness with biscuity finesse.
❙ Now–2002 ⓔⓔⓔ 🍾160F

PANNIER 1990 EGÉRIE   **90**

The best Egérie yet, with a lovely purity of fruit and a degree of finesse absent from any Pannier wine prior to this date.
❙ Now–2005 ⓔⓔⓔ 🍾175F

PARIGOT

Burgundy, France

PARIGOT, CRÉMANT BLANC NV CRÉMANT DE BOURGOGNE BRUT   **73**

Firm structure, good depth of flavour and a firm mousse.
❙ Now–2000 ⓔ

PARIGOT, CRÉMANT ROSÉ NV CRÉMANT DE BOURGOGNE BRUT   **73**

A plump, fruity wine that is almost fat and hints of strawberries.
❙ On purchase ⓔ

PASSAVANT

See Château de Passavant

PELLETIER

20 rue Jean York, 51700 Passy-Grigny
 (326) 52.65.86 (326) 52.65.86

A small family property just downstream from Ste Gemme, where Krug buys some of its best Meunier.

JEAN-MICHEL PELLETIER NV BRUT TRADITION   **83**

Softer and smoother than the Brut Sélection, with none of the wet-straw character.
❙ On purchase ⓔⓔ 🍾64F

JEAN-MICHEL PELLETIER
1993 CUVÉE ANAËLLE BRUT

Extremely rich, smooth and satisfying. A serious, substantial flavour of some class.
❙ Now–2001 ⓔⓔⓔ ⚲90F

PELORUS

Marlborough, New Zealand
Sparkling wine aficionados will not be surprised to learn that "Mad Harry" Osborne of Kristone in California consults here. The 1990 (90 points) and 1992 (91 points) promise to be sensational in the year 2000, but it was the latest release, 1993, that interested me most.

PELORUS 1993 MARLBOROUGH

The lightest and potentially the best Pelorus vintage so far, this 1993 shows what a strange blessing a cold, rainy harvest can be. The malolactic has just started to dominate the wine, although this will eventually be subsumed by the oakiness, when the two will be trans-formed into the creamy-toasty complexity that is the hallmark of Pelorus.
❙ Now–2003 ⓔⓔ

PENLEY

South Australia, Australia
Kym Tolley's mother was a Penfolds and his father a Tolley, thus the name Penley. His penchant is for red wines, but he also produces some fizz, made mainly from Pinot Noir, which is almost a forgotten variety in Coonawarra, and some 15 per cent Chardonnay.

PENLEY PINOT CHARDONNAY
1991 BRUT

Sharp and zesty with a touch of malolactic complexity.
❙ Now–1999 ⓔⓔ

PENLEY PINOT CHARDONNAY
1990 BRUT

The finesse in this *cuvée* puts it into a different class to the 1991 vintage.
❙ Now–1999 ⓔⓔ

PEREJÓN

See Don Perejón

PÉRIGNON

See Moët & Chandon

PERELADA

Ampurdán-Costa Brava, Spain

CASTILLO PERELADA NV
CAVA BRUT NATURE RESERVA

Sweet, easy fruit.
❙ On purchase ⓔ

PERRIER

69 avenue de Paris
51016 Chélons-en-Champagne
☎ (326) 68.29.51 ⓕ (326) 70.57.16
Joseph Perrier is now part of the large Laurent-Perrier group, but the Champagnes are as individual and interesting as ever.

JOSEPH PERRIER NV
CUVÉE ROYALE BRUT

The basic Cuvée Royale Brut is rich, creamy and complex – this is Joseph Perrier on top form.
❙ Now–2000 ⓔⓔ ⚲120F

JOSEPH PERRIER NV BLANC DE
BLANCS, CUVÉE ROYALE BRUT

Deliciously rich and creamy, the Blanc de Blancs is just starting to pick up biscuity-walnutty complexity.
❙ Now–2002 ⓔⓔ ⚲132F

JOSEPH PERRIER 1990
CUVÉE ROYALE BRUT

I have always liked the rich, intense fruit in this vintage, but the first release was spoilt by an oxidative character, which I was glad to see had disappeared from shipments made in early 1998.
▬ 2000–2005 ⓔⓔⓔ

PERRIER-JOUËT

26/28 avenue de Champagne
51200 Épernay
C (326) 55.20.53 **FAX** (326) 54.54.55

This top-quality *grande marque* Champagne owned by Seagram is back on stunning form after a period when it was in threat of being "Mummified" by its sister brand.

PERRIER-JOUËT NV GRAND BRUT — 86

The Grand Brut has been equalling its original high standards since early 1997, and the current shipment is fresh and elegant in style, with plenty of fruit and a serious edge to the quality.
❦ Now–2000 ⓔⓔ 🍷122F

PERRIER-JOUËT NV BLASON DE FRANCE BRUT — 87

The Blason always has more creamy-Chardonnay influence than the Grand Brut. The previous shipment developed faster than it should have done, but this richer, smoother *cuvée* from the current shipment promises to age well.
❦ Now–2002 ⓔⓔⓔ 🍷148F

PERRIER-JOUËT NV BLASON DE FRANCE ROSÉ BRUT — 87

Full, yet delicate Pinot flavour, with a soft, velvety finish.
❦ Now–2000 ⓔⓔⓔ 🍷162F

PERRIER-JOUËT 1992 BRUT — 88

Lovely and fresh with floral-citrussy notes and a softness of fruit cocooned in crisp acidity, this is one of the most promising 1992s on the market.
➤ 1999–2000 ⓔⓔⓔ

PERRIER-JOUËT 1990 BRUT — 90

A deliciously fruity wine that is still available and continues to develop beautiful toasty bottle-aromas.
❦ Now–2000 ⓔⓔⓔ 🍷144F

PERRIER-JOUËT 1988 BELLE EPOQUE ROSÉ — 90

Quite fat, toasty and mature, but a classy vintage with excellent acidity, and plenty of life yet.
❦ Now–2005 ⓔⓔⓔⓔ 🍷375F

PERRIER-JOUËT 1986 BELLE EPOQUE ROSÉ — 90

One of the lightest Belle Epoque vintages, but still the class shines through. Currently going very toasty.
❦ Now–2000 ⓔⓔⓔⓔ

PERRIER-JOUËT 1985 BELLE EPOQUE ROSÉ — 91

Available from some specialists, this will gradually become indistinguishable from the same vintage of Belle Epoque Brut, as the latter acquires a deeper gold colour, while this *cuvée* drops its colour to go sunset gold.
❦ Now–2005 ⓔⓔⓔⓔ

PERRIER-JOUËT 1995 BELLE EPOQUE BRUT (JEROBOAM) — ⊖

You might think that 2,000 dollars for a Jeroboam of Belle Epoque is over the top, but this price includes an overnight stay for two at Perrier-Jouët's fabulous Maison Belle Epoque in Épernay, where you will be lavishly entertained. There are just 2,000 individually numbered Jeroboams for the entire world, so order one from your local stockist right away if you are interested. Perrier-Jouët is not disgorging the wine until 1999, and, with such a limited number, advertising has been by word of mouth (until now!). I have not tasted the wine, but the lowest-scoring Belle Epoque vintages in the past 20 or so years have all scored 90 points, so the 1995 should be good too. Mind you, if they filled the Jeroboams with water, they would still be a bargain!
➤ Wait and see ⓔⓔⓔⓔ

PERRIER-JOUËT 1990 BELLE EPOQUE BRUT — 94

The vintage has such finesse that it would be all too easy to drink now, but ideally you really should try to keep your hands off it until the Millennium.
➤ 2000–2008 ⓔⓔⓔⓔ 🍷340F

PERRIER-JOUËT 1988 BELLE EPOQUE BRUT — 90

Still quite widely available in specialist outlets, this vintage can appear to disappoint due to the tightness of the wine, but it's chock-a-block full of extract and comes out with food.
➤ 2000–2010 ⓔⓔⓔⓔ

PERRIER-JOUËT 1985 BELLE EPOQUE

Available in specialist outlets, this vintage has developed a lovely toasty richness, yet remains extraordinarily fresh, with even more extract than the 1988.

Now–2005 ££££

PETALUMA
South Australia, Australia
Although Bollinger has a financial interest in Petaluma, the famous *grande marque* keeps its distance from any sparkling wines produced outside of Champagne. Croser is entirely Brian Croser's handwork.

CROSER 1994 BRUT

This vintage seems strangely foursquare if served too cold, but has soft, gentle fatness with nice vanilla-fruit finesse on the finish when not over-chilled.

On purchase ££

PHANTOM
See Saxenburg

PHILIPPONNAT
13 rue du Pont, 51160 Mareuil-sur-Aÿ
☎ (326) 52.60.43 ☏ (326) 52.61.49
In November 1997 Bruno Paillard purchased Philipponnat from the ailing Marie Brizard empire on behalf of the up-and-coming BCC (Boizel Chanoine Champagne) group. The deal included Abel Lepitre, but the jewel in the crown was Clos des Goisses, a single-vineyard Champagne that is on par with the exquisite Salon.

PHILIPPONNAT NV LE REFLET

Clos des Goisses grapes have been blended with Chardonnay to make one of the most elegant, ready-drinking non-vintage *cuvées* on the market.

On purchase £££ ☙163F

CLOS DES GOISSES 1991 PHILIPPONNAT

For Clos des Goisses, this has always been very easy to drink when young, with a delicious pineapple-fruit palate that is years away from this Champagne's truly complex potential.

Now–2018 ££££

CLOS DES GOISSES 1990 PHILIPPONNAT

Pure acacia aroma and elegant, with intensely flavoured fruit on the palate, it is a shame to drink this now, yet very hard to resist.

Now–2030 ££££

CLOS DES GOISSES 1989 PHILIPPONNAT

Fat aromas with tight flavours on the palate, this *cuvée* has only recently started to develop richness and complexity.

1999–2020 ££££

CLOS DES GOISSES 1988 PHILIPPONNAT

Not fat like the 1989, but very rich indeed, with an aromatic finesse that will one day make a profoundly complex, utterly beguiling mature Champagne.

1999–2025 ££££ ☙364F

CLOS DES GOISSES 1986 PHILIPPONNAT

Not the class of 1985 Clos des Goisses, but great finesse and quality for the year.

Now–2005 ££££

CLOS DES GOISSES 1985 PHILIPPONNAT

Classic Clos des Goisses, with a huge, rich, deep flavour and slow-building complexity beginning to form.

2000–2020 ££££

PIBALEAU
Loire, France

PASCAL PIBALEAU NV BRUT, CRÉMANT DE LOIRE

Very fresh fruit with a juicy-ripe pear flavour make this a soft-styled apéritif.

On purchase £

PICAMELOT

Burgundy, France

Maison Louis Picamelot has been making sparkling Burgundy since 1926, and this experience is evident in the fact that one of its *cuvées* came equal second in the line-up of Crémant de Bourgogne.

CRÉMANT DE BOURGOGNE, CUVÉE JEANNE THOMAS NV BRUT, LOUIS PICAMELOT

Toasty-oaky fruit aromas of some finesse, with excellent acidity on the palate.
❙ Now–2000 ⓔ

PICAMELOT NV CRÉMANT DE BOURGOGNE BRUT

An elegant fizz that is full of perfumed fruit that seems to be Pinot Noir, but is different than any other Crémant de Bourgogne in the tasting.
❙ On purchase ⓔ

PIPER-HEIDSIECK

See Heidsieck

PISONI

Trentino, Italy

Well-established as one of the best producers of sparkling wine under the Trento DOC.

PISONI BRUT 1992 TRENTO ⓻

Succulent and appealing fruit on the nose becomes much firmer on the palate.
❙ Now–1999 ⓔⓔ

PLANTAGENET

Western Australia, Australia

Named after the shire in which it is situated, Plantagenet was the first to cultivate the Mount Barker area and is its leading winery today, although so far I much prefer its still wines.

PLANTAGENET 1992 BRUT

This sweet and sour, malty *cuvée* is softer, riper and more accessible than Plantagenet's 1993.
❙ On purchase ⓔ

PLATZER

Austria

A small grower in Sud-Osteiermark who produces one of Austria's few interesting sparkling wines.

WEINHOF PLATZER PINOT CUVÉE

Pure Pinot Blanc with elegant fruit, a firm mouse and well-balanced acidity.
❙ Now–1999 ⓔⓔ

PLOYEZ-JACQUEMART

Ludes, 51500 Rilly-la-Montagne
☎ (326) 61.11.87 ℻ (326) 61.12.20

L. d'Harbonville, the prestige *cuvée* from this small, highly respected house, has leaped forward two or three levels of quality as from the 1988 vintage.

L. D'HARBONVILLE 1990 BRUT, PLOYEZ-JACQUEMART

Very rich apricot with high acidity and a tangy finish. It is currently not showing the charm, excitement or focus of the previous two vintages, but based on the development of those *cuvées* and the undisputed greatness of the year, I must at least reserve judgement.
➡ Wait and see ⓔⓔⓔ

L. D'HARBONVILLE 1989 BRUT, PLOYEZ-JACQUEMART ⑨①

Creamy new oak mingling with beautiful toasty aromas, and excellent acidity.
➡ 2000–2005 ⓔⓔⓔ

L. D'HARBONVILLE 1988 BRUT, PLOYEZ-JACQUEMART ⑨⓪

Intense, high-acid fruit that is as clear as a bell, and destined for lemony-toasty Burgundian-style stardom.
❙ Now–2008 ⓔⓔⓔ 🍾235F

POJER & SANDRI

Trentino, Italy

A sparkling wine from a Trentino producer, who makes an excellent range of still wines.

POJER & SANDRI NV CUVÉE '93–'94, EXTRA BRUT

Immaculate presentation and nice, fresh, apricot aromas on the nose, but it lacks the depth and acidity for a top score.
❚ On purchase ⓔ

POL ROGER

1 rue Henri Lelarge, 51206 Épernay
⚫ (326) 59.58.00 FAX (326) 55.25.70
The "Pol" Star in Champagne's firmament is in stunning form.

WHITE FOIL NV BRUT

The non-vintage is fresh, with supple fruit. It is as clean as a whistle, with a touch of class and is always perfect for current drinking.
❚ Now–1999 ⓔⓔ

POL ROGER 1990 BRUT

This is already so seductively soft and exquisitely perfumed with such an impeccable balance and cushiony mouse that it is difficult to accept just how much there is in this wine to develop.
❚ Now–2010 ⓔⓔⓔ 🍷180F

POL ROGER 1989 BRUT

Like Pol Roger's 1983 and 1992 Brut, the 1989 was not released on all the usual markets, and when exported its distribution was often restricted. In the United Kingdom, for example, the 1989 *cuvée* was exclusively sold by the Oddbins chain. The 1989 was initially very fruity, but like the 1983 it quickly developed a creamy walnutty-biscuit complexity beyond its years.
❚ Now–2005 ⓔⓔⓔ

POL ROGER 1988 BRUT

The Stevensons' house Champagne – need I say more?
❚ Now–2018 ⓔⓔⓔ

POL ROGER 1990 BRUT CHARDONNAY

I once said that it is almost perverse that a traditional Pinot-dominated house can produce such a sublime *blanc de blancs* as this *cuvée*, and I have to say that this is the most sumptuous and creamy vintage yet. This wine lasts a fraction of Pol Roger's classic vintage blend, and although interesting to follow up to 15 years of age, Chardonnay Brut is often at its best when first released, or at least within a year or two.
❚ Now–2002 ⓔⓔⓔ

POL ROGER 1990 BRUT ROSÉ

A soft, sensual experience, with a panoply of pristine red-fruits on the finish. Pure delight.
❚ Now–2002 ⓔⓔⓔ

POL ROGER CUVÉE PR 1988 RÉSERVE SPÉCIALE

Richness of fruit in abundance, with class, complexity and fabulous finesse.
❚ Now–2025 ⓔⓔⓔⓔ

POL ROGER CUVÉE SIR WINSTON CHURCHILL 1988 BRUT

Pol Roger has always refused to reveal the composition of this *cuvée*. Most vintages appear to be less Pinot-dominated than the Cuvée PR, even though the opposite would have seemed more fitting. This, however, has a concentrated Pinot character and is so youthful that it would be infanticide to broach just yet.
▬ 2003–2030 ⓔⓔⓔⓔ

POL ROGER CUVÉE SIR WINSTON CHURCHILL 1985 BRUT

Luscious fruit interwoven with fine acacia floweriness when young, this is now a wine of magnificent richness and finesse.
❚ Now–2025 ⓔⓔⓔⓔ

POMMERY

5 Place du Général Gouraud, 51053 Reims
⚫ (326) 61.62.63 FAX (326) 61.62.99
Pommery's winemakers have made some of the finest *cuvées* in Champagne when they are allowed to select according to quality not quantity.

Pommery NV Brut Royal

Simple, fruity, recognizable Pommery style, with a slightly cumbersome finish.
❙ On purchase ⓔⓔ 🍾120F

Pommery NV Brut Royal Apanage

A huge leap forward for Pommery, with its stricter selection and higher Chardonnay content. Fabulous depth of crisp-mellow flavour, with a lovely slow build-up of fresh yet mature complexity.
❙ Now–2001 ⓔⓔⓔ 🍾150F

Pommery NV Brut Rosé

Very pale *blanc de noirs* colour, with true *brut* crisp dryness, but very fruity.
❙ Now–2000 ⓔⓔ 🍾160F

Pommery 1991 Brut, Grand Cru

Firm toasty fruit with a full finish that lacks the finesse of the best Pommery vintages.
❙ Now–1999 ⓔⓔⓔ 🍾160F

Pommery 1990 Brut, Grand Cru

Very rich and very good, but not in the same class as Pommery's 1989 vintage.
❙ Now–2005 ⓔⓔⓔ

Pommery 1989 Brut, Grand Cru

Atypically big for Pommery, but has a finesse that many 1989s lack. A great wine.
❙ Now–1999 ⓔⓔⓔ

Pommery 1988 Louise, Brut

Ten years old and not yet together, but the excellent depth and richness guarantee a slow-maturing Champagne of great complexity and finesse.
▬ 2000–2006 ⓔⓔⓔⓔ 🍾350F

Pommery 1989 Louise, Rosé Brut

Classy toasty aromas pervade every molecule of this richly flavoured, beautifully balanced *cuvée*. Lovely fruit and acidity.
❙ Now–2002 ⓔⓔⓔⓔ

PONGRÁCZ
See Bergkelder

QUARTET
See Roederer Estate

RAIMAT
See Codorníu

RATZENBERGER
Mittelrhein, Germany.

Weingut Ratzenberger 1993 Bacharacher Kloster Fürstental Riesling Sekt Brut

Really good, crisp style with lots of satisfying depth and length to the fruit.
❙ On purchase ⓔⓔ

Weingut Ratzenberger 1994 Bacharacher Kloster Fürstental Riesling Sekt Brut

Succulent peachy fruit. Bottle-fermented.
❙ On purchase ⓔⓔ

RAVENTÓS I BLANC
Penedès, Spain
Josep Maria left his family's firm, Codorníu, to set up his own house in 1986. The classy presentation stands out among other Cavas.

Cava Gran Reserva Personal 1992 Brut Nature, Raventós i Blanc

Some malolactic complexity peeping through a richness of fruit that is going biscuity.
❙ Now–1999 ⓔ

Cava Gran Reserva 1993 Cava Brut Nature, Raventós i Blanc

Lighter than the Gran Reserva Personal, in a much easier, less complex style, with none of the malolactic aromas showing.
❙ On purchase ⓔ

RAVENTÓS ROSELL
Penedès, Spain

This offshoot of the Raventós family owns 60 hectares of vines and established its own Cava enterprise as recently as 1985.

JOAN RAVENTÓS ROSELL 1994 CAVA BRUT NATURE

No Joan Raventós wines were submitted this year, but the 1994 tasted last year had lots of fat, delicious fruit to last until now, plus an intriguing blown-wheat aroma.
On purchase Ⓔ

REBECCA VINEYARD
Tasmania, Australia

Joe Chromy recently sold Heemskerk and Jansz to Pipers Brook, but although this included the Rochecombe Vineyard, it did not include the RV brand, which will now be sourced from Rebecca Vineyard. Hopefully, Rebecca is every bit as stunning.

RV TASMANIA 1995 REBECCA VINEYARD, HEEMSKERK

An easy-drinking, fruit driven *cuvée* formerly from the same stable as Jansz, and utterly beguiling it is too, with beautifully bright Pinot fruit and the most succulent of finishes. Seductive stuff!
Now–2000 Ⓔ

RENAUDIN

Domaine des Conardins, 51530 Moussy
☎ (326) 54.03.41 ℻ (326) 54.31.12
Small, consistently high quality, very expressive Champagnes. The owner, Dominique Tellier, also makes good Kosher Champagne.

R. RENAUDIN NV GRANDE RÉSERVE BRUT

A richly flavoured *cuvée* with intense fruit and a fresh, biscuity complexity.
Now–2000 ⒺⒺ

R. RENAUDIN 1987 BRUT ROSÉ

Not many *rosé* Champagnes benefit from 11 years ageing, but this is now proudly vintaged. An old gold colour, this has matured gracefully, with lots of finesse, and is packing a lot of flavour, spreading out beautifully on the finish, like a peacock's tail.
Now–1999 ⒺⒺⒺ

R. RENAUDIN 1985 RÉSERVE SPÉCIALE C.D. BRUT

This is still very much a fruit-driven wine, without any sign of complex bottle-aromas, but makes very rich current drinking.
Now–2000 ⒺⒺⒺ

RESS
Rheingau, Germany

RESS & COMPAGNIE 1991 SPÄTBURGUNDER SEKT BRUT

Tastes like winegums with bubbles!
On purchase ⒺⒺ

RESS & COMPAGNIE 1994 RIESLING SEKT BRUT

A fine structure with a high concentration of fruit. Bottle-fermented.
On purchase ⒺⒺ

RIBEAUVILLÉ
Alsace, France

Best known for its Clos du Zahnacker, a classic blend from a region renowned for its pure varietal wines.

RIESLING, CRÉMANT D'ALSACE NV BRUT, CAVE VINICOLE DE RIBEAUVILLÉ

Good Riesling fruit spoilt by a whiff of sulphur, but this will go toasty with time, and the wine has the acidity to take that.
Now–1999 Ⓔ

RIENTH
Württemberg, Germany

WEINGUT GERHARD RIENTH 1995 FELLBACHER GOLDBERG RIESLING SEKT BRUT

Nice, easy-going, fresh and fluffy style. Bottle-fermented.

On purchase ££

ROBERT

25 avenue de la République
51190 Le Mesnil-sur-Oger
☎ (326) 57.52.94 ✉ (326) 57.59.22

I was disappointed that only one of the numerous wines submitted survived my blind tastings, as Alain Robert usually makes some of Le Mesnil's greatest grower Champagnes. The 1985 is, however, a wonderful exception.

ALAIN ROBERT 1985 SÉLECTION, BLANC DE BLANCS

Layers of toasty over-ripe peachy fruit, with exquisitely high acidity.

Now–2003 £££ 🍾163F

(LOUIS) ROEDERER

21 Boulevard Lundy, 51053 Reims
☎ (326) 40.42.11 ✉ (326) 47.66.51

Roederer's prestige *cuvée*, Cristal, is a licence to print money in the USA, and the Champagnes produced are of the highest quality.

LOUIS ROEDERER NV BRUT PREMIER

The non-vintage Brut Premier is always a good bet, but currently on stunning form. One of the very best non-vintage *cuvées* of the tasting, it even has the same vanilla mid-palate smoothness found in Charles Heidsieck.

Now–2002 ££

LOUIS ROEDERER 1990 BRUT

Fresh, zesty, creamy-almondy fruit with a very lively mousse. Currently not in the class of Roederer's Blanc de Blancs, but it will gain body, depth and complexity over the next few years.

2000–2005 £££

LOUIS ROEDERER 1990 BLANC DE BLANCS BRUT

Louis Roederer's best-kept secret, this *cuvée* is the least-known, greatest bargain in the range. Wonderfully rich and succulent with classy, complex, creamy-walnutty fruit.

2000–2005 £££

LOUIS ROEDERER 1991 ROSÉ BRUT

Always very pale with a youthful yet oxidative aromas, this *cuvée* has the acidity to let the palate catch up with the rest of the wine.

1999–2001 £££

LOUIS ROEDERER CRISTAL 1990 BRUT

Full and smooth, and, despite the excellent high acidity, there is already a considerable depth of flavour, with lots of Pinot-rich, biscuity complexity coming through on the finish.

Now–2015 ££££

LOUIS ROEDERER CRISTAL 1989 BRUT

The complexity in this *cuvée* started to emerge in 1996, since when it has shown remarkable finesse for the year.

Now–2010 ££££

LOUIS ROEDERER CRISTAL 1988 BRUT

The richness in this wine is just beginning to swell, but it still needs further ageing in order to allow it to develop mellow post-disgorgement bottle-aromas.

2000–2010 ££££

LOUIS ROEDERER CRISTAL 1985 BRUT

The 1985 still tastes so young that it appears to be relatively simplistic, but that is, of course, the hallmark of the greatest Cristal *cuvées*.

2000–2015 ££££

LOUIS ROEDERER CRISTAL 1985 ROSÉ BRUT

The soft, silky, strawberry fruit here is so sublime that this might well turn out to be the best Cristal Rosé since the first and legendary 1974 vintage.

Now–2005 ££££

LOUIS ROEDERER CRISTAL "2000" 1990 BRUT (METHUSELAH)

A different blend to the 1990 Cristal, and not really Roederer in style. Cristal "2000" has a bit more Chardonnay than the regular Cristal, but the selection of *crus* (Mesnil and Avize) emphasizes this grape, producing a leaner structure with crisp, ripe-green-apple fruit. Evolution in this size of bottle is so slow that I suspect most will be gone long before the *cuvée* is ready. They sell for $2,000, which is more than the cost of eight bottles of the 1990.

 2010–2030 ⓔⓔⓔⓔ

(THÉOPHILE) ROEDERER

20 rue Andrieux, 51058 Reims
☎ (326) 40.19.00 📠 (326) 47.66.51
The wines are made and stored separately from Louis Roederer's, but while the raw materials determine Théophile Roederer's lower quality and simpler style, the brand benefits from Roederer "know-how" and is an alternative for any Louis customers who are strapped for cash.

THÉOPHILE ROEDERER NV BRUT ROSÉ

Very pale salmon-gold with rare richness for such a light-bodied wine.
❗Now–2000 ⓔⓔ

ROEDERER ESTATE

Mendocino, California, USA
The Premier Grand Cru of American sparkling wine, Roederer Estate is owned by the French Champagne house Louis Roederer, which prefers to call the wine Quartet on export.

ROEDERER ESTATE NV BRUT

Apart from the 1986-based release, this *cuvée* is always so tight, firm and youthful when first released that it often tastes like green cooking apples, but after two or three years bottle-age, it quietly develops a lovely creamy-biscuit complexity. It is California's greatest sparkling wine.
 2000–2003 ⓔⓔ

ROEDERER ESTATE NV BRUT ROSÉ

The current *cuvée* has lots of very delicate, soft-fruit flavours.
❗Now–2000 ⓔⓔ

ROEDERER ESTATE L'ERMITAGE 1991 BRUT

Full, yet soft and deliciously fruity wine with lots of youthful complexity.
❗Now–2001 ⓔⓔ

ROGER

See Pol Roger

ROHART

Loire, France

VOUVRAY, COEUR DE CUVÉE 1995 BRUT, ALAIN ROHART

Too assertively Chenin for my personal taste, but very good for its type, with a rich finish. Should please Loire purists.
❗Now–1999 ⓔⓔ

VOUVRAY, TÀTE DE CUVÉE NV BRUT, ALAIN ROHART

Rich, lively, perfumed fruit.
❗Now–1999 ⓔ

ROLET

Arbois, France
These are the favourite non-Champagne guzzlers of a Dr Patricia Norman, who is so passionate about the health benefits of drinking wine that she spends more time selling it than practising medicine.

ROLET NV CRÉMANT DU JURA, BRUT ROSÉ

Bruised plums on the nose, with contrasting perfumed fruit on the front to middle palate, and Victoria plums on the finish. All character and no finesse, but who gives a fig, or a plum for that matter?
❗On purchase ⓔ

ROLET NV CRÉMANT DU JURA, BRUT

An oxidative bent with no finesse, but the wine is not unpleasant, rather it is strangely chock-a-block full of character.
❦ On purchase ⓔ

ROSELL
See Raventos Rosell

ROTARI
Trentino, Italy

ROTARI RISERVA 1993 BRUT, TRENTO ⓻⓪

Fresh and fruity, with good acidity, but unfortunately the fruit peters out shortly after mid-palate, otherwise this would have scored higher.
❦ On purchase ⓔⓔ

ROVELLATS
Penedès, Spain

ROVELLATS CAVA GRAN RESERVA NV BRUT NATURE ⓻⓪

Light, clean and easy.
❦ On purchase ⓔ

ROY
See Tour du Roy

ROYER
120 Grande Rue, 10110 Landreville
☎ (325) 38.52.16 ℻ (325) 29.92.26
I was pleased with this *cuvée*, which again emphasizes the potential of Chardonnay in the Aube area, which is closer to Chablis than it is to the rest of Champagne, and has the same soil as Chablis.

ROYER PÈRE NV BLANCS DE BLANCS, CUVÉE PRESTIGE BRUT

Despite a foamy mousse, this is a jump up from the Cuvée de Réserve, with its rich yet elegant fruit flavour.
❦ Now–1999 ⓔⓔ ⚐82F

RUGGERI
Italy
Half the wines submitted by this producer passed the test, but the style seems to be either too amylic or too heavily influenced by malolactic, and so the wines lack finesse.

RUGGERI NV CHARDONNAY BRUT

The nose is restrained, but what shows through is fine, and has more finesse than the fresh, fruit on the palate. It has a correct lean structure.
❦ On purchase ⓔ

RUGGERI NV PROSECCO DI VALDOBBIADENE EXTRA DRY ⓻⓪

Just as amylic as all the other boring Prosecco, but this has a much greater intensity of flavour.
❦ On purchase ⓔ

RUGGERI SUPERIORE DI CARTIZZE NV PROSECCO DI VALDOBBIADENE DRY ⓻⓷

An amylic wine, but with some finesse, much more fruit than other Prosecco and some Muscat-like freshness.
❦ On purchase ⓔ

RUHLMANN
Alsace, France
I will always remember the beautiful balance of acidity in this producer's 1988 Crémant d'Alsace.

RUHLMANN 1995 CRÉMANT D'ALSACE BRUT

A fresh, fat, fruity fizz that needs a little tweaking in its structure and acidity.
❦ On purchase ⓔ

RUINART

4 rue des Crayères, 51100 Reims
📞 (326) 85.40.29 📠 (326) 82.88.43

Champagne lovers know Ruinart very well, but in terms of global awareness this continues to be a sleepy little *grande marque* that could easily double its production without harming its reputation for quality. Sales have crept up in recent years.

RUINART "R" NV BRUT

As rich and as satisfying as always.
❗Now–2000 ⓔⓔ

RUINART "R" NV BRUT ROSÉ

Recently relaunched in a new bottle-shape with an impressively lighter, fresher, easier-drinking style.
❗Now–2000 ⓔⓔ

RUINART "R" 1990 BRUT

A quick developer, but absolutely beguiling, this *cuvée* has lovely toasty aromas and a touch of vanilla to the fruit, with excellent acidity to keep it going.
❗Now–2002 ⓔⓔⓔ

RUINART "R" 1992 BRUT

So young and fruity, but this *cuvée* has a Chablis-like character that will quickly go toasty, so if you do not like those mellowing bottle-aromas, drink this up now.
❗Now–2002 ⓔⓔⓔ

DOM RUINART 1990 BLANC DE BLANCS

It's unusual for Dom Ruinart to be approachable before it enters its toasty stage, but this is already stunning, a lovely, fat, creamy-rich *cuvée*, yet it has not even started to develop the slightest complexity. This could turn out to be on par with the 1979 (94 points).
❗Now–2008 ⓔⓔⓔⓔ

DOM RUINART 1988 BLANC DE BLANCS

After a somewhat sultry start this *cuvée* has developed into an exotically creamy Champagne that is quite wonderful, yet strangely it is not reminiscent of either Dom Ruinart or 1988!
❗Now–2008 ⓔⓔⓔⓔ

DOM RUINART 1986 BLANC DE BLANCS

Starting to go really toasty. Not a top Dom Ruinart, but an exceptional 1986.
❗Now–2008 ⓔⓔⓔⓔ

DOM RUINART 1985 BLANC DE BLANCS

Big, rich and seductively toasty, yet there is so much undeveloped extract that this vintage still has miles to go.
❗Now–2010 ⓔⓔⓔⓔ

DOM RUINART 1986 ROSÉ

The 1986 Rosé has lovely red fruit richness now. When mature, this *cuvée* always develops into the quintessence of Pinot Noir, even though it is basically a Dom Ruinart *blanc de blancs* to which 20 per cent Pinot Noir vinified as a red wine has been added. It is a really lovely Champagne, but not quite in the same class as the 1981 (94 points).
❗Now–2005 ⓔⓔⓔⓔ

RUSSLER

Rheingau, Germany

WEINGUT FRIEDEL RUSSLER 1995 WALLUFER WALKENBERG RIESLING SEKT BRUT

Satisfying depth of fresh Riesling fruit for a non-dosage wine. Bottle-fermented.
❗On purchase ⓔⓔ

WEINGUT FRIEDEL RUSSLER 1995 WALLUFER WALKENBERG RIESLING SEKT EXTRA TROCKEN

Good tangy fruit with a hint of peach. Bottle-fermented.
❗On purchase ⓔⓔ

STE. MICHELLE

Washington, USA

This winery showed great promise for sparkling wine in the late 1970s, but it has struggled ever since to make something decent, let alone anything that is exciting.

DOMAINE STE. MICHELLE NV BRUT

Better than its Blanc de Blancs, this is more serious in structure, with classic floral aromas and a certain scented complexity to the fruit.
❗ On purchase ££

ST. URBANSHOF
Mosel-Saar-Ruwer, Germany

WEINGUT ST. URBANSHOF 1992 RIESLING SEKT BRUT

A very soft and gentle expression of Riesling fruit, with some finesse.
❗ On purchase ££

SALINGER
See Seppelt

SALON

Le Mesnil-sur-Oger, 51190 Avize
📞 (326) 57.51.65 📠 (326) 57.79.29
This is the only wine in the world that is not made every year – in non-vintage years the wine will end up either in one of Delamotte's *cuvées* or used by the parent company Laurent-Perrier. Salon is made exclusively from Chardonnay grown in Le Mesnil-sur-Oger from mid-slope vines over 40 years old, and it is this restricted yield that determines Salon's extraordinary intensity of fruit. The wines need at least 10 years ageing, and do not start to interest aficionados until 20 or 30 years old, when they develop a majestic depth and length, with complex aromas and flavours that typically include coconut, macaroons, walnuts, vanilla and coffee. Only 32 vintages of Salon have ever been produced, and for those who look out for old vintages at auction the very greatest are 1971 (97 points), 1961 (96 points) 1955 (96 points), 1947 (100 points), 1928 (100+ points!).

SALON 1988

Firm, well structured and definitely in the muscular mould. Initially, the very pale 1988 had an edge over the 1990, but the latter vintage has since demonstrated its superiority (95 points), although it will be a long time before it is released. This is still, however, a great vintage, with complex, citrussy fruit that is so tight that it will take time – even for Salon – to unfold, but when it does it will be stunning.
🍾 2003–2028 ££££ 🥂420F

SALON 1985

Very fine, elegant and pure. An absolute delight now, but capable of maturing gracefully for another 30 years or more.
❗ Now–2025 ££££

SALON 1983

It is fascinating to compare this with the 1982, which is a completely different vintage of almost the same age made with the same philosophy. The 1983 was initially firm and very *brut*, with a prune-like character that gave way to a creamy-coconutty, hazelnut-walnut complexity after a spurt of maturation in the mid-1990s. Great intensity, but evolving relatively fast for Salon, and not in the same class as the 1982. Almost impossible to score, but 88 illustrates the difference in quality relative to other Salon vintages.
❗ Now–2013 ££££ 🥂500F

SALON 1982

When recently disgorged this vintage is austere, with a mouth-puckering lemony-toastiness, but if given a few years in bottle, it slowly assumes a luscious peachy fruitiness, with toasty-vanilla aromas and a silkiness on the finish, yet heaps of acidity to keep it fresh. As the disgorgement date makes a vast difference to such a slow-developing Champagne, it should really be indicated on every bottle.
🍾 2003–2028 ££££ 🥂580F

SANDORA
Penedès, Spain
New joint venture between two Champagne groups, Seagram and Vranken-Lafitte.

SANDORA NV CAVA BRUT

Not bad, but not special either, and only just scrapes in because its 35 per cent Chardonnay content provides some mouthfill, although it is rather soapy and youthful. The balance is Parellada, and this is the worst of all three traditional varieties to blend with Chardonnay on a two-to-one basis, although the wine should improve a little in bottle, but only over a matter of months, not years.
▼ On purchase Ⓔ

SAUMUR

Loire, France
I cannot believe this cooperative makes as many _cuvées_ as it sent me, but not one of the Saumur _cuvées_ survived the blind tasting, whereas most of the Crémant de Loire did.

CRÉMANT DE LOIRE BLANC BRUT SPÉCIAL 1994 CAVE DES VIGNERONS DE SAUMUR

The only 1994 Loire fizz I could heartily recommend, this is the year when CVS Crémant de Loire came good, jumping from 15/85 Chenin/Chardonnay to 50/50. The freshness and finesse stand out, with a lovely ripe sweetness of fruit on the finish.
▼ Now–1999 Ⓔ

CRÉMANT DE LOIRE, BLANC BRUT SPÉCIAL NV CAVE DES VIGNERONS DE SAUMUR

One of the best Loire sparkling wines I have tasted, and immeasurably superior to another half-and-half Chenin/Chardonnay _cuvée_ also produced by this cooperative , which just goes to prove that it is not necessarily the grape varieties or producer that matters, but rather where and how those varieties are grown, and how they are processed.
▼ On purchase Ⓔ

CRÉMANT DE LOIRE, BLANC BRUT SPÉCIAL 1995 CAVE DES VIGNERONS DE SAUMUR

The 50 per cent Chardonnay gives this Crémant de Loire real mouthfill.
▼ Now–1999 Ⓔ

CRÉMANT DE LOIRE ROSÉ BRUT NV CAVE DES VIGNERONS DE SAUMUR

A very fresh fizz with lively raspberry fruit, made from Cabernet Franc.
▼ On purchase Ⓔ

CRÉMANT DE LOIRE ROSÉ SEC NV CAVE DES VIGNERONS DE SAUMUR

This pure Cabernet _rosé_ is fat, but fresh, lively and really quite _brut_ for a _sec_.
▼ On purchase Ⓔ

MOUSSEUX ROUGE DEMI-SEC NV CAVE DES VIGNERONS DE SAUMUR

A deep, dark, sweet-raspberry flavoured fizz made totally from Cabernet Franc.
▼ Now–2000 Ⓔ

SAVISA

Paarl/Stellenbosch, South Africa
Large Swiss-owned export-oriented company with numerous labels.

JACQUES GERMANIER BRUT NV CAP CLASSIQUE, SONOP

A sharp, fresh, zingy fizz in an embossed skittle-shaped bottle.
▼ Now–1999 Ⓔ

SAXENBURG

Stellenbosch, South Africa
A rapidly rising star in South Africa's red wine firmament.

LE PHANTOM BRUT NV CAP CLASSIQUE

High acidity gives the fruit a sharp tang.
▼ Now–2000 Ⓔ

SCHALES

Rheinhessen, Germany
Eiswien as the base for a sparkling wine is a new concept but here is no doubting the quality of the raw material.

SCHALES SILVANER TROCKEN 1991 PREMIUM SEKT

Amazing botrytis-like aroma, which follows through onto the palate. Just like drinking a fine Auslese with bubbles
❦ On purchase ⓔⓔⓔⓔ

SCHALLER

Alsace, France
Edgard Schaller is better known for his varietal wines, particularly Riesling Grand Cru Mandelberg, but he makes a creditable *crémant*.

SCHALLER, BLANC DE NOIR NV CRÉMANT D'ALSACE BRUT

Firm, crisp fruit and a sturdy structure. It should develop.
❦ Now–1999 ⓔ

SCHARFFENBERGER

Mendocino, California, USA
Scharffenberger's wines have gained tremendously in elegance and finesse since the early 1990s, particularly the Blanc de Blancs.

SCHARFFENBERGER NV BRUT

Fine, elegant, rich and smooth, with a lovely creamy-biscuit complexity beginning to build.
❦ On purchase ⓔ

SCHARFFENBERGER 1991 BLANC DE BLANCS

Light, soft and creamy with a silky mousse of minuscule bubbles.
❦ Now–1999 ⓔⓔ

SCHELL

Ahr, Germany

WEINGUT OTGER SCHELL 1993 RECHER HARDTBERG RIESLING SEKT HALBTROCKEN

Sweet, succulent Riesling fruit.
❦ On purchase ⓔⓔ

SCHLOSS

See Hambacher Schloss

SCHLOSS ORTENBERG

Baden, Germany
Established in 1950 as a viticultural school, Schloss Ortenburg currently produces 125 cases of Sekt per year.

WEINGUT SCHLOSS ORTENBERG NV PINOT SEKT BRUT

Extremely ripe and rich, this *cuvée* was marked down because it is not just on the sweet side of *brut,* but so richly sweet as to make a nonsense of the so-called *brut* style. On the other hand, if you are looking for a *brut* that tastes like a Halbtrocken then you might like to look upon this as scoring closer to 80 points. Bottle-fermented.
❦ On purchase ⓔⓔ

SCHLUMBERGER

Loire, France

ROBERT DE SCHLUMBERGER NV TOURAINE BRUT

Although the deep flavour and high acidity of Robert de Schlumberger's non-vintage Touraine Brut would seem to suggest a wine fit for ageing, it most definitely is made for ready drinking.
❦ On purchase ⓔ

SCHMITGES

Mosel-Saar-Ruwer, Germany

WEINGUT HEINRICH SCHMITGES 1994 ERDENER HERRENBERG RIESLING SEKT BRUT

Crisp, fresh and focused Riesling fruit. Bottle-fermented.
❦ On purchase ⓔⓔ

SCHRAM

See Schramsberg

SCHRAMSBERG

Napa, California, USA

Until Domaine Chandon was set up in 1973, Schramsberg was the only producer of serious quality bottle-fermented sparkling wine in the whole of the USA. Jamie Davies' aim (formerly shared by his late brother Jack) is to produce rich, complex sparkling wines that are fully mature and expressive of the sun-blessed *terroir* of the Golden State. Much as I respect this decision, I would like to see Schramsberg release much younger wines, particularly on export markets.

SCHRAMSBERG 1991 BLANC DE BLANCS

Very fat, and really quite heavy, yet still quite fresh.
❙ On purchase ⓔⓔ

J. SCHRAM 1991

Rich and toasty.
❙ On purchase ⓔⓔ

SCHWACH

Alsace, France

BERNARD SCHWACH BRUT RESERVE NV CRÉMANT D'ALSACE

This wine scrapes through as an outside bet on how it might develope, based solely on its structure and acidity.
❙ Now–2000 ⓔ

SEAVIEW

South Australia, Australia

Part of Southcorp, Seaview's basic range generally has the edge over that of its sister Seppelt brand.

EDWARDS & CHAFFEY 1993 PINOT NOIR CHARDONNAY BRUT, SEAVIEW

For lovers of toasty fizz only, this *cuvée* has now been at its peak for a couple of years, but it keeps on going thanks to very good acidity.
❙ On purchase ⓔ

SEAVIEW ROSÉ NV BRUT

Creamy strawberry and lavender fruit with a soft mousse.
❙ On purchase ⓔ

SEAVIEW PINOT NOIR CHARDONNAY 1994 BRUT

So smooth and creamy, the richness of fruit in this *cuvée* builds up gently in the mouth to a wonderfully satisfying flavour. This sparkling wine is all about fruit now, but it will become increasingly toasty as the months go by.
❙ Now–2000 ⓔ

SEAVIEW PINOT NOIR CHARDONNAY 1993 BRUT

The big, rich, toasty fruit in this *cuvée* is indicative of how the 1994 will go.
❙ Now–1999 ⓔ

SEAVIEW NV BRUT

Seaview's standard Brut is fresher, fluffier and better than the standard Brut made by its sister Seppelt brand, but, then again, at this end of the market this *cuvée* is also significantly more expensive.
❙ On purchase ⓔ

SEAVIEW PINOT NOIR CHARDONNAY 1995 BRUT

The real richness of fruit to be found in this blend of Chardonnay and Pinot Noir is just beginning to go toasty.
❙ On purchase ⓔ

SEAVIEW BLANC DE BLANCS 1995 BRUT

Unfortunately, there is a touch of oxi-dativeness already showing on the finish of this wine, which would normally exclude such a *cuvée* from this guide. On the other hand, I cannot bring myself to ignore Seaview's previous track record, which has been excellent, and so I will reserve judgement for now.
➤ Wait and see ⓔ

SEDLESCOMBE

Robertsbridge, England, UK

Roy Cook is the winemaker at this proudly organic vineyard.

SEDLESCOMBE ORGANIC 1994 BRUT

The wine was made and estate-bottled at Sedlescombe, but disgorged and dosaged at Chapel Wines in Tenterden. Its fresh garden-herb aroma is unusual, but gives way to rich fruit on the pale. A curiosity.
❗ On purchase ⓔ

SEGURA VIUDAS

Penedès, Spain

This is Freixenet's top-performing Cava brand.

RESERVA HEREDAD NV CAVA BRUT, SEGURA VIUDAS

Lots of satisfying fruit-laden flavour that promises to go toasty.
❗ Now–1999 ⓔ

SELOSSE

22 rue Ernest Vallée, 51190 Avize
📞 (326) 57.53.56 📠 (326) 57.78.22

Anselme Selosse is fastidious about quality in the vineyard and winery, but there are raw, floral, estery notes in most of the wines. They would benefit from one more year on their sediment, plus another year after disgorgement, before shipping.

JACQUES SELOSSE NV GRAND CRU BLANC DE BLANCS, EXTRA BRUT 85

Young, flowery Chardonnay. Needs time.
 1999–2001 ⓔⓔⓔ

JACQUES SELOSSE NV GRAND CRU BLANC DE BLANCS BRUT 85

Vinified in large oak *tonneaux*. It needs time to bring out the richness lurking beneath very young, floral aromas.
 1999–2001 ⓔⓔⓔ

JACQUES SELOSSE NV ORIGINE, GRAND CRU BLANC DE BLANCS BRUT 90

Vinified in small *barriques*, this is as oaky as expected, although how much the exotic, peachy fruit can be put down to wood, rather than ripeness of fruit, is anyone's guess.
❗ Now–2000 ⓔⓔⓔ

JACQUES SELOSSE NV GRAND CRU ROSÉ BRUT 85

Pale apricot colour, creamy-oaky aroma, smooth creamy-oaky fruit, still developing.
 1999–2001 ⓔⓔⓔ

JACQUES SELOSSE NV CUVÉE EXQUISE, SEC 88

Typical Selosse oaky-floral aroma, with extraordinarily tropical fruits and an exotic creamy-fruity sweetness that in purely taste terms is more *demi-sec* than *sec*. An excellent accompaniment to fresh raspberries gratiné.
❗ Now–2000 ⓔⓔⓔ

JACQUES SELOSSE 1989 GRAND CRU BLANC DE BLANCS BRUT 89

A well-structured wine that is already rich and fleshy, yet has huge extract, and awaits further development.
 2000–2005 ⓔⓔⓔ

JACQUES SELOSSE 1988 GRAND CRU BLANC DE BLANCS BRUT 85

Vinified in large oak *tonneaux*. Marked on the finish by the acidity of the 1988 vintage, this is another floral-rich *cuvée* that needs time.
 1999–2001 ⓔⓔⓔ

SENEZ

6 Grande Rue, 10360 Fontette
📞 (326) 29.60.62

CRISTIAN SENEZ 1990 FONTETTE BRUT ⊖

A freshly poured glass had an unpleasant plastic aroma, which I could not get past my nose to put inside my body, but this goes away after ten minutes or so, and the palate has a curious coconutty taste.
 Wait and see ⓔⓔⓔ 🍷120F

CRISTIAN SENEZ 1990 GRANDE RÉSERVE BRUT

Too exotic for me, but just saying that will make some people want to try it.
🍷 On purchase ⓔⓔⓔ ❄120F

CRISTIAN SENEZ 1989 BRUT

This wine has an almost woody (not overtly oaky) richness that promises to develop, and could well result in a much higher-scoring wine with time, but was the best of the three Senez wines tasted as far as current enjoyability goes.
🍷 Now–1999 ⓔⓔⓔ ❄110F

SEPPELT

Victoria, Australia
There are better sparkling wines than Seppelt's Great Western, but none that offers better value.

SEPPELT GREAT WESTERN NV BRUT

This clean, fresh, citrussy-zesty fizz is definitely at the bottom end of the Australian bottle-fermented bubbly market, yet consistently makes a decent mouthful, although it definitely is not for keeping.
🍷 On purchase ⓔ

SEPPELT 1994 BLANC DE BLANCS BRUT

Fresh, crisp, zesty-lemony fruit with a firm mouse of small bubbles.
🍷 Now–2000 ⓔ

SEPPELT 1992 SPARKLING SHIRAZ

A heady wine with a big oaky-Shiraz aroma, although less oak-dominated than Yalumba's sparkling Cabernet Sauvignon. Bags of fruit and a rich, raisiny complexity make this the ideal accompaniment to almost any dish containing blue cheese.
🍷 Now–2000 ⓔ

SEPPELT GREAT WESTERN NV ROSÉ

I find this easier to drink than Seppelt's sister Seaview Rosé. A nicely structured fizz with fine, creamy-rich fruit supported by a firm mousse.
🍷 On purchase ⓔ

SEPPELT 1993 PINOT NOIR CHARDONNAY

This fat, fresh and sassy wine is better than the 1991, which was being sold at the same time on some markets.
🍷 Now–1999 ⓔ

SEPPELT 1994 SPARKLING SHIRAZ

Fresh fruity Shiraz with a touch of oak, this is very much in the same mould as the 1992 vintage.
🍷 Now–2000 ⓔ

SEPPELT 1993 SPARKLING SHIRAZ

Very fruity style with a nice touch of oak, but not the complexity of the 1992.
🍷 Now–2000 ⓔ

SEPPELT 1985 SHOW SPARKLING SHIRAZ

This massive, blackcurrant-flavoured blockbuster is ripe in every sense of the word, and not for the weak-hearted or indeed anyone other than an out-and-out sparkling Shiraz fanatic.
🍷 Now–2000 ⓔ

SALINGER 1992 BRUT

The austere, citrussy fruit in this wine is typical of a young Salinger, which needs time to develop finesse.
🍷 Now–2001 ⓔⓔ

SALINGER 1991 BRUT

Fine and very fresh, with fluffy fruit and high acidity balance.
🍷 Now–2001 ⓔⓔ

SALINGER 1990 BRUT

This vintage of Salinger has really quite exceptional finesse for an eight-year-old fizz from Australia.
🍷 Now–2001 ⓔⓔ

SERRA

Penedès, Spain
Jaume Serra utilize one of Chile's highest-profile winemakers, Ignacio Recabarren, as consultant.

CRISTALINO NV CAVA BRUT

Fresh, fruit-driven style.
🍷 On purchase ⓔ

SHADOW CREEK

See Chandon California

SIEUR D'ARQUES

Limoux, France

DAME D'ARQUES TRADITION NV BLANQUETTE MÉTHODE ANCESTRALE

This unusual sparkling wine has been made by the ancient Blanquette de Limoux method, which involves no second fermentation, but a continuation of the first. The result should be labelled at least *demi-sec*, perhaps even *doux*, for it is lusciously sweet, with just six per cent of alcohol (which is a similar strength to sweet Italian Asti), but it is wonderfully soft with a silky-sweet finish. It is the perfect accompaniment to foie gras. I very much hope that we will see more *méthode ancestrale* on export markets in the future.
❚ On purchase ⓔ

SIEUR D'ARQUES 1991 CRÉMANT DE LIMOUX BRUT

This *cuvée* had the most finesse of all the dry Limoux tasted this year. It also had the tiniest bubbles and the most accessible fruit.
❚ On purchase ⓔ

SIFFERT

Alsace, France
It is Siffert's Pinot Noir Coteaux du Haut-Koenigsbourg that usually stands out, but this *crémant* shows some promise.

SIFFERT NV CRÉMANT D'ALSACE BRUT

There is a beautiful Riesling aroma in this Crémant d'Alsace, but the fruit is rather fat and the structure, although firm, could be leaner. With more acidity this would have scored higher.
❚ On purchase ⓔ

SIMONSIG

Stellenbosch, South Africa

The first producer of *méthode cham-penoise* sparkling wine in South Africa, Simonsig has a very large production and cuts its cloth to meet the price. Note that this often means that the more expensive the wine, the better the bargain.

KAAPSE VONKEL BRUT 1993 CAP CLASSIQUE, SIMONSIG

I tasted two totally different versions of this wine within days of each other: one was too oxidative for the age and weight, and would not have qualified for entry into this guide; the other had a good, clean fruit-driven style that should pick up some biscuitiness by Christmas 1998 (80 points).
➤ Wait and see ⓔ

KAAPSE VONKEL BRUT 1992 CAP CLASSIQUE, SIMONSIG

Classic biscuity aromas, lovely lean structure, fine mousse of tiny bubbles.
❚ Now–2000 ⓔ

SIPP MACK

Alsace, France
As Sipp Mack is such a great producer of still Riesling wines, both generic and *grand cru*, I will give this the benefit of the doubt.

SIPP MACK NV CRÉMANT D'ALSACE BRUT

Strangely fat yet tart fruit here, with fresh, terpene aromas suggesting some Riesling content.
❚ On purchase ⓔ

SOLDATI LA SCOLCA

Gavi, Italy
These wines tend to lean more towards heavy and characterful rather than light and elegant, and could do with more finesse at times.

SOLDATI LA SCOLCA NV BRUT

Hints of toast and lemon run through the bouquet onto the palate, which is rich and mature, yet firm, with a crisp finish.
On purchase Ⓔ

SOLDATI LA SCOLCA NV BRUT, GAVI

Creamy-malo nose with soft fruit, some peachiness and a creamy-menthol aftertaste. Soft mousse, fine bubbles.
On purchase Ⓔ

SOLDATI LA SCOLCA NV PAS DOSÈ, GAVI

Very ripe, fruity aromas with good acidity to highlight the palate.
On purchase Ⓔ

SOLDATI LA SCOLCA 1986 BRUT MILLESIMATO

Gets a high score (for Italian sparkling wine) for survival, which is due to its high acidity, and has matured into an exotic, coconutty concoction with apricots and custard on the finish.
On purchase ⒺⒺ

SOLEIL DU MATIN
See Môreson

SOLJANS
Henderson, New Zealand
Until the relatively recent launch of Soljans' classic _brut_-style Legacy, this traditional winery in New Zealand was known only for its sweet, aromatic Vivace Spumante.

SOLJANS ESTATE LEGACY 1995 METHODE TRADITIONNELLE

This fresh and sprightly fizz is totally fruit-driven.
On purchase ⒺⒺ

SOUNIT
Burgundy, France

CRÉMANT DE BOURGOGNE, CUVÉE CHARDONNAY NV ALBERT SOUNIT

Although this has a typically amylic aroma, there is some finesse, which could be an indication that this character will dissipate after a while. A dry, light style, with fine acidity.
On purchase Ⓔ

SOUTIRAN
3 rue des Crayères, 51150 Ambonnay
📞 (326) 57.08.18 📠 (326) 57.81.87
This grower shows good potential, but needs to tame down the oxidative characteristic found in a lot of its sparkling wines.

PATRICK SOUTIRAN NV BRUT ROSÉ, GRAND CRU

Despite this _cuvée_ having a distinctly oxidative style, the fruit is very smooth on the palate, and the mousse has a seductive, cushiony quality
On purchase ⒺⒺ 🍾88F

PATRICK SOUTIRAN 1992 PRECIEUSE D'ARGENT BRUT, GRAND CRU

Rich and biscuity, but rather rustic.
On purchase ⒺⒺⒺ 🍾109F

SOUTIRAN-PELLETIER
3 rue de Crilly, 51150 Ambonnay
📞 (326) 57.07.87 📠 (326) 57.81.74
Soutiran-Pelletier produces rich and smooth Champagnes that have both complexity and finesse.

A. SOUTIRAN-PELLETIER NV BRUT, GRAND CRU

Mature and biscuity.
On purchase ⒺⒺ 🍾81F

A. SOUTIRAN-PELLETIER NV BLANC DE BLANCS CHARDONNAY BRUT, GRAND CRU

Lovely rich creamy-biscuity fruit on the palate, complexity showing on finish.
Now–2000 ⒺⒺ 🍾87F

SPECHT

Alsace, France

SPECHT NV CRÉMANT D'ALSACE BRUT

This has a rich, succulent fruit, with a cushiony mousse.
🍷 On purchase ⓔ

SPYOPOULOS

Greece
This fully organic, family-owned winery has just released the best sparkling wine produced in Greece.

ODE PANOS NV BRUT

Pale, fresh and clean as a whistle; elegant, creamy fruit of pears and apple. The only Greek fizz worth drinking without first having to drown it in orange juice!
🍷 On purchase ⓔ

STEIN

Nahe, Germany

WEINGUT STEIN 1995 SCHWARZRIESLING WEISSHERBST SEKT BRUT

A smooth *rosé* of some finesse. *Cuve close.*
🍷 On purchase ⓔⓔ

STOEFFLER

Alsace, France

CHARLES STOEFFLER BLANC DE BLANCS 1994 CRÉMANT D'ALSACE BRUT

Rather sweet, but satisfying, fruity style.
🍷 On purchase ⓔ

STOFFEL

Alsace, France

STOFFEL NV CRÉMANT D'ALSACE BRUT

Fresh and fruity with a seductively soft, cushiony mousse, minuscule bubbles and refreshingly ripe acidity.
🍷 On purchase ⓔ

STRAUB

Alsace, France
Jos. Straub is best known for his very rich Vendange Tardives under the Domaine de La Tour label.

JOS. STRAUB, CUVÉE JEAN-SÉBASTIEN NV CRÉMANT D'ALSACE BRUT

Toasty aromas mixed with coffee grinds on the nose, with toasty fruit on the palate, but it needs a leaner structure (without losing ripeness) to score higher.
🍷 On purchase ⓔ

STUART

See Marie Stuart

SYLVAIN GAUDRON

See Domaine Sylvain Gaudron

SZIGETI

Austria
One of the best dryish Muscat fizzes produced anywhere.

SZIGETI GRÜNER VELTLINER BRUT

Fresh, simple, but elegant fruit.
🍷 On purchase ⓔ

SZIGETI MUSKAT OTTONEL EXTRA DRY

Delicate aromatic fruit on the nose, and with moreish floral-fruity Muscat fruit on the palate.
🍷 On purchase ⓔ

TAITTINGER

9 Place Saint-Nicaise, 51061 Reims
(326) 85.45.35

Champagne Taittinger is currently a *grande marque* in high gear.

TAITTINGER NV BRUT RÉSERVE. (88)

This light yet luscious *cuvée* has been on top form since early 1997, and the current shipment has lovely creamy fruit with an elegant balance. Drink the Brut Réserve now while it is young, fresh and delightfully elegant, or wait a year or two for it to become creamy, biscuity and wonderfully complex.

Now–2000 ££ 135F

TAITTINGER 1990 BRUT (89)

The 1990 Brut is gorgeously fat and creamy, with biscuity fruit.

Now–2002 £££

COMTES DE CHAMPAGNE, BLANC DE BLANCS 1990 BRUT, TAITTINGER (94)

Absolutely wonderful now, full of rich, ripe Chardonnay fruit, with a hint of toastiness in the background, but this has a way to go to fulfil its true potential.

Now–2010 ££££

COMTES DE CHAMPAGNE, ROSÉ 1991 BRUT, TAITTINGER (90)

I first tasted this *cuvée* in 1995, when its bright cherry fruit flavour was simple and undeveloped, as all Comtes de Champagne are when young, and it still has a way to go before it will lengthen and deepen into a feast of soft red fruits.

2000–2005 ££££

TALTARNI

Victoria, Australia

Dominique Portet reckons the breakthrough in the quality of his sparkling wines came when he began sourcing some of his grapes from Tasmania, which always accounts for at least 20 per cent of every blend and is exclusively used for Clover Hill.

TALTARNI CHARDONNAY PINOT NOIR NV BRUT (78)

A correct lean structure here, tending towards the austere, yet with some generosity of style.

Now–2000 £

TALTARNI BRUT TACHE NV CHARDONNAY PINOT NOIR BRUT (85)

This delightful *rosé* offers a delicious, soft mouthful of fruit, cushioned by a fluffy-fresh mousse, with a nice finesse derived from the balance between the extremes of richness and acidity.

Now–2000 £

CLOVER HILL 1994 TASMANIA BRUT (–)

This has more malty autolysis on the nose than the 1993, but with the same green Chablis-like fruit on palate that has typified other vintages of this Tasmanian *cuvée*. Opinion reserved for another year.

Wait and see ££

TARLANT

51480 Oeuilly
(326) 58.30.60 FAX (326) 58.37.31

A family of vignerons since 1687, the Tarlants' vineyards are spread across five Marne Valley villages, but centred on Oeuilly and Boursault, ten kilometres west of Épernay. Half the range is classically presented, while the other half is labelled with cheap transparent transfers. Only one wine was submitted this year, but it easily qualified, despite the coconutty aromas (which some people enjoy, and others dislike).

TARLANT NV CUVÉE LOUIS BRUT (86)

This was so chock-a-block full of coconutty-oak that when the covers came off I was not surprised to discover that it had indeed been fermented in new oak *barriques*, although I was amazed that the oak was Vosges. I cannot imagine anyone in Champagne seriously considering to use American oak, but that is what the coconutty character suggests.

Now–1999 ££ 136F

TATACHILLA
South Australia, Australia

An old-established winery, Tatachilla has been through many changes in ownership. Recently, Michael Fragos, the senior winemaker, and Daryl Groom, his consultant who has worked in California, have rapidly built up a brilliant reputation for big, rich red wines, and, judging by the wines below, they are clearly quite adept at putting bubbles into bottles as well.

TATACHILLA NV BRUT

Although soft and creamy, this *cuvée* does have the capacity to age. Very good value.
❚ Now–2000 ⓔ

TATACHILLA NV SPARKLING MALBEC

This highly perfumed *cuvée* has some finesse, and is drier than most Australian sparkling reds.
❚ Now–2000 ⓔ

TELMONT

1 avenue de Champagne, 51480 Damery
☎ (326) 58.40.33 Ⅸ (326) 58.63.93
Not a consistent range, but always something of interest, and invariably it turns out to be good value.

J. DE TELMONT NV GRANDE RÉSERVE BRUT

More tutti-frutti than amylic, with a rich fruitiness on the palate.
❚ On purchase ⓔⓔ ☕68F

J. DE TELMONT 1990 BLANC DE BLANCS BRUT ⊖

At the moment, this has a strangely per-fumed nose with a terpene-like four-square quality on the palate, as if the base wine had been kept as a reserve and bottled later than Spring 1991. I have no idea if that is what happened, but cannot recommend the wine at this stage. How-ever, there is an interesting peachiness that makes me want to follow its evolution, thus judgement is reserved.
▬▶ Wait and see ⓔⓔⓔ ☕80F

TEMPÉ
Alsace, France

ANDRÉ TEMPÉ NV CRÉMANT D'ALSACE BRUT

Fresh amylic style, but with more finesse than most, and good acidity.
❚ On purchase ⓔ

TENER
See Banfi

THAMES VALLEY VINEYARD
Twyford, England, UK

Owned by Jon Leighton, this is also the home to John Worontschak and The Harvest Group, one of the most progressive contract winemaking companies in the UK.

ASCOT NV BRUT

Some flowery finesse in this rises above the English wine aromas. There is creamy-vanilla fruit with some fatness yet also finesse on the finish, and a medium-firm mousse of tiny bubbles.
❚ On purchase ⓔ

CLOCKTOWER GAMAY NV

Fine, flowery autolytic aromas with excellent acidity. It certainly tastes younger than the 1992-based blend it is, but if anything this should mean that it will age very gracefully. At the moment, however, it shows elegant fruit neatly underpinned by excellent acidity, which itself is enhanced by a firm mousse of tiny bubbles.
❚ On purchase ⓔ

THANISCH
Mosel-Saar-Ruwer, Germany

Currently owned and run by Margaritt Müller-Burggraef, who is the fourth generation of female managers.

WWE. DR. H. THANISCH 1992 RIESLING SEKT BRUT

Apricoty fruit with some vanilla creaminess. Bottle-fermented.
🍷 On purchase ⓔⓔ

THIENOT

14 rue des Moissons, 51100 Reims
☎ (326) 77.50.10 🖷 (326) 77.50.19
A high-tech winery just outside Reims.

ALAIN THIENOT NV BRUT

Very fresh and fruity.
🍷 On purchase ⓔⓔ 🍾99F

THÜNGERSHEIM

Franken, Germany

WINZERGENOSSENSCHAFT THÜNGERSHEIM NV RÜCKER SCHALK, RÜCKER JESUITENBERG PINOT NOIR SEKT TROCKEN

Elegant Pinot fruit. Bottle-fermented.
🍷 On purchase ⓔⓔ

TORELLÓ

Penedès, Spain

ALIGUER 1994 CAVA BRUT

Flowery-amylic, but it has some finesse.
🍷 On purchase ⓔ

AUGUSTÍ TORELLÓ MATA 1994 CAVA BRUT RESERVA

Sweet and creamy, but lacks acidity.
🍷 On purchase ⓔ

KRIPTA BRUT NATURE 1992 GRAN RESERVA CAVA

This prestige *cuvée* comes in a replica Roman bottle, which has no flat bottom and therefore must be kept in an ice-bucket once opened. This vintage is better than the 1991, being cleaner and better focused, with sweet vanilla fruit on the palate, but it needs far more acidity
🍷 On purchase ⓔⓔ

TORNAY

2 rue Colbert, 51150 Bouzy
☎ (326) 57.08.58

BERNARD TORNAY NV BRUT CARTE D'OR

Interesting creamy-fruit on nose, with ripe, exotic, toasty fruit on the palate. Just finishes a bit rustic, and could do with a bit of finesse.
🍷 Now–1999 ⓔⓔ

TORRES

Chile
Hopefully the current shipment heralds a return to the promise shown by the first *cuvées* of Brut Nature,

MIGUEL TORRES NV BRUT NATURE

The best Miguel Torres Brut Nature for a very long time, this *cuvée* is light, elegant and delightful, with a long, deliciously fruity finish.
🍷 Now–1999 ⓔ

TOUR DU ROY

Bordeaux, France
One of the oldest producers of sparkling wine in Bordeaux.

TOUR DU ROY NV CUVÉE PRESTIGE, CRÉMANT DE BORDEAUX BRUT

Creamy rich aroma and sweet fruit, with good acidity.
🍷 On purchase ⓔ

TRIOLET

22 rue des Pressoirs, 51260 Bethon
☎ (326) 80.48.24 🖷 (326) 81.16.42
A top Sézannais producer, with complex wines that would be even better if the oxidative character could be toned down.

MARCEL TRIOLET NV SÉLECTION BRUT

The *cuvée* I tasted was pure 1990, with mature, oxidative-biscuity aromas and a sweetness of ripe fruit on the palate. Very rich, creamy fruit on the finish.
❚ On purchase ⓔⓔ

MARCEL TRIOLET NV BRUT 85

This *cuvée* has a minimum of four years' bottle-age and as much mature, oxidative-biscuitiness as the Brut Sélection, but without the same intensity of fruit.
❚ On purchase ⓔⓔ

TWEE JONGEGEZELLEN

Tulbagh, South Africa
The presentation might be rather garish, and the wines may be relatively cheap, but Krone Borealis has an established track record for *cuvées* that age extremely well, typically requiring four years to develop a fine, creamy-biscuit complexity.

KRONE BOREALIS BRUT 1994 CAP CLASSIQUE

A strange high-tone character places a question mark in my mind about this *cuvée,* but it might merely be going through a developmental phase, and if it is like other vintage, it should be drinking nicely by Christmas 1998.
▬► Wait and see ⓔ

KRONE BOREALIS BRUT 1993 CAP CLASSIQUE 87

Two years ago this was an easy-drinking wine, with deliciously gentle fruit that fell somewhere between the New and Old Worlds in character. Last year it had picked up some biscuit complexity, and now it has lovely toasty aromas. Nicely underpinned by fine acidity, the 1993 is still fresh and has a way to go yet.
❚ Now–2001 ⓔ

KRONE BOREALIS BRUT 1992 CAP CLASSIQUE 86

The 1992 had a malty-biscuit complexity two years ago, but the biscuitiness was barely perceptible.
▬► 1999–2000 ⓔ

KRONE BOREALIS BRUT 1990 CAP CLASSIQUE 87

Fresh and breezy fruit with a lovely, mature, creamy-biscuity complexity.
❚ Now–2000 ⓔ

UNION CHAMPAGNE

7 rue Pasteur, 51190 Avize
📞 (326) 57.94.22 📠 (326) 57.57.98

Super-cooperative of 1,200 growers, mostly on the Côte des Blancs. Much of its production is sold on to the *négoce* (Champagne houses). Of the remainder, Union Champagne sells about a million bottles under various labels, mainly De Saint Gall, and also Pierre Vaudon and Lechere.

PIERRE VAUDON NV BRUT, PREMIER CRU 82

A light, buttery-malo aroma, and sweet, easy-drinking, ripe fruit on the palate.
❚ Now–1999 ⓔⓔ

PIERRE VAUDON 1990 BRUT, PREMIER CRU 85

A lovely creamy-biscuit richness makes this splendid value for money.
❚ Now–2003 ⓔⓔⓔ

VALLFORMOSA

Penedès, Spain

VALLFORMOSA NV CAVA SEMI SECO 77

Not terribly sweet, but it has plenty of fruit, with a refreshing citrussy flavour.
❚ On purchase ⓔ

VARINELLES

See Domaine des Varinelles

VAUDON

See Union Champagne

(DE) VENOGE

30 avenue de Champagne, 51204 Epernay
☎ (326) 55.01.01 FAX (326) 54.73.60

Now part of the Remy-Cointreau group and playing a confusingly similar role to Champagne Ferdinand Bonnet. The kitsch Champagne des Princes bottle does not do justice to the quality of the wine inside.

DE VENOGE NV BRUT CORDON BLEU 85

A quaffing fruity style that quickly develops a creamy richness.
Now–1999 ££

DE VENOGE NV ROSÉ PRINCESSE 83

Not so appealing as when it was sold as Crémant Rosé, but a light, refreshing style nonetheless.
On purchase ££ ♈150F

DE VENOGE 1990 BRUT 90

Rich with creamy-biscuity fruit and lifted by toasty-floral aromas, this is probably the best straight vintage from this house.
Now–2005 £££ ♈156F

DE VENOGE CHAMPAGNE DES PRINCES 1990 BRUT ⊖

Not in the same class as the straight vintage, but the 1989 and 1985 went through strange stages, and this *cuvée* has produced some memorable vintages before.
Wait and see £££ ♈290F

VERNIER

See Masachs

VESSELLE

16 rue des Postes, 51150 Bouzy
☎ (326) 57.00.15 FAX (326) 57.09.20

Georges Vesselle is a grower with excellent vineyards and he has always been one of the most intelligent commentators on the industry as a whole.

GEORGES VESSELLE NV BRUT ROSÉ, GRAND CRU 84

Very pale-apricot colour, with lots of Pinot aroma and flavour, but could do with a touch more finesse.
On purchase ££ ♈103F

GEORGES VESSELLE NV BRUT GRAND CRU 82

Perfumed Pinot aromas, but the fruit on the palate will lengthen with bottle-age.
Now–1999 ££ ♈100F

GEORGES VESSELLE 1988 BRUT GRAND CRU 87

Lovely toasty aromas overlaying rich Pinot fruit. Brilliant at the table, particularly with simple meat dishes.
Now–1999 £££

VEUVE CLICQUOT

12 rue du Temple, 51100 Reims
☎ (326) 40.25.42 FAX (326) 40.60.17

Part of the LVMH group, Veuve Clicquot produces Champagne of extraordinary quality for such a large house. Big is truly beautiful here.

VEUVE CLICQUOT NV BRUT 88

Why Veuve Clicquot insists on calling this vivid orange-labelled *cuvée* Yellow Label is beyond me, but the quality is not beyond anyone. A very fruity, but serious, certainly not quaffing, style of Champagne that needs two or three years more bottle-age to bring out a wonderful Christmas-cake complexity.
Now–2002 ££ ♈150F

VEUVE CLICQUOT 1990 BRUT 93

The difference in freshness and development between this and the 1989 is striking, and it is not as if the grapes in 1989 were riper, as is often suggested. This was much the riper year, with higher alcohol levels even than 1976. There is a long way to go before it switches from fruit-driven mode to a more mellow and complex style. Chardonnay currently dominates, although it represents just a third of the blend, as it does in most Veuve Clicquot vintages.
Now–2020 £££

VEUVE CLICQUOT 1989 BRUT 90

Full and rich, with creamy-biscuity complexity, and chewy-vanilla fruit that dries off towards the end, then comes back sweet and ripe on the aftertaste.
❚ Now–2009 ⓔⓔⓔ

VEUVE CLICQUOT 1989 ROSÉ 86

Big, rich, rooty Pinot Noir fruit.
❚ Now–2001 ⓔⓔⓔ

VEUVE CLICQUOT 1989 RICH RÉSERVE 90

A *demi-sec* of impeccable quality, softer and more luscious than the superb 1988, but with just as much depth and finesse.
❚ Now–2009 ⓔⓔⓔ

VEUVE CLICQUOT 1990 GRANDE DAME BRUT 95

Beautifully ripe fruit of great finesse. Very young now, it will quickly go toasty, but with lots of life and freshness ahead. Possibly on par with the magnificent 1975.
❚ Now–2020 ⓔⓔⓔⓔ

VEUVE CLICQUOT 1989 GRANDE DAME BRUT 94

Fat and sassy fruit with a lovely mellow biscuity richness on the finish.
❚ Now–2010 ⓔⓔⓔⓔ 🍇450F

VEUVE CLICQUOT 1988 GRANDE DAME BRUT ROSÉ 95

A stunning first vintage, this ranks with Laurent-Perrier's 1982 and 1985 Alexandra Rosé as one of the greatest pink Champagnes of all time. Extraordinarily luscious for the vintage, but quite how there can be so much fruit without being at all fat is a mystery. With so much finesse, ageing this will be fascinating.
❚ Now–2010 ⓔⓔⓔⓔ

VEUVE –

For all other brands beginning with Veuve, see under main name

---

VIGNERONS DE –

See under main name

VILLA –

See under main name

VILLIERA

Paarl, South Africa
Owned by the Grier family, who used to employ Champenois Jean-Louis Denois as consultant.

VILLIERA TRADITION BRUT ROSÉ NV CAP CLASSIQUE 71

Soft, perfumed aromas, full, fattish fruit, lifted by a soft mousse of small bubbles.
❚ On purchase ⓔ

VILLIERA TRADITION CARTE ROUGE BRUT NV CAP CLASSIQUE 82

Classic *méthode champenoise* creamy-rich fruit, mellowed by nicely understated malolactic. This *cuvée* includes Pinotage and Chenin Blanc.
❚ Now–2000 ⓔ

VILLIERA TRADITION PREMIERE CUVÉE 1990 CAP CLASSIQUE 80

There is no autolytic finesse to be found, but this *cuvée* is recompensed by its lovely peachy fruit.
❚ On purchase ⓔ

VILMART

4 rue de la République
51500 Rilly-la-Montagne
📞 (326) 03.40.01 📠 (326) 03.46.57
The greatest grower Champagne continues to excel.

VILMART NV GRANDE RÉSERVE BRUT 85

A good value, fresh and fruity style.
❚ On purchase ⓔⓔ

VILMART NV BLANC DE BLANCS BRUT 86

The yummiest, glugiest, creamiest fruit-driven *cuvée* in the range.
❚ On purchase ⓔⓔ

VILMART NV GRANDE CELLIER BRUT

Classic structure with fine fruit and a slow-building biscuitiness, this is where the complexity and true ageing potential in the Vilmart range begins.

 Now–2003 ££ 90F

VILMART 1991 GRANDE CELLIER D'OR BRUT (90)

Although not quite the same quality as Vilmart's Coeur de Cuvée, Grand Cellier d'Or is more classic and, relative to most vintage Champagnes, offers extraordinary value for money.

Now–2005 £££

VILMART 1990 GRANDE CELLIER D'OR BRUT (92)

An exquisite depth of fruit with brilliant acidity and deep, mellow biscuity-complex aromas continuing to build. Buy it in magnums, drink one at the Millennium, and keep the rest for five years or more.

Now–2010 £££ 100F

VILMART 1991 COEUR DE CUVÉE (91)

Coeur de Cuvée means "heart of the *cuvée*", and that is literally what this is: from every 2,000 litres of *vin de cuvée* Vilmart plucks out the best 800 litres and vinifies it in small *barriques* of new oak. They got a bit carried away with this vintage, which was far too oaky when first released. It would have benefited from 10 years' yeast contact to absorb as much of the oakiness as possible. This is nevertheless the best 1991 I have tasted, and more post-disgorgement ageing should bury the more obvious oaky traits.

 2000–2010 ££££ 186F

VILMART 1990 COEUR DE CUVÉE (99)

One of the three greatest Champagnes made in the last 25 years, this *cuvée* has a fabulous, rich, creamy-brioche nose. Its fruit is incredibly luscious because the huge ripe acidity has been skilfully balanced by a generous dosage.

Now–2015 ££££

VILMART 1989 COEUR DE CUVÉE (89)

This has lost the heavy oxidative character that spoilt the wine when first released, and its true finesse is now in full bloom.

Now–2006 ££££

VILMART 1990 CUVÉE DU NOUVEAU MONDE IIIE MILLÉNIUM BRUT

The new oak in this special *cuvée* is so dominant that it tastes like an Australian Chardonnay with bubbles, and having now tasted it five times I am convinced that the oakiness is increasing. It is so far off the wall for Champagne, and the base wine so unlike anything else in the Vilmart range, that I must reserve judgement for a few years.

 Wait and see ££££ 175F

VITTEAUT-ALBERTI
Burgundy, France

L. VITTEAUT-ALBERTI, BLANC DE BLANCS NV BRUT, CRÉMANT DE BOURGOGNE (86)

You can taste the selection in this lovely fruit-driven wine, which is not too *brut* and has a silky-soft mousse.

On purchase £

VIUDAS
See Segura Viudas

VRANKEN
42 avenue de Champagne, 51200 Epernay
(326) 53.33.20 FAX (326) 51.87.07
This group includes Charles Lafitte, René Lallement, Demoiselle, Sacotte, Charbaut, Barancourt, and the recently acquired Heidsieck & Co Monopole.

DEMOISELLE NV BRUT (82)

This used to be amylic, but the current *cuvée* is lovely and fresh, with fruit and charm, and not a hint of peardrops. Much preferred to the Demoiselle 1990.

On purchase ££

CHARLES LAFITTE 1990 BRUT (86)

A surprisingly rich, biscuity Champagne of some quality for this secondary brand.

On purchase £££

WACHTENBURG
Pfalz, Germany

WACHTENBURG 1995 WACHEN HEIMER BISCHOFSGARTEN PINOT NOIR BLANC DE NOIRS

Very moreish strawberry fruit that suggests an exaggeration of Pinot Noir.
❙ On purchase ⓔⓔ

WEINGARTNER –, WEINGUT –, WEINHOF –
For brands prefixed with any of these words (Ger. cooperative/wine estate), see under main name

WESTHALTEN
Alsace, France

CUVÉE MARÉCHAL LEFEBVRE, WESTHALTEN NV CRÉMANT D'ALSACE BRUT

Light and fruity now, but will go toasty.
❙ Now–1999 ⓔ

HEIM IMPÉRIAL D'ALSACE NV CRÉMANT D'ALSACE BRUT

Once a producer in its own right, Heim is now just a label belonging Westhalten. This fizzy Chablis-style *crémant* could develop, but I am not certain.
◄■ Wait and see ⓔ

WICKHAM
Shedfield, England, UK
Surprisingly good, classic *brut*-style wine from the Kerner grape.

WICKHAM PREMIÈRE CUVÉE 1993 BRUT

The classic flowery finesse of autolysis on the nose, plus some class and a serious hint of vanilla-complexity of fruit to finish.
❙ Now–1999 ⓔⓔ

WILHELMSHOF
Pfalz, Germany

WILHELMSHOF 1995 SPÄTBURGUNDER BLANC DE NOIRS SEKT BRUT

An impeccable balance of succulent fruit and sherbetty ripe acidity. Bottle-fermented.
❙ On purchase ⓔⓔ

WINZERVEREIN –
For brands prefixed by this (Ger. cooperative), see under main name

WINZERSEKT
Rheinhessen, Germany
This cooperative is dedicated to the production of Sekt.

WINZERSEKT 1994 PINOT NOIR ROSÉ SEKT EXTRA SEKT TROCKEN

Finely structured fruit with nice acidity and a soft, cushiony mousse. A food wine. Bottle-fermented.
❙ On purchase ⓔⓔ

WOLFBERGER
Alsace, France
Brand name of the Eguisheim cooperative, the largest producer in Alsace.

WOLFBERGER RIESLING NV CRÉMANT D'ALSACE BRUT

Petrolly Riesling aroma follows onto the palate, with nice honeyed-petrol richness, but finishes a bit too soft.
❙ On purchase ⓔ

WOLFBERGER ROSÉ NV CRÉMANT D'ALSACE BRUT

Nice cherry-Pinot aromas, with soft fruit lifted by the effervescence on the palate, but needs more acidity for a higher score.
❙ On purchase ⓔ

WOLFBERGER, BLANC DE NOIRS NV CRÉMANT D'ALSACE BRUT

This scrapes in because even though the sample I received was corked, the sweet, ripe fruit was evident.
❚ On purchase ⓔ

WOLFBERGER, CHARDONNAY NV CRÉMANT D'ALSACE, EXTRA BRUT

Not much Chardonnay character, unless you stretch the apricot fruit to the peachy richness of New World Chardonnay, and bring it back to Alsace. It could also do with some finesse, but it is better than many other Crémant d'Alsace.
❚ On purchase ⓔ

WOLFBERGER, PRESTIGE NV CRÉMANT D'ALSACE

This *cuvée* still has the best balance of all Wolfberger sparkling wines, the fruitiness and lovely ripe acidity benefiting from a certain amount of Riesling in the blend.
❚ Now–1999 ⓔ

WOLFBERGER, TOKAY PINOT GRIS NV CRÉMANT D'ALSACE BRUT

Despite a need to tweak the structure to a leaner bent, this pure varietal fizz is quite interesting, and promises to develop well.
❚ Now–1999 ⓔ

WOOLDINGS

Whitchurch, England, UK
Owner-winemaker Charles Cunningham is so serious about perfecting sparkling wine that he organizes field trips to Champagne for himself and other English fizz producers.

WOOLDINGS 1994 BRUT

Creamy-rich and tangy, like the 1992. Still needs a touch more finesse, but a resounding success compared to the 1993.
❚ Now–1999 ⓔⓔ

WYNDHAM ESTATE

New South Wales, Australia

WYNDHAM CUVÉE 1995 BRUT

Trying to be broad and complex, and halfway getting there, but needs more acidity for a higher score.
❚ On purchase ⓔ

XENIUS
See COVIDES

YALDARA
South Australia, Australia
These bubblies are firmly aimed at the budget end of the market.

YALDARA NV BRUT

The fruit is too exotic for a *brut*-style fizz, but if the wine is thoroughly chilled, it reduces the exotic effect.
❚ On purchase ⓔ

YALDARA NV BRUT

Fresh, soft, raspberry fizz.
❚ On purchase ⓔ

YALUMBA
South Australia, Australia
Best known for its simple fruity fizz under the Angas Brut and Angas Rosé labels, Yalumba also produces bottle-fermented sparkling wines under its eponymous brand, and owns Nautilus in New Zealand.

ANGAS NV BRUT

The new shipment appears to be a sea-change in style, even hinting of Chardonnay on the nose though this is just one of 14 grapes used. Very fresh and fattish, with an exotic tropical fruit finish.
❚ On purchase ⓔ

YALUMBA CUVÉE ONE PINOT NOIR CHARDONNAY NV BRUT

There are lovely biscuity aromas on the nose, but this *cuvée* needs time to build a balancing, mellow richness on the palate.
◤ 1999-2000 ⓔ

YALUMBA D 1994 BRUT

I liked the tight, austere flavours and lean fruit structure, all of which promised to open up very slowly into something special, but there was too much sulphur for it to receive a definite score.

Wait and see ££

YALUMBA CUVÉE TWO PRESTIGE NV CABERNET SAUVIGNON

Deep, dark and, according to its back label, "mischievous", this fizzy red wine has a minty Cabernet flavour, with big, oaky overtones.

Now–1999 £

YARRABANK

Victoria, Australia

A recent joint venture between Champagne Veuve Devaux and Yering Station with input from Devaux's winemaker, Claude Thibaut.

YARRABANK 1993 CUVÉE NO 1 BRUT

There is plenty of acidity to keep the tangy-rich fruit in this wine extremely fresh and lively.

Now–2000 ££

YARRA BURN

See Hardy's

YELLOWGLEN

Victoria, Australia

This operation, owned by Mildara-Blass, is where Claude Thibaut gained experience before working at Iron Horse in California.

YELLOWGLEN NV BRUT PINOT NOIR CHARDONNAY

Lovely ripe fruit framed in a nicely lean structure and underpinned by fine acidity with a touch of fatness for good mouthfill.

On purchase £

YELLOWGLEN 1995 BRUT

An early drinking vintage *cuvée* with fine, elegant fruit supported by a nicely structured mousse of tiny bubbles.

On purchase £

ZÄHRINGER

Baden, Germany

A member of Ecovin, a body that adheres to biodynamic wine production.

ZÄHRINGER 1992 VIERLIG PINOT BLANC SEKT BRUT

This wine comes in a tall Rhine bottle with a very classy, understated label. Some botrytis (noble rot) and quite sweet fruit for a *brut*. Very soft mousse.

ZÄHRINGER 1990 ECOVIN SPÄTBURGUNDER ROT SEKT BRUT

This deep, dark red fizz is Germany's answer to Sparkling Shiraz!

ZAMUNER

Veneto, Italy

ZAMUNER 1992 ROSÉ BRUT, SPUMANTE TRADIZIONALE

Fresh, peppery fruit going to cappuccino, with a zesty, uplifting finish.

Now–1999 ££

ZAMUNER 1991 EXTRA BRUT, SPUMANTE CLASSICO

First time I have ever found peanuts on any sparkling wine, but it has good acidity.

On purchase ££

ZARDETTO

Italy

ZARDETTO NV PROSECCO DI CONEGLIANO BRUT

Scrapes in as a fresh, light and fruity fizz for those who don't like their *brut* too dry.

On purchase £

GLOSSARY

A glossary of common technical and
tasting terms used to describe
Champagnes and sparkling wines.

Abbreviations: (Fr.) French (Ger.) German (It.) Italian (Sp.) Spanish.

Accessible Easy to drink.

Acidic Some people confuse this term with bitter. Think of lemon juice as acidic, lemon peel as bitter. The right acidity is vital for sparkling wine.

Aftertaste The flavour and aroma left in the mouth after the wine has been swallowed.

Ages gracefully A wine that retains finesse as it matures.

Aggressive The opposite of soft and smooth.

Amylic The peardrop, banana or bubble-gum aromas of amyl or isoamyl acetate, lots of which can be produced if the first fermentation is conducted at a low temperature. An amylic preponderance is not ideal for classic sparkling wine as it overshadows the subtle aromas of autolysis, and may prevent the development of post-disgorgement bottle-aromas. *See Autolysis, Bottle-aromas.*

AOC (Fr.) Appellation d'Origine Contrôlée, the top rung of the French wine quality system. Champagne is unique in that it does not have to indicate that it is an AOC wine on the label, because the name Champagne is considered sufficient guarantee.

Appellation Literally a "name", this usually refers to an official geographical-based designation for a wine.

Aroma Some people use the word aroma for grape-derived fragrance, and bouquet for more winey odours, especially when developed in bottle, however the two are synonymous in this book.

Aromatic grape varieties Grapes such as the Gewürztraminer, Muscat and Riesling overwhelm the subtle effects of autolysis, and are thus too aromatic for classic *brut* sparkling wines, yet this character often makes them ideal for sweet styles of sparkling wine.

Assemblage (Fr.) The blending of base wines that creates the final *cuvée.*

Asti (It.) A town in Northern Italy that gives its name to a fine sweet sparkling wine.

Atmosphere A measurement of atmospheric pressure. One atmosphere is 15 lbs per square inch (psi). A sparkling wine can be anything up to six atmospheres, or 90 lbs psi. This decreases when the bottle is chilled for serving. A fully sparkling wine of six atmospheres will be just 2.5 atmospheres at 6° C.

Austere A wine that lacks fruit.

Autolysis The breakdown of yeast cells after the second fermentation that creates the inimitable "champagny" character.

Autolytic The smell of a freshly disgorged *brut*-style fizz. This is not "yeasty" but has an acacia-like flowery finesse.

Balance A harmonious relationship between acids, alcohol, fruit, tannin (only in some red sparkling wines) and other natural elements.

Balthazar Large bottle equivalent to 16 normal-sized 75 cl bottles.

Barrel-fermented Some houses, e.g. Krug, ferment in old, well-used oak barrels. A few others, e.g. Selosse and Vilmart, use new oak, a fashion picked up by a number of New World producers, e.g. Pelorus and Kristone.

Barrique (Fr.) Literally means "barrel", but generically used in English-speaking countries for any small oak cask. Often denotes the use of new oak.

Base wines Fully fermented dry wines that when blended together form the basis of a sparkling wine *cuvée.*

Biscuity A desirable aspect of bouquet found particularly in a well-matured Pinot Noir-dominated Champagne. Some top-quality Chardonnay-dominated wines can also acquire a creamy-biscuitness.

Bitterness Either an unpleasant aspect of a poorly made wine or an expected characteristic of undeveloped, concentrated flavours that should, with maturity, become rich and delicious. *See also Acidic.*

Blanc de Blancs (Fr.) A white wine made from white grapes.

Blanc de Noirs (Fr.) A white wine made from black grapes.

Blind, blind tasting An objective tasting where the identity of wines is unknown until the taster has made notes and given scores. All competitive tastings are blind.

Blowzy Overblown and exaggerated.

Blush wine Synonym of *rosé.*

BOB Buyer's Own Brand, under which many retailers and restaurants sell wine.

Body The extract of fruit and alcoholic strength together give an impression of weight in the mouth.

Bottle-age The length of time a wine spends in bottle before it is consumed. A wine that has good bottle-age is one that has sufficient time to mature properly. Bottle-ageing has a mellowing effect.

Bottle-aromas Mellowing aromas created after disgorgement.

Bottle-fermented I use this without discrimination for any sparkling wine that has undergone a second fermentation in bottle, but when seen on a label, it invariably means the wine has been made by the transfer method.

Bouquet *See Aroma.*

Breed The finesse of a wine based on the intrinsic qualities of grape and *terroir* (growing environment) combined with the irrefutable skill and experience of a great winemaker.

Brut (Fr.) Dry. Literally means "raw" or "bone dry", but in practice there is always some sweetness in a sparkling wine.

Buttery Normally caused by diacetyl, which the food industry uses to make margarine taste more like butter. It is fine in still Chardonnays, but the taste detracts from the finesse of sparkling wines.

Caramel An extreme version of buttery.

Cava (Sp.) The generic appellation for *méthode champenoise* wines produced in various delimited areas of Spain, mostly in the Penedès region near Barcelona.

Cave, caves (Fr.) Literally cellar, cellars.

Champagne (Fr.) Specifically a sparkling wine produced in the delimited area of Champagne in Northern France.

"Champagne", "Champaña" The appellation for sparkling wine made in Champagne is protected within the EU, but is sometimes used loosely elsewhere, especially in the

USA, where it is legal to sell domestically produced "champagne". It is also exploited by the Champenois themselves, who call their South American products Champaña.

Champenois (Fr.) The people of Champagne.

Chardonnay One of the greatest sparkling wine grapes for the classic *brut* style.

Charmat (Fr.) *See Cuve close.*

Chef de caves (Fr.) Literally the "cellar manager", but can also mean the winemaker.

Courtier en vins (Fr.) A wine broker who acts as a go-between for growers and producers.

Crayères (Fr.) Chalk-pits in Northern France dug out in Gallo-Roman times.

Creamy Creaminess is most apparent in Chardonnay-based sparkling wines. The sensation, picked up at the back of the throat, is believed to be a combination of the finesse of the mousse (created by the most minuscule of bubbles and their slow release) and a subtle malolactic influence.

Creamy-biscuity *See Biscuity.*

Creamy-caramel malo A lesser, more acceptable version of caramel.

Crémant (Fr.) A sparkling wine with a gentler mousse than normal.

Cru (Fr.) Literally a "growth", *cru* normally refers to a vineyard site, although in Champagne it is a term used for an entire village.

Cushiony A beautifully soft, ultra-fine sensation caused by the minuscule bubbles of a first-rate mousse.

Cuve close (Fr.) A method invented by Eugène Charmat of producing sparkling wine through a second fermentation in a sealed vat or tank. Synonymous with Charmat method or tank method.

Cuvée (Fr.) Originally the wine of one *cuve* or vat, this now refers to a precise blend or specific product, which may be blended from several vats.

Débourbage (Fr.) The settling process that removes bits of skin, pips and so on from the freshly pressed grape juice.

Dégorgement (Fr.) *See Disgorgement.*

Demi-sec (Fr.) Literally "semi-dry", but actually meaning semi-sweet to sweet.

Disgorgement The removal of sediment after the second fermentation.

DOC/DOCG (It.) Denominazione di Origine Controllata/e Garantita. Italian wine quality system based on grape variety and origin. "Garantita" denotes an extra rung of quality.

Dosage (Fr.) The amount of sugar solution added to a sparkling wine after disgorgement.

Doux (Fr.) Literally "sweet", actually very sweet.

Dry straw *See Straw.*

Easy-drinking Probably not a complex wine, but it slips down easily.

English aroma A very fresh herbaceous character.

Explosive A sparkling wine can be literally explosive in the bottle, which is due to defects on the inner surface, or "explosive" in the mouth, which is due to the wine. The latter is often because too much carbonic gas is free (not bound to the wine), although why this sometimes occurs is not fully understood.

Extra-brut Drier than *brut*, possibly no dosage.

Extra-sec (Fr.) Literally "extra-dry", but usually merely dry to medium dry.

Fat Full in body and extract.

Fixed sulphur Sulphur is added to wine primarily as a preservative, to prevent oxidation. Most of the sulphur molecules fix onto other molecules in the wine, especially the oxygen molecules. Sometimes they combine disastrously with other molecules, creating bad smells. However, the toasty bottle-aroma adored by most Champagne aficionados is also possibly a by-product of fixed sulphur. *See also Free sulphur.*

Flowery Floral aromas are found in young sparkling wines and are the precursors to the fuller, deeper, fruitier aromas of maturity. Specific acacia aromas are found in recently disgorged wines of any age.

Foudre (Fr.) A large wooden cask or vat.

Foxy The highly perfumed character of certain indigenous American grapes. It can be sickly sweet and cloying to other nations' palates.

Free sulphur The acrid odour of free sulphur – smelling like a recently extinguished match – will go away with time in bottle, or a swirl of the glass. *See also Fixed sulphur, Sulphur.*

Frizzante (It.) Semi-sparkling or slightly fizzy: the equivalent of *pétillant.*

Frizzantino (It.) Very lightly sparkling: the same as *perlant.*

Fruity Although wine is made from grapes, it will not have a fruity flavour unless the grapes have the correct combination of ripeness and acidity. Simple fruity fizz is fine if it is cheap, but fruit alone is insufficient for a classic sparkling wine.

Full Usually refers to body, e.g. full-bodied. But a wine can be light in body yet full in flavour.

Fully fermented A wine that is allowed to complete its natural course of fermentation and so yield a totally dry wine.

Fully sparkling A wine with a pressure of 5–6 atmospheres.

Grande marque (Fr.) Literally a great or famous brand.

Herbaceous A green-leaf or white-currant characteristic that is usually associated with under-ripeness, particularly with aromatic grape varieties.

Jeroboam Large bottle equivalent to four normal-sized 75 cl bottles.

Lees The sediment that accumulates in a vat or bottle during fermentation.

Light A qualification of body.

Liqueur d'expédition (Fr.) Solution of sugar and wine added to a sparkling wine after disgorgement.

Liqueur de tirage (Fr.) The bottling liqueur – made of wine, yeast and sugar – which induces the mousse.

Magnum Large bottle equivalent to two normal-sized 75 cl bottles, the ideal volume for ageing Champagne.

Malolactic/Malo A biochemical process that turns the hard malic acid of unripe grapes into soft lactic acid and carbonic gas.

Méthode champenoise (Fr.) The process developed by the Champenois that converts a fully fermented still wine into a sparkling wine through the induction of a second fermentation in the same bottle in which it is sold (*see pp10–11*).

Methuselah Large bottle equivalent to eight normal-sized 75 cl bottles.

Mono-cru Champagne made from a single *cru*.

Mousse The thousands of fine bubbles in a sparkling wine.

Mousseux (Fr.) Sparkling, foaming etc.

Nebuchadnezzar Large bottle equivalent to 20 normal-sized 75 cl bottles.

Négociant (Fr.) Commonly used to describe large wine-producing companies.

Non-dosage (Fr.) A sparkling wine that has received no dosage of *liqueur de tirage*.

Non-vintage (NV) In theory a blend of at least two different years, but many producers, particularly in Champagne, grade their *cuvées* on selection, often selling a pure vintage *sans année* (without year).

Oaky The aromatic quality picked up from new oak, usually consisting of the creamy-vanilla aroma of vanillin, a natural oak aldehyde and also the principal aromatic component in vanilla pods.

Organic A generic term for wines that are produced with the minimum amount of sulphur, from grapes grown without chemical fertilizers, pesticides or herbicides.

Oxidation, oxidized From the moment grapes are pressed or crushed, oxidation sets in. It is an unavoidable part of fermentation and essential to the maturation process: "oxidative" denotes a certain maturity. To say a wine is "oxidized", however, means that it has been subjected to too much oxidation and has an unwanted sherry-like character.

Oxidative A wine that openly demonstrates the character of maturation on the nose or palate. The longer it takes to appear in a wine, the more finesse the wine will have.

Peppery A somewhat incongruous taste associated with sparkling wine. If detected as just a flicker in a young blend, it can add to the wine's future complexity, but be wary of a dominant pepperiness.

Perlant (Fr.) Lightly sparkling.

Perlwein (Ger.) Cheap, semi-sparkling wine made by carbonating a still wine.

Pétillance, pétillant (Fr.) A wine with enough carbonic gas to create a light sparkle.

Pinot Noir (Fr.) Black grape variety used in Champagne.

Récoltant-manipulant (Fr.) A grower who produces Champagne exclusively from his or her own vineyards.

Rehoboam Large bottle equivalent to six normal-sized 75 cl bottles.

Remuage (Fr.) The process whereby the sediment is encouraged down to the neck of the bottle in preparation for disgorgement.

Reserve wines Older wines added to a non-vintage blend to create a sense of maturity.

Rich, richness A balanced wealth of fruit and depth on the palate and finish.

Rooty Usually refers to a certain rooty richness found in Pinot Noir. Not vegetal, which is a negative term.

Rosado (Sp.) Pink.

Rosé (Fr.) Pink.

Saignée (Fr.) The process of drawing off surplus liquid from the press or vat in order to produce a *rosé* wine from the free-run juice. In cooler wine regions, the remaining mass of grape pulp may be used to make a darker red wine than would normally be possible because of a greater ratio of solids to liquid.

Salmanazar Large bottle equivalent to 12 normal-sized 75 cl bottles.

Sassy Used to describe fruit in a wine that is lively, jaunty, breezy etc.

Sboccatura (It.) Disgorged.

Sec (Fr.) Literally dry, but effectively medium to medium-sweet.

Sekt (Ger.) Sparkling wine produced in Germany, usually by the *cuve close* method.

Soft An atractive smoothness caused when fruit has the upperhand over acidity. This is very desirable, but a wine that is too soft will lack acidity.

Solera (Sp.) System of continually replenishing an established blend with a small amount of new wine.

Sprightly fruitiness A positive outcome of ultra-fruitiness accentuated by volatile acidity. The term is used in this book instead of "VA fruitiness".

Spumante (It.) Literally just "sparkling", but normally refers to a fully sparkling wine. *See Fully sparkling.*

Straw Straw-like aromas often blight sparkling wines. Sometimes the aroma is reminiscent of dry straw, other times wet straw, sometimes it is simply straw-like. The aroma possibly comes from the yeast, or rotten grapes, or the reaction of yeast on rotten grapes.

Structure The structure of a wine is based on the balance of its solids (tannin, acidity, sugar, and extract or density of fruit flavour) with the alcohol, and how positively the form feels in the mouth.

Sulphur, SO₂ A preservative used primarily to prevent oxidation. *See also Free sulphur, Fixed sulphur.*

Tank method Another term for *cuve close*.

Terpene A terpene character may indicate Riesling in the blend, but is more likely to be due to the base wine being kept unduly long in tank.

Toasty The slow-developing bottle-induced aroma associated with Chardonnay.

Transfer method Decanting under pressure from one size bottle to another, not the ideal of *méthode champenoise*.

VA Volatile acidity.

VA fruitiness Ultra-fruitiness accentuated by volatile acidity. This can be a positive factor, but volatile acidity has such negative connotations that I have used "sprightly fruitiness" instead.

Vanilla *See Oaky.*

Vin de cuvée (Fr.) Made only from the first and therefore the best pressing.

Vin de garde (Fr.) Wine that is capable of great improvement if left to age.

Vin de taille Made from the second pressing.

Vintage The harvest or wine of a single year.

Volatile acidity This has a sweet vinegary aroma and if too obvious may be deemed a fault. But a certain amount of volatile acidity is essential for fruitiness, and high levels can sometimes be a positive factor. *See Sprightly fruitiness, VA fruitiness.*

Wet straw *See Straw.*

UK STOCKISTS

A listing of major stockists of
Champagnes and sparkling wines in the
UK, including a key to where to find
over 500 major brands.

Where to Find Major Brands in the UK

Brands are in bold type, with the names simplified for easy indexing. Only regularly stocked products are included, and not all are recommended in the A–Z listing this year. Note that stockists do not necessarily carry the full range of a brand, and are bound to de-list brands from time to time. For full details of stockists, see pp183–191.

Abell & Cie Edward Sheldon; **Agusti Torello Mata** The Wine Society; **Aigle** Nicolas, Christopher Piper; **Ailerons et Baie** Pavilion; **Alasia** Valvona & Crolla; **Albecourt** Lay & Wheeler; **Albert Étienne** Safeway; **Alderic** John Arkell; **Aldridge Estate** George Hill, Christopher Piper, The Wright Wine Co; **Aliança** Booths; **Aliguer** Selfridges; **Aneri** Valvona & Crolla; **Antech** The Wine Society; **Antoine** Champagne Exchange, Quellyn Roberts; **Aquese** Christopher Piper; **Araldica** Somerfield, Valvona & Crolla, Villeneuve; **Argyle** Booths, Rodney Densem, Harrods, Harvey Nichols, Terry Platt; **Arione** Averys, Oddbins; **Arnaud** Stones of Belgravia; **Arnould (Michel)** T&W, Tanners; **Arnould (Patrick)** Tesco; **Aubac** Brian Coad; **Auran** Morris & Verdin; **Aurigny** Morrisons; **Ayala** Majestic, Nicolas, Quellyn Roberts

Backsberg Terry Platt; **Bailli** The Vintry; **Bailly (Caves de)** La Reserve; **Bailly (Charles)** Hedley Wright, Quellyn Roberts, Smedley; **Bailly (Coopérative de)** Somerfield, Stevens Garnier; **Balachat** Charles Hennings; **Baldovino** Terry Platt, Waters; **Barnaut** Satchells; **Baron** Charles Hennings, Unwins, Waters; **Baron de Beaumont** Waitrose; **Baron de Beaupré** S.H. Jones; **Baron de Marck** Lay & Wheeler; **Barramundi** Asda, Booths, Co-op, Cooperative, Morrisons; **Bass Tuba-Bava** The Nobody Inn; **Bauchet Père & Fils** Châteaux Wines; **Bauchet** Majestic; **Baudry** Villeneuve; **Bauget-Jouette** High Breck; **Baumard** Eldridge Pope, Mark Reynier; **Beaumet** Le Pont de la Tour; **Beaumont des Crayères** John Armit, Oddbins, Mark Reynier; **Beck** Fortnum & Mason, John Harvey; **Beerens** Bibendum; **Bellavista** Valvona & Crolla; **Belle Fleur** Waters; **Berger** B.H. Wines, Justerini & Brooks, Yapp Brothers; **Berlucchi** Mitchells, Roberson, Valvona & Crolla; **Bernard-Massard** B.H. Wines, Eldridge Pope; **Besserat de Bellefon** Nicolas, Pallant; **Billecart-Salmon** Widely available; **Billiot** Adnams,

Bibendum, Raeburn; **Binet** Berry Bros & Rudd; **Blin** Charles Hennings, Oddbins, Villeneuve; **Blue Lake Ridge** Asda; **Bluff Hill** Marks & Spencer; **Bochingen** Amathus; **Boeckel** Allez Vins!; **Bohemia Regal** Waitrose; **Bollinger** Widely available; **Bonaval** Adnams, Shaws of Beaumaris; **Bonnamy** Nicolas; **Bonnet (A)** Richard Harvey, Le Pont de la Tour; **Bonnet (F)** Kwik Save, Oddbins; **Bonval** Ramsbottom; **Borelli** Mitchells, Stevens Garnier; **Bortoli** Richard Harvey, The Wright Wine Co; **Bortolotti** Harrods; **Boschendal** Terry Platt; **Bosio** Majestic; **Botter** Forth; **Boucheron** The Wine Treasury; **Bourgeois Père et Fils** Safeway; **Bourillon d'Orléans** Morris & Verdin; **Boursault** Fuller's; **Bouvet-Ladubay** Widely available; **Breban** The Wine Schoppen; **Bracieux** Co-op; **Brédif** S.H. Jones; **Bredon** Waitrose; **Breuer** Direct Wine; **Breze** B.H. Wines; **Brigand** Raeburn; **Brochet-Hervieux** Holland Park; **Brossault** Booths, Budgens, Fuller's; **Brouette** Nicolas; **Brown Brothers** Co-op, Rodney Densem, Direct Wine, Hall Batson, Penistone Court, Christopher Piper, Terry Platt, John Stephenson, Stevens Garnier, The Wright Wine Co; **Brummel** The Wright Wine Co; **Brun (Albert Le)** Satchells; **Brun (Daniel Le)** B.H. Wines, Fortnum & Mason, Hedley Wright, The Nobody Inn, Roberson, Shaws of Beaumaris, Smedley; **Brun de Neuville** Waterloo; **Bry** Edward Sheldon

Cadre Noir Waters; **Cairolle** Oddbins; **Calissano** S.H. Jones, Portland; **Callot** Growers & Châteaux; **Camuset** Bibendum, Sainsbury's; **Can Vendrell** Pallant; **Canard-Duchêne** Widely available; **Carneros** Terry Platt; **Carpene Malvolti** Roberson, Valvona & Crolla; **Carrington** See Orlando; **Carr Taylor** Budgens, Ramsbottom; **Casa del Valle** Oddbins; **Casarito** Corkscrew; **Cascina Castelet** Sandiway; **Castell d'Olerdola** S.H. Jones, Lay & Wheeler, Portland; **Castell de Vilarnau** Brian Coad, Corkscrew, John Harvey, Somerfield; **(De) Castellane** Growers & Châteaux, Valvona & Crolla; **Castellblanch** Bibendum, S.H. Jones, Thresher, Waitrose, Waters; **Castelnau** Justerini & Brooks; **Cavalier** Amathus, Booths, Cooperative, Oddbins; **Cavicchioli** Valvona & Crolla; **Cavini** Mitchells; **Cazanove** Hall Batson, The Wright Wine Co; **Champalou** Pallant; **(Domaine) Chandon Australia** See Green Point; **(Domaine) Chandon USA** See Shadow Creek; **Channay**

Morrisons; **Chanoine** Sainsbury's; **Chanson** Averys, S.H. Jones; **Chantelore** Majestic; **Chapel Down** Booths, Fortnum & Mason, Hicks & Don, S.H. Jones, Roberson, Selfridges, Waitrose, Woodhouse; **Charbaut** Penistone Court, Stratford's, The Vintry; **Charnay** Bibendum; **Chartogne-Taillet** Safeway; **Chassenay** Thresher; **Chassey** Corney & Barrow; **Châtelain Desjacques** John Harvey; **Chaudron** Nicolas; **Chevalier de France** Rodney Densem, Nicolas, The Wright Wine Co; **Chevaliers de Malte** Lloyd Taylor; **Chidaine** Pavilion; **Chimere** B.H. Wines, Forth; **Christel (Marguerite)** See Marguerite Christel; **Cinzano** Brian Coad; **Clairveaux** Cooperative; **Clos Naudin-Philippe Foreau** Direct Wine; **Cloudy Bay** See Pelorus; **Clouet** T&W, Tanners; **Cocchi** Penistone Court; **Cockatoo Ridge** Oddbins, Sainsbury's; **Codorníu** Asda, Co-op, Cooperative, Safeway, Somerfield, Woodhouse; **Codorníu Napa** Asda; **Collin et Bourisset** Brian Coad, Selfridges; **Comte de France** Woodhouse; **Comte Royer de Bravard** Hicks & Don; **Coq Rouge Champagne** The Wine Schoppen; **Courbet** Victoria Wine; **Cranswick** Asda; **Cray** Booths, Corkscrew, Sandiway, Shaws of Beaumaris; **Cristalino** Woodhouse

Deakin Estate Bibendum, Oddbins, Ramsbottom; **Debesson** Rodney Densem; **Deinhard** John Arkell, Budgens, John Stephenson; **Delamotte** Corney & Barrow; **Delmas** Pallant; **Delorme** Selfridges, Waterloo; **Delot** Hedley Wright; **Demets** Raeburn; **Demoiselle** Nicolas; **Denois** See Aigle; **Derose** Oddbins; **Desroches** Marks & Spencer; **Deutz** John Armit, Berkmann, B.H. Wines, Forth, Harvey Nichols, Laytons, Mitchells, Nicolas, Penistone Court, John Stephenson; **Deutz-Marlborough** See Montana; **Devaux** Majestic; **Devauzelle** Somerfield; **Deville** Pallant; **Devilliers** Justerini & Brooks; **Dinet-Peuvrel** Holland Park, The Wine Treasury; **Divinoude** Nicolas; **Dom Pérignon** See Moët & Chandon; **Dopff Au Moulin** Harrods, Terry Platt, Roberson; **Drappier** Amathus, B.H. Wines, Anthony Byrne, Corkscrew, Satchells, Thresher; **Dubois-Martin** Smedley; **Duc de Breux** B.H. Wines, Stevens Garnier; **Duchatel** Unwins; **Dulac** B.H. Wines; **Dumont** Fuller's; **Dumont (Daniel)** Ramsbottom, Sandiway; **Duval-Leroy** Adnams, Rodney Densem,

Lay & Wheeler, Terry Platt, Portland, John Stephenson, Tanners, Waters

Ellner Lay & Wheeler, The Wine Schoppen; **Epoch** *See* Chapel Down; **Eschenauer** Somerfield; **Espinosa de los Monteros** Somerfield; **Estrand** S.H. Jones, Portland; **Étienne (Albert)** *See* Albert Étienne

Fairview Sandiway; **Faubert** Selfridges; **Faustino Martinez** Amathus, Mitchells, The Ubiquitous Chip; **Férat** Bibendum; **Féraud** Charles Hennings; **Fere** B.H. Wines; **Ferrari** Holland Park, Valvona & Crolla; **Ferrer (Gloria)** *See* Gloria Ferrer; **Fita Azul** Morrisons; **Flavy La Vigneronne**; **Fleuret** Berkmann; **Fleury** Raeburn, The Wine Society; **Fontanafredda** Fortnum & Mason, Harrods, James Nicholson, Roberson, The Ubiquitous Chip, Valvona & Crolla; **Foreau** Adnams, Gelston Castle; **Forget-Brimont** Brian Coad, Tesco; **Freixenet** Widely available

Gailen Nicolas; **Gallimard** B.H. Wines, Shaws of Beaumaris; **Gallo** Asda, Budgens, Co-op, Cooperative, Forth, Mitchells, Safeway, Sainsbury's, Victoria Wine; **Gancia** Amathus, Co-op, Hall Batson, Hedley Wright, Nicolas, Quellyn Roberts, Valvona & Crolla; **Ganioud** The Wine Society; **Gardet** Ballantynes of Cowbridge, Hicks & Don, The Nobody Inn, La Vigneronne; **Gardin** Hicks & Don; **Gareoult** High Breck; **Gatinois** Haynes Hanson & Clark; **Gaucher** John Arkell, Stevens Garnier; **Gauthier** Pallant; **Geoffroy** Tanners; **Germain** Budgens; **Gianni** Morrisons; **Gilbert** Corney & Barrow; **Gimonnet** Oddbins; **Gioiosa** Valvona & Crolla; **Gloria Ferrer** George Hill, Majestic, Terry Platt, Shaws of Beaumaris, John Stephenson; **Gobillard** Lay & Wheeler; **Golan Heights** Averys; **Gonet** B.H. Wines, Somerfield; **Gosset** Widely available; **Goulet** Harrods, Nicolas; **Gramey** Mitchells; **Grandin** Cooperative, Stevens Garnier; **Grand Marque (Saumur)** S.H. Jones; **Grant Burge** Corkscrew; **Gratien (Alfred)** Fortnum & Mason, Sainsbury's, The Wine Society; **Gratien & Meyer** Richard Harvey, George Hill, Morrisons, Oddbins, Quellyn Roberts, C A Rookes, The Wine Society, The Wright Wine Co; **Great Western** Victoria Wine, Woodhouse; **Green Point** Widely available; **Gregoletto** Harvey Nichols; **Gremillet** Christopher Piper, Sandiway; **Guidon** Selfridges

Hardys Mitchells, Nicolas, Safeway, John Stephenson, Villeneuve; **Harlin** Oddbins; **Heemskerk** Tesco; **Heidsieck (Charles)** Widely available; **Heidsieck Monopole** John Arkell, Champagne Exchange, Rodney Densem, S.H. Jones, Oddbins; **Heidsieck (Piper)** *See* Piper Heidsieck; **Henkell** Amathus, Booths, Mitchells, Morrisons, Satchells, Unwins; **Henriet** La Bouteille d'Or; **Henriet-Bazin** La Bouteille d'Or; **Henriot** Anthony Byrne, Justerini & Brooks, Nicolas, Penistone Court; **Hérard (Paul)** Lloyd Taylor, Morrisons, James Nicholson; **Hérard (Philippe)** High Breck, Edward Sheldon, Lloyd Taylor; **Hollick** Lay & Wheeler; **Hosthomme** The Nobody Inn, Selfridges; **Huet** Bibendum, Justerini & Brooks, Raeburn, The Wine Society; **Huguenot Hills** Somerfield; **Hunter's** Harrods, Justerini & Brooks, Majestic; **Hurlingham** Justerini & Brooks; **Husson** Growers & Châteaux, Budgens

Igé Fuller's; **Inviosa** The Nobody Inn

J Wine Co Harvey Nichols; **Jackson** Hedley Wright, Portland, Sandiway; **Jacquart** Booths, Majestic, Selfridges, John Morris & Verdin, Sandiway; **Jacquart (André)** Sandiway; **Jacquesson & Fils** James Nicholson, Selfridges, Yapp Brothers; **Jarry** Yapp Brothers; **Jeanson** Oddbins; **Jeeper** The Wine Schoppen; **Juvé y Camps** Berry Bros & Rudd, Fortnum & Mason, Harrods, Laymont & Shaw, Roberson, Satchells, Selfridges, Shaws of Beaumaris, Ubiquitous Chip, Villeneuve, The Wright Wine Co

Killawarra Fuller's, Charles Hennings, Lay & Wheeler, Lloyd Taylor, Pallant; **Kripta** Selfridges; **Kriter** Selfridges, John Stephenson; **Krone Borealis** Waitrose; **Krug** Widely available

Laborie Charles Hennings The Wright Wine Co; **Lafitte** Budgens, Nicolas; **Lallement** Gelston Castle; **Lamiable** High Breck; **Lamoure** B.H. Wines, Stevens Garnier, Unwins; **Landiras** Somerfield; **Langlois** Rodney Densem, Majestic, Villeneuve; **Lanson** Widely available; **Lanvin** Hall Batson; **Larmandier** Tanners; **Laurent-Perrier** Widely available; **Lechere** Ballantynes of Cowbridge; **Lemoine** Hedley Wright, Quellyn Roberts, Smedley; **Lenoble** Brian Coad, James Nicholson; **Lenz Moser** Forth; **Lepitre** Harvey Nichols; **Leprince** Mark Reynier; **Liards** *See* Berger; **Lilbert** T&W; **Lindauer**

See Montana; **Listel** Booths, Satchells, Edward Sheldon; **Longridge** Brian Coad, Hedley Wright, Ramsbottom, Roberson; **Lonsdale Ridge** Bibendum; **Lorent** Averys; **Lorentz** Forth; **Louis St Croix** Averys; **Lourmel** Asda; **Lugny** Haynes Hanson & Clark, Oddbins, Christopher Piper, Waitrose

Madeba Cellars Lay & Wheeler, Oddbins, Safeway, Sainsbury's, Unwins, Victoria Wine; **Magenta** The Wright Wine Co; **Mailly Grand Cru** Friarwood; **Maire** Averys; **Malard** Thresher; **Mandois** Somerfield; **Mann** Lay & Wheeler; **Mansard** Champagne Exchange, Forth; **Marca** Tesco, Victoria Wine, Waitrose; **Marchesini** B.H. Wines; **Marguerite Christel** Hall Batson; **Marie Stuart** Hall Batson; **Marino** Co-op; **Marlin Bay** Marks & Spencer; **Marqués de Alella** Harvey Nichols; **Marqués de Monistrol** Amathus, Berkmann, Budgens, Raeburn, Stevens Garnier; **Marquis de la Tour** Victoria Wine; **Marquis d'Estrand** *See* Estrand; **Martini** Widely available; **Martinolles** B.H. Wines, Stevens Garnier; **Marwood** Corkscrew; **Mascaro Monarch** Terry Platt; **Masse** Champagne Exchange, Somerfield; **Massing** Tesco; **Mauler** Selfridges; **Maxim's** Growers & Châteaux; **Mazegrand** Stratford's, The Vintry; **Medot** Harvey Nichols; **Melton** Adnams, Harrods, Harvey Nichols, Hedley Wright, Sandiway; **Mercier** Widely available; **Mesnil** Adnams, Richard Harvey, S.H. Jones, Justerini & Brooks, Raeburn, Ramsbottom, Thresher; **Meyer-Fonné** Lay & Wheeler; **Mignon** Pallant; **Mills Reef** Forth; **Mionetto** Reid; **Miraucourt** George Hill; **Mirru** Mirru *See* Hunter's; **Mitchell** Lay & Wheeler; **Moët & Chandon** Very widely available; **Moncontour** B.H. Wines, James Nicholson, Stevens Garnier; **Monluc** Satchells; **Monmousseau** Nicolas; **Montana** Widely available; **Montarlau** Pallant, Woodhouse; **Montaudon** Mitchell's, Satchells; **Mont Marcal** Booths; **Monteau** Victoria Wine; **Montoy** Thresher; **Morton Estate** Berkmann; **Motte** Asda; **Mottura** Penistone Court; **Mounier** Penistone Court; **Mountadam** The Wright Wine Co; **Muller** Forth, Somerfield; **Mumm** Widely available; **Mumm Cuvée Napa** Widely available; **Muré** Nicolas

Nautilus Amathus, B.H. Wines, Majestic, James Nicholson; **Nederburg** Eldridge Pope; **Neufchatel** John Arkell, Hall Batson, The Wright Wine Co; **Noirot** S.H. Jones; **Northbrook Springs** Charles Hennings; **Nottage Hill** Fuller's;

Nutbourne Manor Charles Hennings; **Nyetimber** Charles Hennings, Pallant, Reid

Ode Panos Greek Wine Centre; **Omar Khayyam** Adnams, Amathus, Budgens, Co-op, Mitchell's, The Nobody Inn, Christopher Piper, John Stephenson; **Ondarre** Averys; **Orlando** B.H. Wines, Rodney Densem, Forth, S.H. Jones, Quellyn Roberts, Selfridges, The Ubiquitous Chip, Unwins; **Orpale** See St Gall; **Oudinot** Marks & Spencer

Paillard Berkmann, Champagne Exchange, Nicolas, Yapp Brothers; **Paleine** Holland Park; **Palmer** Justerini & Brooks, Somerfield; **Pannier** Direct Wine, Oddbins; **Pannier (Rémy)** Forth, Majestic; **Parxet** Direct Wine, Fortnum & Mason, Nicolas, The Wine Schoppen; **Pasqua** Waters; **Pelcino** Waters; **Pelorus** Widely available; **Penley** Lay & Wheeler, Villeneuve, The Wine Treasury; **Pérignon (Dom)** See Moët & Chandon; **Perlino** Victoria Wine; **Perrier (Joseph)** B.H. Wines, Fuller's, Hall-Batson, Hicks & Don, Roberson, Shaws of Beaumaris, Edward Sheldon, Stevens Garnier, Stones of Belgravia, Stratford's, Tanners, Woodhouse; **Perrier (Laurent)** See Laurent-Perrier; **Perrier-Jouët** Widely available; **Perrone** Harvey Nichols, Reid; **Petaluma** B.H. Wines, Fortnum & Mason, Harrods, Harvey Nichols, Sebastopol, Shaws of Beaumaris; **Philipponnat** Stevens Garnier; **Pilton Manor** Harrods; **Piper-Heidsieck** Widely available; **Plantagenet** Stevens Garnier; **Pol Acker** Cooperative, Safeway; **Pol Pasquier** Fuller's; **Pol Rémy** Majestic; **Pol Roger** Widely available; **Pommery** Bibendum, Champagne Exchange, Rodney Densem, Fuller's, Lay & Wheeler, Majestic, Morris & Verdin, Oddbins, Le Pont de la Tour, Roberson, Selfridges, Edward Sheldon, Stratford's, Villeneuve; **Pongracz** Amathus, B.H. Wines, Corkscrew, Charles Hennings, Majestic, Mitchell's, Quellyn Roberts, Sandiway, Selfridges, John Stephenson, Stevens Garnier, Waters; **Poniatowski** Waters; **Praisac** Thresher; **Prieure** Waterloo

Quartet Widely available

Raventos Waterloo; **Raventos L'hereu** Waterloo; **Raventos Rosell** Hedley Wright; **Raymond** Kwik Save; **Redbank** Hicks & Don, Roberson; **Reichscrat Von Buhl** James Nicholson; **Reminger** Morrisons; **Rennesson** The Vintry; **Reynier** Eldridge Pope; **Rheinach**

B.H. Wines, Fuller's; **Rialto** Cooperative; **Richeville** Waters; **Richmond** Terry Platt; **Richmond Royal** Waters; **Riva del Brun** The Wine Schoppen; **Rivetti** Adnams; **Robart** Valvona & Crolla; **Robe d'Or** S.H. Jones; **Robert (J.P.)** S.H. Jones; **Roederer (Louis)** Widely available; **Roederer (Théophile)** Berry Bros & Rudd, Brian Coad, Villeneuve; **Roederer Estate** See Quartet; **Rolet** La Bouteille d'Or; **Rolleston Vale** George Hill, Penistone Court, Portland, Villeneuve; **Rosemount** Forth, Majestic; **Rowlands Brook** Haynes Hanson & Clark, S.H. Jones, Lay & Wheeler, Portland; **Royal Marquissac** Nicolas; **Royal St Charles** Pallant; **Ruelle Pertois** Roger Harris; **Ruggeri** Selfridges, Valvona & Crolla; **Ruinart** Amathus, John Arkell, Berry Bros & Rudd, Andrew Bruce, Harrods, John Harvey, Justerini & Brooks, Lay & Wheeler, Mitchell's, Nicolas, Selfridges, John Stephenson, Thresher, La Vigneronne, Villeneuve; **Rumigny** T&W; **RV** Growers & Châteaux; **Rymill Estate** Raeburn

Sacred Hill Pallant, Stevens Garnier; **Saint-Ceran** Lay & Wheeler; **Saint Flavy** Hicks & Don; **St Gall** Marks & Spencer; **St Honore** Thresher; **Ste Michelle** Hedley Wright; **Salon** Corney & Barrow, Fortnum & Mason, Harvey Nichols, Le Pont de la Tour, Selfridges; **San Carlo** Corkscrew, Forth; **Sandro** Waterloo; **Santa Carolina** Morrisons; **Sarcey** Justerini & Brooks; **Saumur (Caves de)** Nicolas; **Saumur (Vignerons de)** Yapp Brothers; **Scharffenberger** Asda; **Schlumberger** Mitchell's, Penistone Court; **Schramsberg** Adnams, Lay & Wheeler, Roberson; **Seaview** Widely available; **Sécade** Nicolas, The Wright Wine Co; **Segura Viudas** Direct Wine, Oddbins; **Selaks** Stevens Garnier; **Selosse** Ramsbottom, Sandiway; **Seltz** Waterloo; **Seppelt** Widely available; **Serafina & Vidotto** Hicks & Don; **Serres** John Arkell; **Servin** Rodney Densem; **Shadow Creek** Widely available; **Signat** Eldridge Pope; **Silver Ridge** Co-op; **Silver Swan** Waitrose; **Simon, André (Champagne)** Corkscrew, Mitchell's, Portland, Satchells; **Simon, André (Mousseux)** Budgens, Corkscrew, John Stephenson; **Simonsig Kaapse Vonkel** Corney & Barrow, The Nobody Inn, Tesco; **Sonoma Pacific** Berry Bros & Rudd, Pallant; **Soutiran-Pelletier** Allez Vins!, Holland Park; **Sorevi** Stevens Garnier; **Stary Pizenec** Rodney Densem; **Sumarroca** The Wine Society; **Sunnycliff** Haynes Hanson & Clark, S.H. Jones, Lay & Wheeler, Portland

Taittinger Widely available; **Taltarni** Widely available; **Tarlant** Laytons; **Teixidor** Corkscrew, George Hill, Penistone Court; **Telmont** Majestic; **Thienot** Le Pont de la Tour; **Thiers** Yapp Brothers; **Tollana** Averys; **Törley** Wines of Westhorpe; **Tornay** La Bouteille d'Or; **Torre del Gall** Adnams, Amathus, Averys, Budgens, Fuller's, Hall Batson, Harvey Nichols, Lay & Wheeler, Mitchell's, Terry Platt, Quellyn Roberts, Raeburn, John Stephenson, Victoria Wine, Villeneuve; **Torrerossa** Majestic; **Torres** Amathus, Direct Wine, Ramsbottom; **Triolet** Gelston Castle; **Trouillard** Penistone Court; **Trudel** Waitrose; **Turckheim** Unwins; **Tyrrell's** The Wright Wine Co

Vaillant Booths; **Val Brun** Hedley Wright, Smedley; **Valdivieso** Bibendum, Sainsbury's; **Valentin** Friarwood; **Vallformosa** B.H. Wines, Forth, Mitchell's; **Van Lovern** Villeneuve; **Varichon et Clerc** Corney & Barrow, Lay & Wheeler, Reid, Unwins; **Vaudon** Haynes Hanson & Clark; **Vauzelle** Amathus; **Venoge** Amathus, Nicolas, Waters; **Verdier** Cooperative; **Vesselle (Georges)** Nicolas, Stones of Belgravia; **Veuve de Bomonde** Corkscrew, Hedley Wright, Shaws of Beaumaris, John Stephenson; **Veuve Borodin** Roberson; **Veuve Chapelle** Averys; **Veuve Clicquot Ponsardin** Very widely available; **Veuve Corbin** Waterloo; **Veuve Delaroy** Bibendum; **Veuve Fourny** Christopher Piper, Shaws of Beaumaris; **Veuve Honorain** Co-op; **Veuve Lorin** Berry Bros & Rudd; **Veuve Noiziers** Cooperative; **Veuve Oudinot** Mitchell's, Penistone Court; **Veuve Truffeau** Marks & Spencer; **Veuve Valmante** Terry Platt, Waters; **Veuve du Vernay** Widely available; **Viardot** La Bouteille d'Or; **Villa Pigna** Tesco; **Vilmart** Direct Wine, Fortnum & Mason, Gauntleys, Selfridges, Shaws of Beaumaris; **Viña Manquehue** Hedley Wright

Windy Peak Brian Coad; **Wissembourg** George Hill, James Nicholson; **Wolf Blass** Mitchell's; **Wunsch et Mann** Penistone Court

Yaldara Booths, Brian Coad, Hedley Wright, Majestic, Oddbins, Terry Platt, Satchells, Shaws of Beaumaris; **Yalumba** Widely available; **Yellowglen** Majestic, Mitchell's, Oddbins, John Stephenson

Zonin Booths

Major Stockists in the UK

OWN LABELS
All the stockists were asked to submit their own-label Champagnes and sparkling wines to the author for tasting, if they have any. Recommended own-labels (scoring 70 or above) are listed in italics below the entries.

PRICES
The retail prices in this section are inclusive of VAT.

KEY
✉ Mail order available
Recommended own-labels
🔵 Author's overall rating out of 100 (*see p67*)

Adnams

The Crown, High Street,
Southwold, Suffolk IP18 6DP
📞 01502 727222
FAX 01502 727223 ✉
Want to go back in time? Then visit sleepy Southwold and stay at The Crown, which also belongs to Adnams. It has one of the best wine lists in the country, with a first-class range of Champagnes through to innovative New World sparkling wines.

Adnams' own non-vintage Spécial Cuvée Duval-Leroy is a fine example. Its fresh, elegant, pineapple aromas are seductive, and the fruit on the palate has a wonderfully fluffy feel, and a zesty, invigorating finish. It is light-bodied but not lightweight.
Adnams Spécial Cuvée Champagne NV Brut, Duval-Leroy £13 🔵

Allez Vins!

PO Box 1019,
Long Itchington, Rugby,
Warwickshire CV23 8ZU
📞 01926 811969
FAX 01926 811969 ✉
John and Ann Bouttal specialize in regional French wines from quality-minded growers such as Soutiran-Pelletier in Champagne.

Amathus Wines

377 Green Lanes,
London N13 4JG
📞 0181 886 3787/1864
FAX 0181 882 1273 ✉
The really useful feature of the service offered by Amathus is that, unlike most retail or wholesale operations, it tends to list the whole range and prices of *cuvées*, bottle sizes and vintages of the producers it deals with.

John Arkell Vintners

Arkell's Brewery Ltd,
Stratton St Margaret, Swindon,
Wiltshire SN2 6RU
📞 01793 823026
FAX 01793 828864 ✉
Nick Arkell runs the wine division of his family's brewery, which owns 95 licensed outlets, and supplies 400 free houses, pubs, hotels and restaurants. The excellent-value Bernard Gaucher is the house Champagne.

John Armit Wines

5 Royalty Studios,
105 Lancaster Road,
London W11 1QF
📞 0171 727 6846
FAX 0171 727 7133 ✉
An upmarket, beautifully produced list, with a small selection of Champagne but no sparkling wines. The highly reputed Beaumont des Crayères cooperative is the house Champagne.

Asda

Asda House, South Bank,
Great Wilson Street,
Leeds LS1 5AD
📞 0113 243 5435
FAX 0113 241 7766
One of the country's leading supermarket groups, Asda has over 200 branches, and a good-value range of own-label fizz. It is one of the few places to sell Scharffenberger, albeit not its top-performing Blanc de Blancs.

The own-label non-vintage Brut Réserve Cuvée Speciale, with its creamy-biscuit richness and fine structure, is a steal at the price.
Asda Champagne NV Brut Réserve, Cuvée Speciale £11.99 🔵

Averys

Orchard House, Southfield Road,
Nailsea, Bristol BS19 1JD
📞 01275 811100
FAX 01275 811101 ✉
A wide range of alternative sparkling wines, including a red Burgundy, and such obscurities as fizz from Israel and Vin Fou ("Mad Wine") from the Arbois.
Averys Champagne 1989 Bicentennial Cuvée Brut £22.10 🔵

Ballantynes of Cowbridge

3 Westgate, Cowbridge,
South Glamorgan CF71 7AQ
📞 01446 774840
FAX 01446 773044 ✉
Ballantynes has a small range of Champagnes from Gosset, Gardet and Lechere, including Cuvée Orient Express, in case you can't afford the real thing.

Berkmann Wine Cellars

12 Brewery Road,
London N7 9NH
📞 0171 609 4711
FAX 0171 607 0018 ✉
Primarily a supplier to London restaurants, but also a general wholesaler and retailer, with a very strong list – particularly in Burgundy – although relatively few bubblies. It is a long-time supporter of Champagne Bruno Paillard and was recently appointed an agent for Deutz.

Berry Bros & Rudd

3 St James's Street,
London SW1A 1EG
📞 0171 396 9600
FAX 0171 396 9611 ✉
A stockist of a classic range of *grande marque* Champagnes, and shippers of Champagne Binet since 1887. It is also a good source for Théophile Roederer.

The own-label non-vintage UK Cuvée, with its sprightly fruitiness and rich finish, is better on its own than with food.
Berry Bros & Rudd Champagne NV United Kingdom Cuvée, Brut, Binet £15.25 🔵

B.H. Wines

Boustead Hill House,
Boustead Hill, Burgh-by-Sands,
Carlisle CA5 6AA
📞 01278 576711
FAX 01278 576711 ✉
An interesting, well thought-out list of Champagne and other fizzies, majoring in Drappier and Pol Roger. Also one of the very few places in the UK that stocks Daniel Le Brun vintage.

Bibendum

113 Regents Park Road,
London NW1 8UR
📞 0171 722 5577
FAX 0171 722 7354 ✉
The Oddbins of the independent wine merchant sector, Bibendum stocks a bewildering

range of brilliant wines of almost every description. It has yet to give Champagne and sparkling wine its full attention.

Booths

4 Fishergate, Preston
Lancashire PR1 3LJ
☎ 01772 251701
🖷 01772 255642

Since the arrival of wine buyer Chris Dee, this Yorkshire-based supermarket chain of 24 outlets has been giving the very best of the big national chains a run for their money.
Booths Champagne NV Brut
£12.69 **65**

Bottom's Up

See Thresher Group

La Bouteille d'Or

Queen's Lodge
Queen's Club Gardens
London W14 9TA
☎ 0171 385 3122/01264 781518
🖷 0171 833 9391 ✉

Those lucky enough to be on Patricia Norman's mailing list know that she only sells Champagne from a select group of quality-minded growers, which at present includes Henriet-Bazin, Viardot and Tornay.

Andrew Bruce

Fourth Floor, 22 Hans Place,
London SW1X 0EP
☎ 0171 225 1982
🖷 0171 225 0366 ✉

This stockist is a good source for major Champagne names such as Ruinart and Pol Roger.

Budgens

9 Stonefield Way, Ruislip,
Middlesex HA4 0JR
☎ 0181 422 9511
🖷 0181 422 1596

This supermarket group has over 100 stores, but just one wine buyer, Tony Finnerty, who has no staff whatsoever, and even has to wash up his own glasses after a tasting. When its own brand, Brossault (which is made by Bonnet), is on form, Budgens' aggressive pricing policy can make it one of the best Champagne bargains available.

Anthony Byrne Fine Wines

Unit 1–7, Ramsey Business Park,
Stocking Fen Road, Ramsey,
Cambridgeshire PE17 1UR
☎ 01487 814555
🖷 01487 814962 ✉

A fabulous selection of great

wines from star producers, and UK agents for Champagnes Henriot and Drappier.

Cave Cru Classé

Unit 13 The Leathermarket,
Weston Street,
London SE1 3ER
☎ 0171 378 8579
🖷 0171 378 8544 ✉

This Bordeaux specialist also stocks Pol Roger, Krug and Salon, plus various vintages of Dom Pérignon and Dom Pérignon Rosé going back to 1966.

The Champagne Exchange

See Classic Wines & Spirits

The Champagne House

28 Longmoore Street,
London SW1V 1JF
☎ 0171 828 4615
🖷 0171 828 4615 ✉

A low-profile Champagne specialist for private customers only.

Chateaux Wines

Paddock House,
Upper Tockington Road,
Tockington,
Bristol BS12 4LQ
☎ 01454 613959
🖷 01454 613959 ✉

David and Cheryl Miller have a small list with a faithful following. My personal selection in terms of Champagne is Laurent-Perrier or, for those on a budget, Bauchet.

Classic Wines & Spirits

Vintners House, Third Avenue,
Deeside Industrial Park,
Deeside, Chester CH5 2LA
☎ 01244 288444
🖷 01244 280008 ✉

Every year Classic Wines & Spirits issues a special *Champagne Exchange* brochure chock-full of fizzy finds, including some top-draw *grande marque* Champagnes at bargain prices.

Brian Coad Fine Wines

66 Cole Lane, Stowford Park,
Ivybridge, Devon PL21 0PN
☎ 01752 896545
🖷 01752 691160 ✉

The entire range of Théophile Roederer is sold at Brian Coad.

Co-op

New Century House,
Manchester M60 4ES
☎ 0161 827 5353
🖷 0161 827 5117

The Co-op has almost 2,500 stores owned by 30 regional soci-

eties, but, as they vary enormously in size, the range of products offered differs from shop to shop.
Veuve Honorain NV Blanc de Noirs Brut £10.69 **63**

Cooperative

Sandbrook Park, Sandbrook Way,
Rochdale OL11 1SA
☎ 01706 713000/891628
🖷 01706 891207

Some 290 superstores that are completely separate from the Co-op societies (*see above*), although all share a hard-core of Co-op own-label wines supplied by CWS (Co-operative Wholesale Society), including Veuve Honorain.

Corkscrew Wines

Arch 5, Viaduct Estate, Carlisle
Cumbria CA2 5BN
☎ 01228 43033
🖷 01228 43033 ✉

An interesting selection of Champagnes and sparkling wines, including cultish New World offerings such as Roederer Estate's Quartet and Cloudy Bay's Pelorus.

Corney & Barrow

12 Helmet Row,
London EC1V 3QJ
☎ 0171 251 4051
🖷 0171 608 1373 ✉

A City wine merchant with an impeccable list of Champagnes, including various vintages of Dom Pérignon going back, at the time of writing, to 1952. However, apart from Pelorus, the range of sparkling wine alternatives is pretty dull, but then who in the City drinks sparkling wine anyway (except maybe Pelorus)?

Rodney Densem Wines

Regent House, Lancaster Fields,
Crewe Gates Farm Estate, Crewe
CW1 1SS
☎ 01270 212200
🖷 01270 212300 ✉

Rodney Densem has a small but well-chosen list of Champagnes, plus some interesting fizz from other places, including Argyle Brut from Oregon, and Green Point from Australia.

Direct Wine Shipments

5–7 Corporation Square,
Belfast BT1 3AJ
☎ 01232 243906
🖷 01232 240202 ✉

The best wine merchant in Belfast (and perhaps the UK) offers an excellent range, including the star-performing Champagne Vilmart.

Eldridge Pope & Co plc
Weymouth Avenue,
Dorchester,
Dorset DT1 1QT
☎ 01305 251251
℻ 01305 258300 ✉
With one of the best and biggest wine lists in the country, Eldridge Pope also owns Reynier London (a separate company from Mark Reynier Fine Wines), which is a faithful long-term shipper of De Venoge. It also sells all the famous Champagne names.
Reynier NV Brut £12.04 ⑧⓪
The Chairman's Champagne 1990 Blanc de Blancs Brut £19.92 ⑥⑦

Forth Wines
Crawford Place, Milnathort,
Kinross-shire KY13 7XF
☎ 01577 863668
℻ 01577 864810 ✉
The exclusive agent for Champagne Mansard, and stockist of the usual range of *grande marque* names, plus a fair selection of dependable sparkling wines.

Fortnum & Mason
181 Piccadilly,
London W1A 1ER
☎ 0171 734 8040
℻ 0171 437 3278
Plenty of famous names, some of which are at surprisingly affordable prices. It is also a good place to go for large bottle formats, *rosés* and sparkling wines.

Friarwood
26 New Kings Road,
London SW6 4ST
☎ 0171 736 2628
℻ 0171 731 0411 ✉
This upmarket wine merchant recently acquired then dropped the excellent-value De Castellane Champagne agency, but is still the only source for the equally great-value Mailly Grand Cru.
Friarwood Champagne NV Brut Réserve, Premier Cru, Le Royal Coteau £13.71 ⑥③

Fuller's
Griffin Brewery,
Chiswick Lane South,
London W4 2QB
☎ 0181 996 2000
℻ 0181 995 0230 ✉
World-famous amongst the hop-worshippers for its London Pride, Fuller's also has an increasingly impressive wine selection, which it offers through mail order and more than 70 wine shops.

Gauntleys of Nottingham
4 High Street, Exchange Arcade,
Nottingham NG1 2ET
☎ 0115 941 7973
℻ 0115 590 9519 ✉
This is *the* source when it comes to Champagne Vilmart.

Gelston Castle Fine Wines
45 Warwick Street,
London SW1V 2AJ
☎ 0171 821 6841
℻ 01556 504183 ✉
An excellent source of grower Champagnes (Triolet and Lallement), and one of the very best Vouvray producers (Foreau).

Greek Wine Centre
46–48 Underdale Road,
Shrewsbury,
Shropshire SY2 5DT
☎ 01743 364636
℻ 01743 367960 ✉
The ebullient Jordanis Pertridis has at long last found a Greek fizz of international quality: Ode Panos.

Growers & Châteaux
Hartland House, Church Street,
Reigate, Surrey RH2 ODA
☎ 01737 214957
℻ 01737 214958 ✉
A recent venture by Peter and Jan Wharam, who are agents for Maxim's (which is made by De Castellane), and will look after De Castellane itself until a new importer is found. Also included on the list are a couple of grower Champagnes, and the stunning new RV *cuvée* from Tasmania.

Hall Batson & Co
168 Wroxham Road,
Norwich, Norfolk NR7 8DE
☎ 01603 415115
℻ 01603 484096 ✉
A few interesting Champagnes and sparkling wines. House Champagne under the Lanvin label is from the same stable as Charles de Cazanove.

Roger Harris Wines
Loke Farm, Weston Longville,
Norfolk NR9 5LG
☎ 01603 880171
℻ 01603 880291 ✉
The world's foremost Beaujolais specialist focuses on Ruelle Pertois in terms of Champagne.

Harrods
87–135 Brompton Road
London SW1X 7XL
☎ 0171 730 1234
℻ 0171 225 5823

As expected, Harrods lists all the *grande marques*. The world's most famous store also boasts a large range of own-label Champagnes that would appear to be over-priced, but, as they were not submitted for tasting, it is impossible to say whether they are a cut above most BOBs (Buyer's Own Brands) and hence worth the premium.

John Harvey
12 Denmark Street,
Bristol BS1 5DQ
☎ 0117 927 5010
℻ 0117 927 5002 ✉
A small, traditional selection of *grande marque* Champagnes.

Harvey Nichols
109–125 Knightsbridge,
London SW1 7RJ
☎ 0171 201 8596
℻ 0171 235 8589 ✉
This store's wine department supplies the wines for its own Fifth Floor Café, as well as the Oxo Tower Restaurant, Bar & Brasserie. They employ 12 young sommeliers who are keen to spot interesting new wines for their fashion-conscious clientele. This, plus the recent launch of a mail order service, has put the Harvey Nichols range of wines ahead of that offered by other so-called "top people's" shops.

Richard Harvey Wines
Bucknowle House, Bucknowle,
Wareham, Dorset BH20 5PQ
☎ 01929 480351
℻ 01929 481275 ✉
Champagne Le Mesnil is the best buy at this stockist.

Haynes Hanson & Clark
25 Eccleston Street,
London SW1W 9NP
☎ 0171 259 0102
℻ 0171 259 0103 ✉
Well-selected sparkling wine alternatives, good-value house fizz under the Pierre Vaudon label from Union Champagne, and a quality-focused range of *grandes marques* are what you can expect here.

The Heath Street Wine Company
See La Reserve

Hedley Wright
10-11 Twyford Business Centre,
London Road, Bishops Stortford,
Hertfordshire CM23 3YT
☎ 01279 506512
℻ 01279 657462 ✉

A small range of quality *grande marque* Champagnes and a good range of new classics from the New World are stocked here.

Charles Hennings Vintners
London House, Lower Street,
Pulborough, Sussex RH20 2BW
☎ 01798 872458/873909
℻ 01798 873163 ✉
A long list of *grandes marques*; Pelorus heads a small selection of sparkling wine alternatives.

Hicks & Don
The Brewery, Blandford St Mary,
Dorset DT11 9LS
☎ 01258 456040
℻ 01258 450147 ✉
Sells Gardet, Gosset, Bollinger, Roederer and Joseph Perrier, along with a couple of second-label Champagnes that were not submitted for tasting.

High Breck Vintners
Bentworth House,
Bentworth, Near Alton,
Hampshire GU34 5RB
☎ 01420 562218
℻ 01420 563827 ✉
With the exception of Billecart-Salmon of the highest quality, High Breck Vintners tends to major on the cheaper end of the Champagne market. And it does it rather well, too.

George Hill
59 Wards End,
Loughborough,
Leicestershire LE11 3HB
☎ 01509 212717
℻ 01509 236963 ✉
Buyers will find a few *grande marque* Champagnes here, while the range of sparkling wine alternatives could be described as reliable rather than exciting.

The Holland Park Wine Company
12 Portland Road,
London W11 4LA
☎ 0171 221 9614
℻ 0171 221 9613 ✉
Master of Wine James Handford has a soft spot for Champagnes from Brochet-Hervieux and Soutiran-Pelletier, which he backs up with only the best from Bollinger, Gosset, Roederer and Veuve Clicquot. There is also a small, but extremely well-selected, range of sparkling wine alternatives.

Jeroboams
See Stones of Belgravia

S.H. Jones
27 High Street, Banbury,
Oxfordshire OX16 8EW
☎ 01295 251179
℻ 01295 272352 ✉
S. H. Jones has a good selection of *grande marque* Champagnes, with the excellent Le Mesnil cooperative topping the lesser-known brands, and Quartet and Green Point leading the New World sparklers.

Justerini & Brooks Retail
61 St James's Street,
London SW1A 1LZ
☎ 0171 493 8721
℻ 0171 499 4653 ✉
An excellent range of mostly *grande marque* names, including the incredible 1981 Krug, which I rate as one of the three finest Champagnes produced in the last 25 years. With one of the few merchant own-label Champagnes to rate above 80, and offering Green Point, Quartet, Mirru Mirru and Pelorus as its New World pack, Justerini & Brooks provides its customers with an excellent service indeed.

A good bet is the own-label Sarcey Private Cuvée, made by Boizel. This firm, rich Champagne has a lemony, Chablis-like fruit that promises to go toasty.
Justerini & Brooks, Sarcey Champagne NV Private Cuvée Brut £13.95 **80**

Kwik Save
Warren Drive, Prestatyn,
Clwyd LL19 7HU
☎ 01745 887111
℻ 01745 882504
Although this supermarket chain has no own-label Champagne as such, it tends to use F. Bonnet and its second label Louis Raymond as its house Champagnes.

Lay & Wheeler
6 Culver Street West,
Colchester, Essex CO1 1JA
☎ 01206 764446
℻ 01206 560002 ✉
Everything you would expect from the country's best wine list.

Lay & Wheeler's non-vintage Champagne Extra Quality, made by Duval-Leroy, is very fresh and elegant with fragrant fruit and a touch of vanilla finesse. It makes an ideal pouring Champagne for discerning guests.
Lay & Wheeler Champagne NV Extra Quality Brut, Duval-Leroy £14.24 **68**

Laymont & Shaw
The Old Chapel, Millpool,
Truro, Cornwall TR1 1EX
☎ 01872 270545
℻ 01872 223005 ✉
Juvé y Camps is the fizz stocked by this Spanish wine specialist.

Laytons
20 Midland Road,
London NW1 2AD
☎ 0171 387 2552
℻ 0171 383 7936 ✉
This has never been the cheapest place to buy wine. However, critics seldom argue with the pedigree of its list, and the own-label Champagne is the one wine that regularly manages to combine quality with value.

A good buy is Laytons' own non-vintage Brut Reserve, made by F. Bonnet, and characterized by a fine mousse, flowery finesse and zippy, zingy fruit that will develop a mellowing toastiness.
Laytons Champagne NV Brut Reserve, F. Bonnet £11.95 **84**

Lloyd Taylor Wines
Bute House, Arran Road,
Perth PH1 3DZ
☎ 01738 447878
℻ 01738 447979 ✉
A small selection of Champagnes and sparkling wines, with Paul Hérard providing the best value.

Majestic Wine Warehouse
Odhams Trading Estate,
St Albans Road, Watford,
Hertfordshire WD2 5RE
☎ 01923 298200
℻ 01923 819105
A chain of 65 wine warehouses. Oeil de Perdrix from Devaux is the best bargain in what is a selection of very good, well-priced Champagnes and sparkling wines.

Marks & Spencer
Michael House,
46–47 Baker Street,
London W1A 1DN
☎ 0171 268 3855
℻ 0171 268 2674
More than 280 department stores offering one of the most under-rated own-label ranges (under the St Michael name) on the market.

The Marlin Bay non-vintage Bottle Fermented Brut Reserve is light, fresh and fruity, and, frankly, unbeatable for the price.

One of Marks and Spencer's pricier offerings is the De Saint Gall 1990 Brut Premier Cru, made by Union Champagne, notable for its creamy and complex nature, which has a vanilla-rich apricot ripeness of fruit.

Marlin Bay NV Bottle Fermented Brut Reserve, St Michael £4.39 **70**

Malvasia Prosecco Vino Spumante NV Brut, Zonin, St Michael £4.99 **73**

Bluff Hill NV Brut, St Michael £6.99 **70**

South African Sparkling Wine NV Pinot Noir Chardonnay Brut, Madeba, St Michael £6.99 **70**

Australian Sparkling Shiraz 1993 Bottle Fermented, Dry, Seppelt, St Michael £9.99 **78**

Oudinot NV Cuvée Brut, St Michael £9.99 **80**

Oudinot 1990 Brut Grand Cru, St Michael £12.99 **80**

De St Gall NV Brut Premier Cru, St Michael £13.99 **85**

De St Gall Blanc de Blancs NV Premier Cru Brut, St Michael £15.99 **82**

De St Gall 1990 Brut Premier Cru, St Michael £18.99 **86**

Cuvée Orpale 1985 Blanc de Blancs Brut Grand Cru, St Michael £22.50 **85**

Mitchell's Wine Merchants

354 Meadowhead, Sheffield, South Yorkshire S8 7UJ

☎ 0114 274 5587

✉ 0114 274 8481 ✉

John Mitchell is a friendly Yorkshire wine merchant who knows what he likes. In this case it's Champagne Montaudon, although he also stocks many other brands.

Morris & Verdin

Unit 10 The Leathermarket Weston Street, London SE1 3ER

☎ 0171 357 8866

✉ 0171 357 8877 ✉

This quality-minded wine merchant focuses its attention on André Jacquart, which is a grower Champagne with no connection to the cooperative-produced Champagne Jacquart.

Morrisons

Junction 41 Industrial Estate, Carr Gate, Wakefield, West Yorkshire WF2 OXF

☎ 01924 870000

✉ 01924 875120

A Northern-based supermarket chain of 80 or so stores, which is beginning to move South, and is just starting to get into own-label fizz. Great choices for value

include Paul Hérard and Nicole d'Aurigny. However, the list of sparkling wines could do with some pepping up.

James Nicholson

27a Killyleagh Street, Crossgar, Co Down BT30 9DG

☎ 01396 830091

✉ 01396 830028 ✉

Impeccable quality from Billecart-Salmon and Roederer, while Quartet and Pelorus provide the New World challenge.

Nicolas UK

157 Great Portland Street, London W1N 5HP

☎ 0171 436 9338

✉ 0171 637 1691

France's premier wine shop chain has 14 branches in London, but is noticeably lacking in New World fizz, having just one such product, Hardy's (but at least that is one more than Nicolas's shops in France offer). There are a number of good to very good *grandes marques*, plus a scattering of excellent lesser-known brands such as Bruno Paillard. Among the interesting second labels are Chaudron from Georges Goulet. Own-label wines were not submitted for tasting.

The Nobody Inn

Doddiscombleigh, Near Exeter, Devon EX6 7PS

☎ 01647 252394

✉ 01647 252978 ✉

A country tavern with a wine list to die for, including the sublime 1979 Krug, if you can afford it.

The own-label house Champagne is an attractive, fruity wine.

The Nobody Inn, House Champagne NV Gardet Brut £13.83 **82**

Oddbins

The Ark, 201 Talgarth Road, London W6 8BN

☎ 0181 944 4400

✉ 0181 944 4411

When it comes to High Street chains, Oddbins has no peers. Its 230 or so stores stock an amazing range of Champagnes and sparkling wines, and the seven Fine Wine Stores boast an even greater range. There are multiple-purchase bargains galore: they practically give the stuff away!

Pallant Wines

17 High Street, Arundel, West Sussex BN18 9AD

☎ 01903 882288

✉ 01903 882801 ✉

A few well-chosen *grandes marques*, supported by a number of good-value brands from Marne & Champagne. Pallant Wines is also one of just three stockists of Nyetimber, Britain's only world-class sparkling wine; the others being Reid Wine and Charles Hennings.

Pavilion Wine Company

Finsbury Circus Gardens, London EC2M 7AB

☎ 0171 628 8224

✉ 0171 628 6205 ✉

Just Bollinger, Krug and Ruinart as far as Champagne is concerned, but I think I could live with being restricted to those three brands.

Penistone Court Wine Cellars

No. 5 The Railway Station, Penistone, Sheffield, South Yorkshire S36 6HP

☎ 01226 766037

✉ 01226 767310 ✉

Pol Roger is the strongest representation at Penistone Court, along with lovely mature gems such as a 1983 Roederer Blanc de Blancs and a 1976 Cuvée Baccarat from Henriot. Austrian fizz is another speciality.

Le Picoleur

See La Reserve

Christopher Piper

1 Silver Street, Ottery St Mary, Devon EX11 1DB

☎ 01404 814139

✉ 01404 812100 ✉

This stockist exclusively ships a grower Champagne called Gremillet, plus a number of *grandes marques*, majoring on Charles Heidsieck, including all three *Mis en Caves* – 1992, 1993 and 1994 – (*see A–Z listing*).

Terry Platt

Ferndale Road, Llandudno Junction, Gwynedd LL31 9NT

☎ 01492 592971

✉ 01492 592196 ✉

Terry Platt stocks a few well-selected famous names, but relies on Duval-Leroy to fulfil the needs of most customers. Indeed, it would be difficult to find a better-value, more expressive Champagne. Argyle and Green Point are the best options from the New World selection.

Le Pont de la Tour
The Butlers Wharf Building,
36d Shad Thames,
Butlers Wharf,
London SE1 2YE
☎ 0171 403 2403
🖷 0171 403 0267 ✉
A dual-function shop and cellar for the Conran Restaurant, Le Pont de la Tour offers an impressive selection of *grande marque* Champagnes, including Billecart-Salmon, Bollinger, Dom Pérignon, Gosset, Krug, Salon and Taittinger Comtes de Champagne.

Portland Wine Company
152a Ashley Road,
Hale, Near Altrincham,
Cheshire WA15 9SA
☎ 0161 962 8752
🖷 0161 905 1291 ✉
Second-label wines from Duval-Leroy and Ellner head up the value section of this stockist, which also has stores in Macclesfield, Cheshire and Sale, Greater Manchester. Quartet, Green Point and Jackson Estate form the cream of the New World offering.

Quellyn Roberts
15 Watergate Street, Chester,
Cheshire CH1 2LB
☎ 01244 310455
🖷 01244 346704 ✉
Apart from standard bottles, Quellyn-Roberts sells Pol Roger non-vintage in quarters, halves, magnums, Jeroboams, Methuselahs and Nebuchadnezzars!

Raeburn Fine Wines
23 Comely Bank Road,
Edinburgh EH14 1DS
☎ 0131 332 5166
🖷 0131 332 5166 ✉
One look at Zubair Mohamed's list and you know he loves wines. His fizz section includes just two I simply wouldn't – not couldn't – drink, and I can't say that about any other range.

Ramsbottom Victuallers
16-18 Market Place,
Ramsbottom, Bury,
Lancashire BL0 9HT
☎ 01706 825070
🖷 01706 822005 ✉
Ramsbottom Victuallers is affiliated with the Village Restaurant, whose awards have included the BBC Best Food Shop, *Good Food Guide* Greater Manchester Restaurant of the Year and *Lancashire Life* Wine Merchant of the Year. As Chris Johnson, the owner,

says: "We studiously avoid *grandes marques* and any other widely available growers."

Reid Wines
The Mill, Marsh Lane,
Hallatrow, Bristol BS18 5EB
☎ 01761 452645
🖷 01761 453642 ✉
The best source of old vintage Champagnes (for example, a 1921 Moët & Chandon), and one of just three stockists of Nyetimber, Britain's only world-class sparkling wine. The others are Pallant Wines and Charles Hennings.

La Reserve
56 Walton Street,
London SW3 1RB
☎ 0171 589 2020
🖷 0171 581 0250 ✉
This is the flagship of a small chain of shops under the Mark Reynier Fine Wines banner. Other branches in London include The Heath Street Wine Company (29 Heath Street, NW3), Le Picoleur (47 Kendal Street, W2) and Le Sac à Vin (203 Munster Road, SW6). They major on Pol Roger and Gosset, and have an interest in old vintages of Bollinger, Krug and Dom Pérignon.
Charles Leprince NV Grande Reserve Brut £14.95 **80**

Mark Reynier Fine Wines
See La Reserve

Reyniers
See Eldridge Pope & Co plc

Roberson
348 Kensington High Street,
London W14 8NS
☎ 0171 371 2121
🖷 0171 371 4010 ✉
An excellent Champagne list that is as long as your arm, but the sparkling wine alternatives could do with a bit of a shake-up.
Veuve Borodin NV White Label, Brut, Boizel £12.95 **84**

C A Rookes
7 Western Road Industrial Estate,
Stratford-upon-Avon,
Warwickshire CV37 0AH
☎ 01789 297777
🖷 01789 297752 ✉
As far as the Champagne sold here is concerned, quality is supplied by Gosset, and value comes from Moutardier, which is run by Englishman Jonathan Saxby. Sparkling wines are primarily limited to Gratien & Meyer.

Le Sac à Vin
See La Reserve

Safeway
Safeway House,
6 Millington Road, Hayes,
Middlesex UB3 4AY
☎ 0181 848 8744
🖷 0181 753 1865
A small range of *grandes marques* for a supermarket group with 450 stores. The best-value choices are Chartogne-Taillet for Champagne, and Edwards & Chaffey for Australian fizz. And don't forget Safeway's May and October Wine Fairs, when special deals abound.
The own-label Bottle Fermented Chardonnay has a delicately rich and creamy aroma, followed by crisp, toasty fruit with a fresh, floral aftertaste.
Sparkling Chenin NV Brut, C.C.V. £3.99 **70**
Australian Quality Sparkling Wine NV Bottle Fermented Brut, Seppelt, Safeway £4.99 **71**
Bottle Fermented Chardonnay NV Brut, Trento, Safeway £5.99 **75**

Sainsbury's
Stamford House, Stamford Street,
London SE1 9LL
☎ 0171 921 7168
🖷 0171 921 6343 ✉
This national chain, with almost 400 stores, has always been strong on own-label Champagne. A home-delivery service is offered via Sainsbury's magazine.
An excellent choice is the own-brand non-vintage Champagne Extra Dry, made by Duval-Leroy: a fresh, light, vibrantly fruity style that just gets better and better.
Sainsbury's Champagne NV Blanc de Noirs Brut £11.99 **80**
Sainsbury's Champagne NV Extra Dry, Duval-Leroy £12.95 **84**
Sainsbury's Champagne NV Brut Rosé, Beaumet £13.95 **82**
Sainsbury's Vintage Champagne 1991 Blanc de Blancs Brut, UVCB £14.95 **85**

Sandiway Wine Company
Chester Road, Sandiway,
Cheshire CW8 2NH
☎ 01606 882101
🖷 01606 888407 ✉
A small but well-selected range of Champagne, including three different growers (Dumont, Jacquart and Selosse), plus an interesting choice of sparkling wines.

Satchells of Burnham Market

North Street, Burnham Market,
Norfolk PE31 8HG
☎ 01328 738272
🖷 01328 738272 ✉
A limited but interesting selection of Champagne (including Barnaut, Albert Le Brun, Drappier and Montaudon) is sold at this wine merchant.
*Louis Masseran NV Brut,
   Satchells £12.95* **63**

Savage Selection

The Ox House, Market Place,
Northleach, Cheltenham,
Gloucestershire GL54 3EG
☎ 01451 850896
🖷 01451 850896 ✉
After asking Master of Wine Mark Savage to taste wines for *The Sunday Telegraph Good Wine Guide* in 1984, I remember how low his scores were compared with those of all the other judges, and commented on how apt his surname was. Since then I have expected the highest standards from any wine he sells, and have never been disappointed. Savage is a long-term shipper of Billecart-Salmon.

Sebastopol Wines

Sebastopol Barn,
London Road, Blewbury,
Oxfordshire OX11 9HB
☎ 01235 850471
🖷 01235 850776 ✉
Sebastopol sells a small but impeccably chosen selection of Champagnes and sparkling wines.

Selfridges

400 Oxford Street,
London W1A 1AB
☎ 0171 318 3730
🖷 0171 491 1880 ✉
A wide range of Champagnes and sparkling wines, including some delightful finds for a department store, such as Vilmart and old vintages of Krug and Dom Pérignon.

Selfridges also produces one of my highest-scoring own-label Champagnes, made by Georges Goulet, a company which used to have a reputation for big, Pinot-dominated Champagnes. It comes as a surprise, therefore, that this *cuvée* is fresh, light and elegant, with a zingy, lemony fruit. However, the structure indicates there is still a way to go.
*Selfridges Millennium Cuvée
   Champagne 1990 Blanc de
   Blancs, Brut £28* **67**

Shaws of Beaumaris

17 Castle Street, Beaumaris,
Isle of Anglesey LL58 8AP
☎ 01248 810328
🖷 01248 810328 ✉
Bollinger, Pol Roger and Vilmart are the *grande marque* names dominating the selection of Champagne at this stockist.

Edward Sheldon

New Street, Shipston-on-Stour,
Warwickshire CV36 4EN
☎ 01608 661409
🖷 01608 6631166 ✉
A small, traditional range of mostly *grande marque* Champagnes is sold at Edward Sheldon. Unfortunately, there are only a couple of interesting sparkling wines amid a selection that could do with an injection of new blood.
*Edward Sheldon Champagne
   NV Extra Quality Dry,
   Cuvée Réservée £13.10* **80**

Smedley Vintners

Rectory Cottage,
Lilley, Luton,
Bedfordshire LU2 8LU
☎ 01462 768214
🖷 01462 768332 ✉
A small range of old classics for devoted followers of Master of Wine Derek Smedley. His favourite Sauvignon Blanc is Jackson Estate, and it's mine too, but Jackson was originally planted for sparkling wine production, and it's about time Derek added it to his portfolio.

Somerfield

Hawkfield Business Park,
Whitchurch Lane,
Bristol BS14 OTJ
☎ 0117 935 9359
🖷 0117 978 0629
Somerfield is a supermarket chain with around 440 stores, whose own-label Champagnes seem to be rather underrated.

Outstanding choices among them include the Prince William Blanc de Blancs Brut, with an attractively creamy fruit, which is good either to drink now or to keep for up to 12 months. Its *rosé* counterpart has a soft, succulent fruit made for easy drinking by Henri Madois.
*Champagne Prince William NV
   Brut Reserve £11.99* **80**
*Champagne Prince William NV
   Blanc de Blancs Brut
   £15.29* **82**
*Champagne Prince William NV
   Rosé Brut £15.29* **86**

John Stephenson

Darwil House,
Bradley Hall Road, Nelson,
Lancashire BB9 8HF
☎ 01282 614618
🖷 01282 601161 ✉
This third-generation, family-run business was established in 1914, the year of one of the great Champagne vintages of the 20th century. Moët still has commercial quantities of 1914, so perhaps John Stephenson should reserve some stock while it can. It would make the most outrageous own-label Champagne for the centennial celebrations.

Stevens Garnier

47 West Way, West Way,
Botley, Oxford OX1 2EW
☎ 01865 263303
🖷 01865 791594 ✉
This stockist sells a good own-label Champagne, but for just a pound more, Bernard Gaucher offers better quality and greater value. Stevens Garnier is one of the few places to stock Clos des Goisses, but its sparkling wine selection is rather lacklustre.
*H. Garnier & Co. Champagne
   NV Brut, Charles de
   Cazanove 12.95* **80**

Stones of Belgravia

6 Pont Street,
London SW1X 9EL
☎ 0171 235 1612
🖷 0171 235 7246 ✉
A small selection of Champagnes, including some interesting ones from Georges Vesselle. Own-label *cuvées* were not supplied for tasting. Wines are also sold through Jeroboams, a sister company with shops in Belgravia, Holland Park and Cirencester, Gloucestershire.

Stratford's Wine Shippers

High Street,
Cookham-on-Thames,
Berkshire SL6 9SQ
☎ 01628 810606
🖷 01628 810605 ✉
A small range of good *grande marque* Champagnes.

T&W Wines

51 King Street, Thetford,
Norfolk IP24 2AU
☎ 01842 765646
🖷 01842 766407 ✉
A range of superb vintages from great *grandes marques*, which are underpinned by the excellent quality-price ratio of Michel Arnould and André Clouet.

Tanners Wines

26 Wyle Cop, Shrewsbury,
Shropshire SY1 1XD
☎ 01743 234455
℻ 01743 234501 ✉
Tanners' own-label Brut Extra Réserve Special – a classic, lean and biscuity Champagne – is superior.
Tanners Brut Extra Réserve Special £13.95 **85**

Tesco

Delamare Road, Cheshunt,
Hertfordshire EN8 9SL
☎ 01992 658190
℻ 01992 658225
The usual smattering of *grande marque* Champagnes, an excellent source of own-label fizz, and branded sparkling wines including goodies like Jansz (but not Rebecca Vineyard).

At the cheaper end of Tesco's own-brand range is the South African Sparkling Sauvignon Blanc 1996: a fresh, fruity wine with tropical undertones. More expensive is the Blanc de Noirs non-vintage Cuvée Spéciale. This is very fruity – in a serious way – with good depth and length, with a building biscuity richness.
Asti NV Sweet, Santero, Tesco 4.99 **71**
Australian Sparkling Wine NV Brut, B. Seppelt, Tesco £4.99 **70**
Cava Brut NV Sant Sadurní d'Anoia, Tesco £4.99 **71**
Cava Rosé NV Brut, Sant Sadurní d'Anoia, Tesco £4.99 **70**
South African Sparkling Sauvignon Blanc 1996 Brut, Tesco £4.99 **70**
Blanquette de Limoux NV Brut, Tesco £6.99 **70**
Robertson W.O. Sparkling Wine NV Brut, Kangra Farms, Tesco £6.99 **78**
Tesco Champagne, Blanc de Noirs NV Cuvée Spéciale, Brut £11.99 **65**
Tesco Champagne NV Special Cuvée, Premier Cru Brut, CM-803 £12.95 **63**
Tesco Champagne, Blanc de Blancs NV Brut, Duval-Leroy £13.99 **60**

Thresher Group

Sefton House, 42 Church Road,
Welwyn Garden City,
Hertfordshire AL8 6PJ
☎ 01707 328244
℻ 01707 371398
This group includes Bottom's Up (87 outlets) and Wine Rack (116 outlets), as well as Thresher Wine Shops (813 outlets), although the latter is not teeming with quite so much Champagne. Bottom's Up and Wine Rack not only stock all three Charles Heidsieck *Mis en Caves* (1992, 1993 and 1994), but also the magnums of 1993, worth laying down for the Millennium.
Jean De Praisac NV Brut, F. Bonnet £12.99 **80**
Thresher Jean-Louis Malard NV Premier Cru Brut £16.99 **60**

The Ubiquitous Chip

8 Ashton Lane, Hillhead,
Glasgow G12 8SJ
☎ 0141 334 5007
℻ 0141 337 1302 ✉
One of the best places to eat and drink in Glasgow is on the bubbly front, but all of its Champagnes are worth buying, including the only own-label I have seen from Pol Roger (not submitted for tasting). As for the other fizz, stick to Pelorus.

Unwins

Birchwood House,
Victoria Road, Dartford,
Kent DA1 5AJ
☎ 01322 272711
℻ 01322 294469 ✉
Unwins has almost 400 shops and an increasing range of excellent Champagnes, some at pretty slick prices, including the best range of own-label currently available on the High Street. F. Duchatel is the house Champagne.

Especially recommended from the selection is the F. Duchatel 1990, which gives full, toasty aromas on the nose, while toastiness is still budding on the palate.
F. Duchatel & Cie NV Brut £11.49 **80**
F. Duchatel & Cie NV Blanc de Blancs, Brut £14.99 **82**
F. Duchatel & Cie NV Brut Rosé £14.99 **80**
F. Duchatel & Cie 1990 Brut £15.99 **84**

Valvona & Crolla

19 Elm Row,
Edinburgh EH7 4AA
☎ 0131 556 6066
℻ 0131 556 1668 ✉
This is an excellent place to buy Italian fizz. It also sells some pretty good Champagnes.

Victoria Wine

Dukes Court, Duke Street,
Woking, Surrey GU21 5XL
☎ 01483 715066
℻ 01483 755234 ✉

The colossus of the High Street, with over 1,500 outlets, including 100 Victoria Wine Cellars, which carry a better choice. There are some good Champagnes and one or two interesting New World bubblies, but the choice and excitement level does not match that encountered elsewhere.

That said, the Millennium Cuvée 1990 Grand Cru, with its full, toasty aromas of some finesse, and beautifully ripe, toasty fruit on the palate, is a star. Made by the Le Mesnil cooperative, it is an elegant, stylish Champagne that will just get better and better.
Charles Courbet NV Speciale Cuvée, Brut £11.99 **80**
Millennium Cuvée 1990 Grand Cru, Brut £21.99 **90**

La Vigneronne

105 Old Brompton Road,
London SW7 3LE
☎ 0171 589 6113
℻ 0171 581 2983 ✉
The list here includes a small selection of top *grandes marques*, with Gardet for value, and the odd old vintage.

Villeneuve Wines

1 Venlaw Court,
Peebles EH45 8AE
☎ 01721 722500
℻ 01721 729922 ✉
A nice range of great *grande marque* Champagnes, including some mature vintages that true aficionados would die for, such as a Bollinger RD 1973. (RD means *Récemment Dégorgé*, or "recently disgorged".)

El Vino Co

Vintage House,
1 Hare Place, Fleet Street,
London EC4Y 1BJ
☎ 0171 936 4948
℻ 0171 936 2367 ✉
A small selection of superb *grande marques*, but the even smaller range of sparkling wines is a little unimaginative.

The Vintry

Park Farm,
Midland, Liphook,
Hampshire GU30 7JT
☎ 01428 741389
℻ 01428 741688 ✉
Started by a group of five like-minded couples from Southern England, The Vintry offers a selection of French-only wines, mostly from English growers or *négociants* resident in France.

Other group members are located in Gillingham, Dorset; Calne, Wiltshire; Newbury, Berkshire; and Curdridge, Hampshire.

Waitrose

Doncastle Road,
Southern Industrial Area,
Bracknell,
Berkshire RG12 4YA
☎ 01344 824694
📠 01344 825255 ✉

Simply the best when it comes to own-label fizz: better than any other supermarket group, High Street chain or independent wine merchant, with lots of exciting branded bubbly too. Mail order is available through Waitrose Direct.

The magnum of own-label non-vintage Champagne is in a class of its own. It consists of sublime fruit interlaced with a toastiness of considerable finesse, and is gently buttressed by an impeccable mousse of the finest bubbles. Some mediocre *grandes marques* cost as much as this for a normal bottle size, making this a sensational bargain for a magnum.

Another good example is Waitrose's Blanc de Blancs NV, made by F. Bonnet, a fat and creamy *cuvée* which has a softer, smoother mousse than most supermarket Champagnes. This is serious stuff indeed.

Less pricey is the own-brand Cava: full, serious-styled with a real flavour and good weight, without being heavy or coarse.

Le Baron de Beaumont NV Chardonnay Brut £4.99 **70**
Cava Brut NV Waitrose £5.25 **76**
Waitrose Champagne Blanc de Noirs NV Brut, NM-122 £11.99 **85**
Waitrose Champagne NV Brut, NM-123 £12.95 **88**
Waitrose Champagne NV Brut £25 per magnum **91**
Waitrose Champagne Blanc de Blancs NV Brut, NM-123 £13.95 **89**
Champagne Waitrose Rosé NV Brut, CM-806 £14.95 **90**
Waitrose Champagne Vintage 1989 Brut, NM-123 £15.95 **85**

Waterloo Wine Co

6 Vine Yard,
London SE1 1QL
☎ 0171 403 7967
📠 0171 357 6976 ✉

As the UK agent for Le Brun de Neuville, the Waterloo Wine Co sells a wide range of its *cuvées*.

Waters of Coventry

Collins Road, Heathcote,
Warwickshire CV34 6TF
☎ 01926 888889
📠 01926 887416 ✉

Duval-Leroy and De Venoge offer the best value in terms of Champagne at this stockist, while Quartet, Green Point and Taltarni lead the way for New World choices.

The Wine Schoppen

3 Oak Street, Heeley,
Sheffield
South Yorkshire S8 9UB
☎ 0114 255 3301
📠 0114 255 1010 ✉

Only a limited selection of *grande marque* Champagnes, but they are of an impeccable quality, with Jeeper and a second label of Ellner for good value.

The Wine Society

Gunnels Wood Road,
Stevenage,
Hertfordshire SG1 2BG
☎ 01438 741177
📠 01438 741392 ✉

The Wine Society is very strong on own-label choices, with two of the Society's Saumurs getting through in preference to Gratien & Meyer's principal label, although the latter's much deeper, darker rouge rated over 80 when the Society's did not. Apparently there is no special selection, but obviously the shipments differ.

Of the Wine Society's stock, I would recommend the Society's Celebration 1995 Crémant de Loire, Gratien Meyer Seydoux – extremely fresh and tangy, with some substance and mouthfill.

Another top choice is the own-label Private Cuvée Champagne NV Brut, produced by Alfred Gratien: serious stuff, with oodles of fruit waiting to burst through. Keep it for two years for a real treat. Of course, not everyone can bear to wait that long.

The Wine Society Brut NV Sparkling Saumur, Gratien Meyer Seydoux £5.75 **72**
The Wine Society Rosé Brut NV Sparkling Saumur, Gratien & Meyer £6.95 **70**
The Society's Celebration 1995 Crémant de Loire, Gratien Meyer Seydoux £7.95 **78**
The Wine Society's Private Cuvée Champagne NV Brut, Alfred Gratien £14.75 **88**
The Wine Society's Private Cuvée Champagne NV Rich, Alfred Gratien £16 **85**

The Wine Treasury

143 Ebury Street,
London SW1W 9QN
☎ 0171 730 6774
📠 0171 823 6402 ✉

House Champagne under the Dinet-Peuvril label was not submitted for tasting, but good-value fizz is available under the Boucheron label from Gardet, plus an interesting new sparkler from Penley Estate in Coonawarra, Southern Australia.

Wines of Westhorpe

Marchington,
Staffordshire ST14 8NX
☎ 01283 820285
📠 01283 820631 ✉

The UK source for Törley sparkling wines, for all those homesick Hungarians out there.

Wine Rack

See Thresher Group

Woodhouse Wines

Blandford Forum,
Dorset DT11 9LS
☎ 01258 452141
📠 01258 450147 ✉

Woodhouse does not sell a wide range, but you *will* find decent prices, such as vintage Joseph Perrier for £19.99.

The Wright Wine Co

The Old Smithy,
Raikes Road, Skipton,
North Yorkshire BD23 1NP
☎ 01756 70886
📠 01756 798580 ✉

Some very keen prices among the non-vintage Champagnes, plus one or two interesting New World sparkling options.

Peter Wylie Fine Wines

Plymtree Manor, Plymtree,
Cullompton, Devon EX15 2LE
☎ 01884 277555
📠 01884 277557 ✉

Great for old vintages, with gems such as, at the time of writing, a 1971 Dom Ruinart, a 1959 Krug and a 1947 Pommery.

Yapp Brothers

The Old Brewery,
Water Street, Mere,
Wiltshire BA12 6DY
☎ 01747 860423
📠 01747 860929 ✉

An excellent source of Champagnes from Bruno Paillard and Jacquesson, Saint Péray from Jean-Louis Thiers, and various Loire bubblies.

Author's Acknowledgments

I am as pleased as Punch to work with Dorling Kindersley on any book, as this publisher is second to none when it comes to design, illustration, presentation and marketing, but I am particularly grateful to Christopher Davis, whose personal enthusiasm for this guide steamrollered it through the normally lengthy acceptance phase that every author has to face.

On the editorial side, my first thanks must go to Rosalyn Thiro, who was on my case daily. From personal knowledge I am only too well aware that, until now, most annual guides have had to skimp on design, forsake colour and be printed on low-grade paper, which leaves me eternally indebted to Anthony Limerick, whose artistic talents have made this book a wine guide any author would be proud of. Also at Dorling Kindersley I must thank Vivien Crump and David Lamb.

My gratitude cannot be properly expressed to the hundreds of producers who at great expense sent me samples from all four corners of the wine world, but I hope they all realise how appreciative I am, even those whose wines failed to pass muster (perhaps a new vintage or a different *cuvée* may qualify in a future edition). I am also greatly obliged to the following, who either organized a large centralized tasting or arranged for an industry-wide shipment of samples to my tasting facility: Maureen Ashley MW (for freelance services on behalf of Italian producers); Luis Avides Moreira (Wines of Portugal); Nelly Blau Picard (UPECB, Burgundy); Daniel Brennan (formerly of Wines from Spain); Stéphane Chaboud (Syndicat des Vignerons de Saint Péray); Tina Cody (Wines of South Africa); Maria do Cé Hespanha (Wines of Portugal); Nicole Dufour (CIVAS, Anjou-Saumur); Mme Faure (Syndicat de Die); Roger Fisher (T&CVA for English and Welsh sparkling wines); Dieter Greiner (Deutsches Weininstitut); Rosemary Hall (Wines of Austria); Sarah Hately (Westbury Blake for Wines of Canada); Graham Hines (Wines from Spain); Jane Hunt MW (formerly Wines of South Africa); Tony Keys (formerly of Australian Wine Bureau); Jon Leighton (Thames Valley Vineyards for English and Welsh sparkling wines); Georgina McDermott (Syndicat des Maisons de Saumur); Lisa McGovern (New Zealand Wine Guild); Steffen Maus (The German Wine Information Service); Françoise Peretti (Champagne Information Bureau); Hazel Murphy and Georgie Beach (Australian Wine Bureau); Emma Roberts (SOPEXA, France); Olivier Sohler (SPCA, Alsace); James S. Trezise (New York Wine & Grape Foundation); Barbara Tysome (German Wine Information Service); Michelle Vernoux (SVR Bordeaux); Emma Wellings (formerly Westbury Blake for Wines of Canada); and Victoria Williams (Wines of Chile).

I must also thank those from individual estates who coordinated the collection, information and samples from other producers, including Colin Cameron (Caxton Tower for Dragon Seal, China); Rémy Gauthier (Varichon & Clerc, Seyssel); Jeff Grier (Villiera Estate, South Africa); Jane Hunter (Hunter's Wines, New Zealand); and Alex and Claire Taylor (Canto Perlic, Gaillac); and, last but not least, Jeff Porter of Evenlode Press, who provided invaluable logistics support.

My sincere apologies for any omissions.

PICTURE RESEARCHERS
Brigitte Arora, Ellen Root

SPECIAL PHOTOGRAPHY AND DESIGN
Andy Crawford, Steve Gorton, Neil Lukas, Dave Pugh

A special thanks to Bernard Higton for the initial design and styling.

Dorling Kindersley would like to thank the following companies for providing items to be photographed:
Codorníu, Matthias Deis, Freiherr zu Knyphausen, Nyetimber, Screwpull International, Vilmart, Winzersekt Sprendlingen

PICTURE CREDITS
t – top; tl – top left; tlc – top left centre; tc – top centre; trc – top right centre; tr – top right; cla – centre left above; ca – centre above; cra – centre right above; cl – centre left; c – centre; cr – centre right; clb – centre left below; cb – centre below; crb – centre right below; bl – bottom left; b – bottom; bc – bottom centre; bcl – bottom centre left; br – bottom right; bra – bottom right above; brb – bottom right below; d – detail

Allsport: Adrian Murrell 56t; **Bellavista:** 48b; **Guido Berlucchi:** 49t, 50b; **Billecart-Salmon:** 39b; **Ca'del Bosco:** 51t; **CBI,** London: 11crb; **Cephas:** Andy Christodolo 2 – 3; Kevin Judd 59t; Alain Proust 61t, 62t; Mick Rock 13t, 16t, 24t, 27c, 35t, 36br, 37t, 44t, 47b, 55b; **Codorníu:** 41tr/cl, 43b; **Corbis:** W. Wayne Lockwood, M. D. 12t; **Culver Pictures:** 52t; **Deutsches Weininstitut:** 46t; **DIAF,** Paris: Jean-Daniel Sudres 1 (insert), 4t, 19t; Daniel Thierry 6t; **E.T. Archive:** 8t, 54t; **Mary Evans Picture Library:** 8b, 9cr/br, 45t, 46c, 47t; **Ferrari:** Joachim Falco 5c; 48t, 51b; **Freixenet:** 40t, 42b, 43t, 40 – 41b; **Hulton-Getty:** 9t; **Gosset:** 21b, 24bl; **Gramona:** 42t; **Charles Heidsieck:** 17, 25cr; De Visu 25t; **Seppelt/Image Library, State Library of New South Wales:** 58b; **Jackson Estate:** 59b; **Jacquesson & Fils:** 26t/b; **Kobal Collection:** 52c; **Krug:** 14t, 27t; **Laurent-Perrier:** 28t; **Moët & Chandon:** 16c, 20b, 29b; **Pol Roger:** 31t/c/b; **Janet Price:** 12b, 32b; **Retrograph Archive,** London: Martin Breese 16b, 29t; **Louis Roederer:** 9bl; Jean-Claude Rouzaud 30t; Michel Jolyot 30b; **Root Stock,** Ludwigsburg: Hendrik Holler 4 – 5b, 36bl, 38b, 44b, 52 – 53b, 54b, 56b, 61b, 62b; **Ruinart:** 18c; *Champagne Ruinart, Rheims,* Alphonse Mucha @ ADAGP, Paris and DACS, London 1998 32r; **Salon:** 33b; **Scope:** Bernard Galeron 31t; Michel Guillard 22b; Eric Quentin 20t; **Southcorp Wines Europe:** 57bl; **SOPEXA (UK):** 39T; **Topham Picturepoint:** Ulf Berglund 60t; **Veuve Clicquot Ponsardin:** 5t, 11cra/b, 34t/b; **Villiera Estate:** 63t/b; **Vilmart & Ciel:** 35b; **Visual Arts Library:** Collection Kharbine-Tapabor 9cl, 18b, 21t, 10, 33t, 55t; **John Wyand:** 64t; **Yalumba:** 57br, 58t

Back Jacket: **Cephas:** Mick Rock top left; StockFood bottom; **The Image Bank:** David de Lossy top right